Book Publishing in Australia

BOOK PUBLISHING IN AUSTRALIA

A Living Legacy

Edited by Millicent Weber and Aaron Mannion

MONASH University Publishing

Book Publishing in Australia: A Living Legacy
© Copyright 2019
Copyright of this collection in its entirety is held by the editors, Millicent Weber and
Aaron Mannion. Copyright of the individual chapters is held by their respective author/s.
All rights reserved. Apart from any uses permitted by Australia's Copyright Act 1968, no
part of this book may be reproduced by any process without prior written permission from
the copyright owners. Inquiries should be directed to the publisher.

Monash University Publishing
Matheson Library and Information Services Building
40 Exhibition Walk
Monash University
Clayton, Victoria 3800, Australia
www.publishing.monash.edu

Monash University Publishing brings to the world publications which advance the
best traditions of humane and enlightened thought.

Monash University Publishing titles pass through a rigorous process of
independent peer review.

ISBN: 9781925835458 (paperback)
ISBN: 9781925835465 (pdf)
ISBN: 9781925835472 (epub)

www.publishing.monash.edu/books/bpa-9781925835458.html

Series: Publishing Series

Design: Les Thomas

Cover image: The spines of books. Shutterstock royalty-free stock photo ID: 789692986.

A catalogue record for this book is available from the National Library of Australia.

Printed in Australia by Griffin Press an Accredited ISO AS/NZS 14001:2004
Environmental Management System printer.

The paper this book is printed on is certified against the Forest Stewardship Council ®
Standards. Griffin Press holds FSC chain of custody certification SGS-COC-005088.
FSC promotes environmentally responsible, socially beneficial and economically viable
management of the world's forests.

Contents

Publishing Legacies

An Introduction

Millicent Weber and Aaron Mannion

Discussion of contemporary publishing implies a point of comparison between the publishing industry of the present and the publishing industry of the past. Technological advances have undoubtedly reshaped the practices of publishing in the twenty-first century. Contrary, however, to early prognostications about the dismal fate of books and reading,[1] Australian independent publishing, and the Australian publishing sector more broadly, demonstrate relative stability and even growth in recent years.[2]

Legacy is a usefully ambivalent concept to invoke in disentangling the relationship between present and past practices. Situated in the present, but reflecting back on the past, legacy refers to both the capital accrued and passed on by predecessors, and the reliance on widespread but superseded practices and technologies. Legacy thus defined both enables and hinders.

Both of these senses of legacy are undoubtedly central to publishing. It is, on the one hand, an industry whose central aim is the production and circulation of objects of cultural value. Books' consecration as canonical occurs as a result of longevity and recognition: the books that are most valuable are those whose cultural legacy is most prominent.[3] And publishing is itself a space governed by pre-existing conventions

---

1   Sven Birkerts, *The Gutenberg Elegies: The Fate of Reading in an Electronic Age* (Boston: Faber & Faber, 1994).

2   David Carter, "General Fiction, Genre Fiction and Literary Fiction Publishing 2000–13," in *The Return of Print? Contemporary Australian Publishing*, eds. Aaron Mannion and Emmett Stinson (Melbourne: Monash University Publishing, 2016), 1–21.

3   See Pierre Bourdieu, *The Rules of Art: Genesis and Structure of the Literary Field*, trans. Susan Emanuel (Cambridge: Polity Press, 1996).

and expectations. Some of these are codified by copyright laws and business contracts; others, like the placement of bibliographical information, are merely conventions of habit.

Twenty-first century books remain largely recognisable as close siblings of the objects produced by Gutenberg—but while books remain remarkably unchanged, the processes of writing, editing, typesetting, printing, distributing, buying, discussing and appraising books continue to develop, sometimes slowly and sometimes dramatically, a trend mapped by Padmini Ray Murray and Claire Squires in their reworking of Robert Darnton's classic "communications circuit".[4] New technologies reshape certain publishing sectors and skip over others, with digital self-publishing for example remaking genres like romance publishing while leaving literary fiction largely untouched.

In a political context, digital tools like Wordpress and Twitter offer widely accessible, low-cost platforms for activists to publish and disseminate their work. But traditional publishing, both mainstream and academic, continues as an important communicative mode for those agitating for social change. Both the VIDA and the Stella Count[5] demonstrate the very real need for feminist interventions in publishing—and publishing industries, Australian and international, are only now beginning to recognise the need for intersectional interventions that address the historical and ongoing marginalisation of other social and cultural groups.[6]

New technologies are being developed by libraries and digital humanists to explore the history of publishing. The first chapter in this

---

4   Padmini Ray Murray and Claire Squires, "The Digital Publishing Communications Circuit," in *Book 2.0* 3, no. 1 (June 2013): 3–23. Robert Darnton, "What Is the History of Books?" *Daedalus* 111, no. 3 (Summer 1982): 65–83.

5   "The Prize Count," The Stella Prize, https://thestellaprize.com.au/the-count/the-prize-count/; "The 2017 VIDA Count," VIDA: Women in Literary Arts, http://www.vidaweb.org/the-2017-vida-count/.

6   Natalie Kon-Yu, "A Testicular Hit-List of Literary Big Cats," in *Overland Literary Journal* 223 (Winter 2016): 14–20; Hannah McGregor, Julie Rak and Erin Wunker, eds., *Refuse: CanLit in Ruins* (Toronto: Book*hug, 2018).

collection, Katherine Bode's "'Large, Vigorous and Thriving': Early Australian Publishing and Futures of Publishing Studies", reports on an innovative study of fiction publishing in nineteenth-century Australian newspapers. Bode's study dramatically reshapes understandings of where and how much colonial Australian fiction was published. It also identifies the possibilities of digital research methods to "redirect and invigorate the future of publishing studies, including by connecting it to new collaborators and publics".

The chapters that follow explore how legacy industry practices are encountered, recycled and remodelled in contemporary contexts. Tracy O'Shaughnessy, Rose Michael and Ronnie Scott in "From Cultural Entrepreneurs to an Apprenticeship Practice" use the frame of apprenticeship to explore how skills are transferred between generations of publishing industry professionals. Using three independent publishers—Arcade Publications (2007–12), The Lifted Brow (est. 2007), and The Bowen Street Press (est. 2016)—as case studies, O'Shaughnessy, Michael and Scott argue that this para-formal mode of mentorship is particularly suitable for knowledge transfer in publishing, replete as it is with "novel ventures and original personalities".

Sophie Masson's "Crowdfunding and Small Publishers" draws attention to the growth of publicly sourced donations and commitments to purchase as viable revenue streams. Masson identifies "credibility, endorsement and preparedness" as key factors in successful crowdfunding ventures, and argues that this contemporary reworking of a patron-like model is particularly well suited to the independent publishing sector, as it rewards projects that are both risky and distinctive.

More strictly codified forms of industry legacy are explored in Katherine Day's "The Publishing Contract: A Complicated Inheritance". Day argues that the publishing contract can be seen as both "an ideological artefact and as a sanctioning instrument", leveraging this analysis to identify how the Australian publishing industry has been impacted by copyright.

Jocelyn Hargrave, in "On the Road to the Standardisation of the Printed Page: The Legacies of John Degotardi and Benjamin Fryer", similarly uses the documentation that governs how publishing occurs to understand the relationship between contemporary publishing and past practice. Degotardi in 1861 and Fryer in 1930 published the only two Australian industry manuals in circulation before *The Style Manual for Authors, Editors and Printers* was first published in 1966. Hargrave explores the legacy of how each contributed to the standardisation of book publishing, arguing that the guidance they provided was instrumental in establishing a thriving Australian print culture.

Millicent Weber's "Scholarly Feminist Presses: Germaine Greer and Stump Cross Books" is the first of several chapters that explore publishing's political and gendered dimensions. With reference to the archive of Greer's own publishing house, Stump Cross Books, this chapter explores the different criteria against which the success of feminist publishers might be measured. Although Stump Cross was a commercial failure, its intellectual legacy can be seen in its editions' scholarly citations and widespread presence in libraries around the globe.

The chapters following explore the way that legacy, value and consecration operate in Australian print culture more broadly, with a particular focus on books' reception. As Michelle Goldsmith notes in "Speculating on Gender: Investigating the Effects of Author and Reader Gender in the Speculative Fiction Field", reception and reader preference are considerations "especially important to authors, publishers and other parties involved in the production and dissemination of books". Goldsmith's work offers a data-rich empirical investigation of the effect of gender on reader taste in the field of speculative fiction, contextualised against research like the VIDA and Stella Counts that identify persistent gender imbalances in how books are valued.

Brigid Magner and Emily Potter's chapter, "Shared Reading in the Victorian Mallee", offers a qualitatively empirical study of reception.

Magner and Potter's research into rural Victorian book groups notes the lack of public profile and recognition for literature from the area of the Mallee, an important reminder of the historically city-centric constitution of the Australian literary canon. This chapter also explores the concept of legacy in relation to local, historical knowledge, and the ways that literature with strong local roots supported social interactions where participants could share their own experiences and understandings of the region.

In "Small Publishers, Symbolic Capital, and Australian Literary Prizes", Emmett Stinson updates his earlier work on the Miles Franklin, discussing the unprecedented prominence of small publishers on Australian literary prize lists in 2017 and 2018. Stinson connects this recent trend with "an institutional reassertion of the value of explicitly literary writing" at a time when popular writing is flourishing—a reminder of the centuries-old tension between aesthetics and popularity that continues to structure value judgements in the industry. This balancing act between different forms of value becomes even more charged in the case of literary prizes, which boost sales but also recognise cultural merit; Stinson's chapter usefully maps out independent publishers' relationship, "tenuous and contingent" as it is, to these different forms of industry success.

The final chapter, Melinda Harvey and Julieanne Lamond's "Literary Prizes and Book Reviews in Australia since 2014", concludes the volume with an overview of the professional mechanisms of reception—book reviewing and prizes. Harvey and Lamond's analysis reveals that the relationship between reviews and prizes "is one of interdependence and amplification", and that both prizes and the assessments of merit made in professional book reviews "are crucial to a book's longevity". This chapter builds directly on the statistical data that Harvey and Lamond have collected in collaboration with the Stella Count; the central role that prizes and reviews play in ensuring a book's success underscores the importance of political actions like the Stella Prize and the Count that work to reveal and counter the industry's persistent power imbalances.

The themes that re-emerge throughout this collection reveal the centrality of two concerns in particular to the study of contemporary publishing. The first is the problem of inequality, power and representation; the second relates to our own interventions as researchers in the publishing industry. Digital technology has, to a certain extent, lowered the barriers for entry into writing and publishing—a trend that is visible, for example, in the recent explosion of self-publishing. Despite this broadening of access, however, inequalities—including those along gender, race and regional lines—persist in structuring participation, representation and valuation in the field of Australian publishing.

Works cited

Birkerts, Sven. *The Gutenberg Elegies: The Fate of Reading in an Electronic Age.* Boston: Faber & Faber, 1994.

Bourdieu, Pierre. *The Rules of Art: Genesis and Structure of the Literary Field.* Translated by Susan Emanuel. Cambridge: Polity Press, 1996.

Carter, David. "General Fiction, Genre Fiction and Literary Fiction Publishing 2000–13." In *The Return of Print? Contemporary Australian Publishing*, edited by Aaron Mannion and Emmett Stinson, 1–21. Melbourne: Monash University Publishing, 2016.

Darnton, Robert. "What Is the History of Books?" *Daedalus* 111, no. 3 (Summer 1982): 65–83.

Kon-Yu, Natalie. "A Testicular Hit-List of Literary Big Cats." In *Overland Literary Journal* 223 (Winter 2016): 14–20.

McGregor, Hannah, Julie Rak, and Erin Wunker, eds. *Refuse: CanLit in Ruins.* Toronto: Book*hug, 2018.

Ray Murray, Padmini, and Claire Squires. "The Digital Publishing Communications Circuit." *Book 2.0* 3, no. 1 (June 2013): 3–23.

The Stella Prize. "The Prize Count." Updated 2018, https://thestellaprize.com. au/the-count/the-prize-count/.

VIDA: Women in Literary Arts. "The 2017 VIDA Count." Updated 2018, http://www.vidaweb.org/the-2017-vida-count/.

CHAPTER I

"Large, Vigorous and Thriving"

Early Australian Publishing
and Futures of Publishing Studies

KATHERINE BODE

This chapter is adapted from a keynote presentation at the Small Press Network's Independent Publishing Conference at the Wheeler Centre in Melbourne in November 2017.

Just as digital technologies have transformed publishing, so too are they transforming publishing studies. As in other disciplines, such as archaeology, by changing the methods and scale of research, digital resources and approaches enable new perspectives on and insights into the history of publishing.[1] With this digital transformation in mind, the chapter's first part identifies three principles that I think are essential to bear in mind when conducting publishing research with large digital collections. In the third and final part, I explore another issue relevant to digital research—data publishing—that has the potential to redirect and invigorate the future of publishing studies, including by connecting it to new collaborators and publics.

---

1   I mention archaeology as a field that seems to generate particularly newsworthy examples of this transformative capacity of digital technologies. Recently reported examples include the Birka Viking, where DNA analysis revealed that a warrior long assumed to be male was female (Amy Ellis Nutt, "Wonder Woman Lived: Viking Warrior Skeleton Identified as Female, 128 Years After its Discovery"), and a crowd-sourcing project in satellite archaeology, where members of the public help to discover previously unknown ancient sites based on satellite imagery (Elizabeth Stinson, "Want to be a Space Archaeologist? Here's Your Chance").

The chapter's second part demonstrates these principles and possibilities with reference to previously unknown features of early Australian fiction publishing in nineteenth-century newspapers. These periodicals are the "large, vigorous and thriving" enterprises of my title, and publishing historians have long known that some of them published fiction.[2] More particularly, they have argued that most of this fiction appeared in major metropolitan newspapers, especially the weekly companions to the major metropolitan dailies—including Melbourne's *Leader*, Sydney's *Australian Town and Country Journal* and Brisbane's *Queenslander*—and that most of these stories (around 80 percent by one estimate) were by British authors.[3] This understanding has contributed to a (perhaps the) key legacy of Australian publishing studies: the notion that Australian publishers—and hence readers—have for most of their history been dominated by British interests, publishers and authors. Summarising this widely held view in the *Cambridge Companion to Australian Literature*, Elizabeth Webby wrote that, "for much of the nineteenth-century and indeed afterwards, Australian readers were mainly interested in books by English authors".[4]

Applying new digital methods to new digital resources—namely, the National Library of Australia's (NLA) mass-digitised collection of historical Australian newspapers—enables a very different version of Australian publishing, literary and reading history. Based on data drawn from Trove Newspapers and published in "To Be Continued… ": The Australian Newspaper Fiction Database, I show that nineteenth-century Australian newspapers were undoubtedly the most successful and

---

2   Elizabeth Morrison, "Serial Fiction in Australian Colonial Newspapers," in *Literature in the Marketplace: Nineteenth-Century British Publishing and Reading Practices*, eds. John O. Jordan and Robert L. Patten (Cambridge: Cambridge University Press, 1998), 308.

3   Ibid., 315.

4   Elizabeth Webby, "Colonial Writers and Readers," in *The Cambridge Companion to Australian Literature*, ed. Elizabeth Webby (Cambridge: Cambridge University Press, 2000), 50.

prolific of Australia's early independent publishers.[5] Not only was fiction publishing much more widespread and actively pursued in Australian newspapers in the nineteenth century than has been recognised, it was cosmopolitan from its origins, encompassing fiction from around the world. At the same time, local writing had a much greater presence, more organised systems of distribution, and a more receptive and substantial market, than literary and publishing historians have understood. From the time Australian newspapers began routinely to publish fiction (the mid-1860s), early Australian fiction publishing was both enmeshed in globalised cultural and economic networks, and distinctively local, adaptive and independent.

Methods and Principles for Digital Publishing Studies

From 2013 to 2016 Carol Hetherington and I worked to identify and explore fiction in Trove's digitised newspapers. While most Australian researchers are familiar with Trove and its newspaper collection, some—perhaps many—are unaware that this is the largest open-access collection of digitised historical newspapers in the world, with significantly more searchable pages than related collections, including Chronicling America, Europeana or Papers Past. Of course, just because a collection is big does not make it complete; nor does it mean the documents it contains are representative of those that once existed.

By comparing the newspapers digitised by Trove with historical records, such as indexes of newspapers created for advertisers, I estimate that, at the time we stopped harvesting from Trove (July 2015), 28 percent of nineteenth-century Australian newspapers had been digitised. This percentage is perhaps lower than a lot of people assume

---

5   *Trove Newspapers*, National Library of Australia, https://trove.nla.gov.au/
    newspaper/; Katherine Bode and Carol Heatherington, "To Be Continued…":
    The Australian Newspaper Fiction Database, http://cdhrdatasys.anu.edu.au/
    tobecontinued/.

when conducting historical research with Trove; and certain types of newspapers were over- or under-represented. For instance, as the collection stood in mid-2015, certain newspapers from Queensland and Western Australia were digitised at a higher rate than for other colonies, while provincial newspapers are generally underrepresented. This recognition that archives and other collections are partial and reflect a particular version of history—created by collection practices, contingent notions of value and meaning, and economic and political considerations—has always been present in publishing studies, and it should not be minimised or obscured when research shifts from analogue to digital collections, regardless of how extensive the latter may be.

My first principle for conducting publishing studies with digital technologies is, thus, an old one: namely, that the collections we work in have histories. We need to know those histories—including the effects of our own engagements with those records—to understand the relationship between the collections we investigate and the publishing context we seek to understand.

After establishing what proportion of historical newspapers have been digitised, and areas of under- and overrepresentation, the task was to find the fiction these periodicals contained. Rather than applying complex text mining and machine-learning algorithms, as the Viral Texts project does to analyse reprinting in historical American newspapers,[6] our analysis of Trove began with arguably the most familiar of all components of digital research infrastructure: the search box. However, we used it in a different way to how keyword searching is typically approached in the humanities.

---

6   Ryan Cordell and David Smith, The *Viral Texts Project: Mapping Networks of Reprinting in 19th-Century Newspapers and Magazines*, http://viraltexts.org/. David Smith et al., "Computational Methods for Uncovering Reprinted Texts in Antebellum Newspapers," *American Literary History* 27, no. 3 (September 2015): E1–E15.

What we did not do was to enter the names or titles of known nineteenth-century authors. The limitations of that approach are (at least) four-fold. First, it would produce lots of irrelevant results, including literary gossip, obituaries and book reviews. Second, it would be very time-consuming, as it would require us to work through bibliographies of fiction and enter hundreds or even thousands of authors or titles into Trove. Third, this approach would be self-confirming, in that it would yield only the authors and titles we expected to be present. Even if we searched for all known authors and titles, this approach would reinforce existing knowledge of fiction. Finally, it would be ahistorical in that it fails to accommodate the common changes in title for, and especially the widespread anonymous and pseudonymous publication of, fiction in early Australian newspapers.

The solution devised in response to these practical and conceptual problems is one that I call the "paratextual method". Paratext, of course, refers to elements—here, textual—that surround, signal and introduce publication events. In nineteenth-century newspapers, as today, paratextual features are very consistent, enabling readers to open the pages and differentiate, at a glance, the advertising from the feature articles, the letters to the editor from the crime reporting, and the sports reporting from the fiction. The paratextual method adapts this mechanism—or technology—for supporting human searching and reading to digital discovery. Thus, into the search box I entered not authors or titles, but words that consistently appeared in the paratexts of fiction in early Australian newspapers, such as "serial", "story", "our author", "tales and sketches", "our novelist" and (most successfully) "chapter".

Because of the way Trove's relevance-ranking algorithm works to privilege articles where words appear in the title, and especially when they recur throughout (as with "chapter"), the vast majority of the initial tens of thousands of results for searches with these terms were fiction. We then used Trove's Application Programming Interface (or API—

a set of protocols for interacting with a computer system, in this case a database) to export the results in large batches. For each search term, this approach was employed until a substantial number of irrelevant records appeared in results: a sign that a particular paratextual term, in its interaction with Trove at a specific point in time, had exhausted its usefulness.[7]

The "paratextual method" embodies a second principle for conducting publishing studies with large digital collections: the need for methodologies that articulate between disciplinary knowledge and the affordances and systems of the digital infrastructure available. In this case, a focus on paratextual search terms reflects an understanding of the newspaper genre, and of fiction publishing in nineteenth-century periodicals. But it can only be systematised—that is, used to investigate a large digital collection in a reliable and consistent way—by virtue of Trove's specific digital affordances: its segmentation of digitised pages into articles, its manual correction of the Optical Character Recognition (OCR) text in article titles, the nature of its relevance-ranking algorithm, and the provision of an API to enable mass searching and harvesting of results.

This analysis of digitised newspapers yielded over 200,000 article records. But it was not simply a matter of extracting the data and beginning analysis, because the format in which the API provides information is not particularly useful for publishing research. Figure 1 is an example of the html records that were extracted, along with associated text files. This example contains a wealth of information in a single field "<heading>", including the story's title ("WYNNUM WHITE'S WICKEDNESS") and information about copyright ("The right of publishing this Novel in the Northern District has been purchased by the Proprietor of the ARMIDALE CHRONICLE") as well as the chapter number and chapter title published in that

---

7   For each term, harvesting was performed multiple times over a two-year period, yielding new results as additional newspapers were digitised.

instalment. Other "<heading>" fields arising from the same "chapter" search contained much more information than this one, including other periodicals in which the work had been published, descriptions of the story (for instance, as "sensational", "original" or "tragic") or signature details (that this story is "by the author of…" other titles). In other records, the "<heading>" field contained only the chapter number.

```
<article id="183169625" url="/newspaper/183169625">
  <heading>
    "WYNNUM WHITE'S WICKEDNESS" (COPYRIGHT), (The right of
    publishing this Novel in the Northern District has been
    purchased by the Proprietor of the ARMIDALE CHRONICLE.) CHAPTER
    VIII-A CHILD'S STORY OF "THE GOLDEN CROSS."
  </heading>
  <category>Article</category>
  <title id="983">The Armidale Chronicle (NSW : 1894 - 1929)</title>
  <date>1895-10-23</date>
  <page>4</page>
  <pageSequence>4</pageSequence>
  <troveUrl>http://trove.nla.gov.au/ndp/del/article/183169625</tro
  veUrl>
  <illustrated>N</illustrated>
  <wordCount>1370</wordCount>
  <correctionCount>0</correctionCount>
  <listCount>0</listCount>
  <tagCount>0</tagCount>
  <commentCount>0</commentCount>
  <identifier>http://nla.gov.au/nla.news-article183169625</identif
  ier>
  <trovePageUrl>http://trove.nla.gov.au/ndp/del/page/21217063</tro
  vePageUrl>
  <pdf>
    http://trove.nla.gov.au/ndp/imageservice/nla.news-page21217063/
    print
  </pdf>
</article>
```

Figure 1: Example html record resulting from a search of Trove Newspapers for "chapter," exported using Trove's API.

These differences in the information presented in particular fields, as well as the inclusion of irrelevant results, meant that significant manual data processing was required to transform what was extracted from Trove into data useful for research. Different instalments of stories also had to be collected under a single title, and Carol also conducted extensive bibliographical research on these records, for instance, to identify changes in the titles of stories or the origins of anonymously and pseudonymously published works. The third and final principle for conducting publishing studies with large digital collections, evidenced by the above example, is that digital research is not the quick or lazy option. Although we hear a lot about how digital resources radically increase access to information, the form in which that information is available is often not one that suits academic research. Extensive work, and once again, significant disciplinary expertise, goes into constructing useful data. As well as taking an enormous amount of time, this process adds considerable value to the resulting data—an issue I will return to with respect to data publishing in the final part of the chapter.

Based on this analysis of Trove digitised newspapers, we discovered over 21,000 novels, novellas and short stories, including unique publications and republications, in nineteenth- and early-twentieth-century Australian newspapers. Other details of that dataset, available through the To Be Continued database, include:

1. 16,648 fictional works published in the nineteenth century, made up of 9,249 works of extended fiction (stories serialised over two or more newspaper issues or amounting to 10,000 words or more in a single issue)[8] as well as 7,399 short stories;

---

8   The majority—98 percent—of the fiction in this category is extended by serialisation. Of the 2 percent of titles that are categorised as extended because consisting of 10,000 words or more, some are novella-length (10,000 to 25,000 words). But others are full novels of 60,000 words or more.

2. 4,515 fictional works in early twentieth-century newspapers (published from the start of the twentieth century until 1914), made up of 3,507 works of extended fiction and 1,008 short stories;

3. 4,146 author names;

4. 5,671 titles where an author's name is not given and, even after extensive bibliographical research, we have not been able to confirm an identity; and

5. 194,108 individual text files (some of these are stories in their own right; a great many comprise instalments that needed to be grouped with other text files).[9]

When one considers that, prior to this analysis, the bibliographical record for fiction in nineteenth-century Australian newspapers numbered in the hundreds, this discovery of almost 17,000 titles represents a significant increase on existing knowledge and confirms the importance of newspapers as sources of fiction for colonial readers.

New Discoveries about Early Australian Publishing

In what follows, I focus on fiction published in the nineteenth century, especially between 1865 and 1899, when 98 percent of the titles discovered in this period appeared. More specifically still, I concentrate on extended fiction, as defined above, because these titles imply a particular mode of publishing and reading. Where stories completed in a single newspaper issue suggest incidental publishing and reading—with such content often selected simply to fill column inches, and likely read in a casual manner—extended fiction

---

9   These figures describe the contents of To Be Continued in November 2017. Since its public launch in March 2018 members of the public have added many hundreds of new stories to the database. I discuss this crowdsourcing component of the project at the end of the chapter.

required deliberate sourcing and publishing by editors, and implies more intensive or committed engagement from readers. This subset is in itself substantial—over 9,200 titles—and exploring it makes possible four findings that transform understandings of publishing in Australia in the nineteenth century, and of the transnational circulation of fiction in this period.

As already noted, publishing historians have recognised nineteenth-century Australian newspapers as fiction publishers for many decades, with the understanding that most of this fiction was British. Among the fiction harvested from Trove, British works were prevalent, comprising about 50 percent of titles where authors' identities were discovered. But the idea that British fiction was essentially all that was published is far from true.

The first key finding from this project is that fiction in nineteenth-century Australian newspapers originated from a much greater and more diverse range of national and proto-national contexts than has been understood. American fiction was widely published, representing around 20 percent of the titles by known authors discovered, and there was also a significant number of French and German titles in translation as well as fiction from other British dominions (Canada, New Zealand and South Africa) and even further afield, such as Austria, Holland, Hungary, Italy, Japan, Russia and Sweden. Much of this fiction was popular, including a substantial amount of British sensation and adventure fiction, and American dime stories, including crimes, romances and westerns. But a surprising number of titles were by literary, even canonical, writers: Honoré de Balzac, Charles Dickens, Benjamin Disraeli, Alexandre Dumas, George Eliot, Thomas Hardy, Victor Hugo, Henry James, Harriet Beecher Stowe, Eugène Sue, William Thackeray, Anthony Trollope, Ivan Turgenev, Mark Twain, Oscar Wilde and Émile Zola are all represented in the To Be Continued database. As with the sheer scale of the fiction published in newspapers, this list of literary writers indicates how different this nineteenth-century reading context was from the one we associate with newspapers today.

Alongside this wide range of international writing was a significant amount of Australian fiction: both known and new. Some notable findings include previously unlisted fiction by Catherine Martin and Jessie Mabel Waterhouse; a new Australian author, John Silvester Nottage, responsible for multiple full-length novels; and new titles by "Captain Lacie" and "Ivan Dexter", in addition to the discovery that both were well-developed pseudonyms for James Joseph Wright. Indeed, although British author of sensation fiction Mary Elizabeth Braddon has been identified as the most widely-published author in the Australian colonies, based on the fiction identified in Trove, Wright—a local author—holds this position. Certainly, he emerges from this analysis as one of Australia's most prolific writers. More significant to understanding the publishing context than these individual literary discoveries is the scale of Australian fiction present. Such stories make up around 25 percent of publications by known authors discovered in this project, with many hundreds of other works by unknown authors indicating—indeed highlighting—an Australian origin.

This brings me to a second key finding arising from analysis of this extensive new collection of fiction: not only was there more local fiction in nineteenth-century Australian newspapers than has been recognised, but it was also accorded significantly more value. This statement might give readers pause: how can I know that readers valued Australian fiction? Local stories could have been published simply because they were cheaper or more readily available than the imported product. However, this claim is supported by paratextual information surrounding these stories, which provides insights into the meanings and values informing both publication and reception. Editors aim to sell newspapers—and fiction was one of the main ways they achieved this aim.[10] So it makes sense that they would foreground features of the fiction that they thought readers would look favourably upon. And in nineteenth-century Australian newspapers, it was routinely the case that local origins of fiction were highlighted.

Some individual examples will serve to give a sense of this local emphasis. For instance, in the 1890s, the *Jewish Herald* assured readers that "A Jewish Wife" was "An Australian Story by an Australian Author" (#13201), while the *Traralgon Record* described "The Dis-Honourable" as "A newly published and fascinating story of Australian life" (#6074).[11] Such emphasis was not limited to the 1890s. In 1887, the *Horsham Times* was one of many newspapers to present "ALMA" as "An Original Australian Story" by a "New South Wales" member of parliament (#4945); and in 1875 in the *Sydney Mail*, the first chapter title for "Investing Uncle Ben's Legacy; or, Mr. McTailing's Mining and Matrimonial Speculations. A Tale of the Mining Era" set the scene firmly in the colonies with: "A failure in Melbourne and a fresh start in Sydney" (#14877). The local origins of this latter story are further emphasised by its attribution to the very Australian-sounding "Old Boomerang", a pseudonym for journalist J. R. Houlding, who emerges from this analysis as the most widely published colonial author of the 1860s and 1870s.

Hundreds of stories simply featured Australia—or places therein— in their titles. Some examples by well-known authors include J. D. Hennessey's "The Bells of Sydney" in 1896 (#6064; #6065), Lilian

---

10 Colonial newspaper editors frequently noted the importance of fiction to their readers. For instance, the editor of the *Barrier Miner* wrote in 1895 that: "The success which has attended the publication of 'The Last Signal' has been so pronounced that the proprietors of the BARRIER MINER have decided to continue, for a time at least, the publication of serial stories; and have just completed arrangements wish [sic] Miss Adeline Sergeant for the publication of her latest brilliant dramatic serial, 'Marjory's Mistake'." "'Marjory's Mistake': Another Original Story for the 'Miner'," *Barrier Miner*, April 22, 1895, 3, nla.gov.au/nla. news-article44167084.

11 I cite fiction in the To Be Continued database using the unique record number. Full bibliographical details and available text files of these stories can be accessed by entering this number into the "Trove ID" field in the search interface for the database.

Turner's "By the Blue Australian Mountains" in 1894 (#7820), and Rolf Boldrewood's "The Wild Australian" in 1877 (#7664). Lesser known or unknown authors did the same, including V. L. Thomas's "An Australian Anarchist" in 1896 (#15438), Ralph De Peveril's "An Australian Settler's Tale" in 1874 (#149; #150), and "Bush Life in Australia: An Original Tale", published anonymously in 1859 (#423). Indeed, so consistently were local origins emphasised that, although Australian titles make up only 25 percent of publications by known authors, "Australia/n" was the third most common word in titles and subtitles across all extended nineteenth-century fiction, after "story" and "tale". Some overseas fiction—particularly from America—was even adapted to make it seem as if it came from Australia. Thus, "Florabel's Lover, or, Rival Belles" by American writer Laura Jean Libbey became "The Rival Belles of Parramatta" in multiple provincial newspapers in 1888 (#3042; #3043; #3044; #3045; #3561; #14589; #14590; #14591; #14592; #14593); and Old Sleuth's "The American Detective in Russia" was serialised in various sites as "Barnes, the Australian Detective" (#6415; #6416; #6417; #6418; #6419; #6420; #6421).

The data represented in Figure 2 provides a broader sense of this foregrounding of local origins. It shows the place with which stories were identified (by titles, by-lines, copyright information and other prominent paratextual and textual features) where the actual nationality of authors is known. For all national or proto-national categories (American, Australian, British and other) the presentation or inscription of fiction was more likely to align with the actual origins of the author than otherwise. But there are significant differences between these categories. American and other fiction was much more likely to be depicted as coming from elsewhere than either British or Australian writing. By contrast, editors were equally likely to represent British and Australian fiction as coming from Britain or Australia, respectively. This trend suggests that British fiction was seen as desirable and of interest to readers, but not necessarily more so than Australian writing.

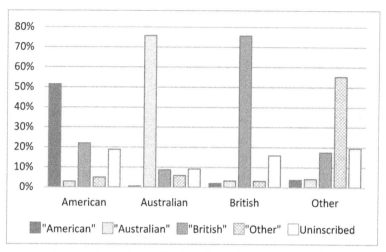

Figure 2. Proportion of titles by authors of known nationalities as nationality was inscribed.

The cultural value accorded to Australian writing is reinforced by the attribution of fiction. If we allow that an editor was more likely to attribute a title to a particular author if that author was seen as prestigious or noteworthy, then trends in attribution can also be used to explore editorial assumptions about colonial readers' interests. In this light, it is significant that British fiction was more likely than most other fiction to be attributed to a named author in nineteenth-century Australian newspapers; but local fiction, especially by men, was the most likely to be attributed. Taken together, such foregrounding of local origins and authors suggests that Australian fiction not only appeared much more frequently in nineteenth-century Australian newspapers than has been recognised; its publication was also foregrounded as interesting and valuable to readers.

The third major finding from this project is, simply put, a new structure and organisation for nineteenth-century Australian publishing and literary culture. Scholars have focused on metropolitan newspapers as fiction publishers, with most assuming that fiction was rare—if present at all—in provincial periodicals.[12] I have found, to the contrary, that more fiction appeared in provincial than in metropolitan newspapers: 55 percent of the extended nineteenth-century fiction publications identified. This proportion is made more remarkable by the underrepresentation of provincial newspapers in Trove, and the fact that they only started publishing fiction in earnest in the 1880s, whereas metropolitan newspapers began in earnest in the 1860s. Thus, the metropolitan newspapers that have received almost all the critical attention emerge as less prolific in their publication of fiction than their neglected provincial counterparts.

More significantly for Australian publishing history, metropolitan newspapers also emerge as less interconnected than provincial ones in how they sourced this fiction. Among the titles identified in Trove's digitised newspapers, it is not uncommon to find two or three, sometimes even four, metropolitan newspapers publishing the same overseas story around the same time. Not infrequently, tracing the publishing histories of these works confirms that they were syndicated by British or American companies and suggests that metropolitan newspaper editors strategically banded together to purchase particular international stories, or purchased stories individually and sold them on to other colonial newspapers. In contrast to these occasional metropolitan groupings, large clusters of provincial newspapers published many of the same titles, around the same time, and often in an identical sequence.

Figure 3 shows two examples of these groupings, in the form of excerpts from network graphs for different periods. In these graphs, a connection (or to use network terminology, an edge) between two newspapers indicates that they published a title or titles in common,

---

12 Two notable exceptions to this tendency are: Elizabeth Morrison, "Retrieving Colonial Literary Culture: The Case for an Index to Fiction in Australian (or Australasian?) Newspapers." Bibliographical Society of Australia and New Zealand Bulletin 13, no. 1 (1989): 27–36; Graham Law, "Savouring of the Australian Soil? On the Sources and Affiliations of Colonial Newspaper Fiction." Victorian Periodicals Review 37, no. 4 (Winter 2004): 75–97.

with the thickness of the line growing as the number of common titles increases. In this force-directed graph, the distance between different newspapers also relates to publishing patterns: specifically, the algorithm forces individual publications (or nodes) closer together the more they share links in common with other newspapers.

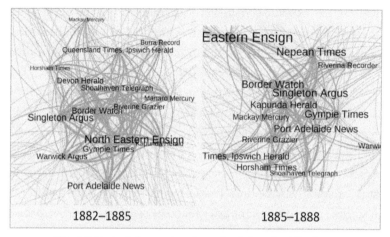

Figure 3. Excerpts from network graphs of shared publications,
1882 to 1885 and 1885 to 1888.

Based on these publishing patterns, detailed examination of publishing histories and newspaper pages identified eleven separate newspaper fiction syndicates operating in the Australian provincial press in the latter part of the nineteenth century. Only one of these had been known to publishing historians previously.[13] These syndicates operated in many cases across multiple colonies and could include seventy or more shared titles, and forty or more individual newspapers; and that is from a collection where under 30 percent of newspapers are digitised, and where provincial newspapers are underrepresented. In all probability,

---

13   Elizabeth Morrison, *Engines of Influence: Newspapers of Country Victoria*, 1840–1890, (Carlton: Melbourne University Press, 2005) 210–12, 253–56.

therefore, these syndicates were much more extensive than we have yet been able to discern. Significantly, when the circulations of these provincial newspapers are combined, the readership of many of these syndicated stories would have been as large as, if not considerably larger than, for fiction published in metropolitan venues.

Some of these syndicates published mostly international fiction, and may have been international enterprises with distribution networks in Australia or colonial enterprises that sourced their fiction primarily from overseas. But others published mostly Australian fiction, and at a scale that makes them—even individually—the most significant publishers of Australian writing in the nineteenth century, and probably up until the latter part of the twentieth century. For instance, in just four years, between 1880 and 1884, one of these syndicates serialised twenty-six Australian novels, plus an additional two that are almost certainly Australian. By comparison, AustLit records indicate that the most prolific local book publisher of this period—George Robertson—in thirty years (from 1860 to 1889) published only nine Australian novels.[14] Put simply, the prevalence of fiction in provincial newspapers and the operations of these syndicates indicate that publishing historians have been looking in the wrong place—to book publishers and metropolitan newspapers—when seeking to understand fiction publishing in the Australian colonies.

The fourth and final finding relates to the contents of these fictions, particularly the Australian titles. When considering thousands of novels and novellas, one cannot just read them: it would take decades. But digital methods offer new ways to explore and understand large collections of text. The approach I used combines a common method in digital literary studies, topic modelling,[15] with a method fairly widespread

---

14 Katherine Bode, *Reading by Numbers: Recalibrating the Literary Field* (London and New York: Anthem Press, 2012), 44.

15 See, for example, Andrew Goldstone and Ted Underwood, "The Quiet Transformations of Literary Studies: What Thirteen Thousand Scholars Could Tell Us," *New Literary History* 45, no. 3 (2014): 359–84.

in other disciplines (such as ecology and economics) but new to the analysis of literary works: decision trees. Both use machine-learning algorithms to sort data. The first sorts words from a large corpus into groups based on the likelihood that these words will appear in the same documents. The second identifies which of these word clusters or topics are most likely to appear in or to characterise fiction of a specific category (in this case, author nationality).

I combine these methods so as to align corpus-wide topics—lexically contextualised but separate from the literary works these word associations arise from—with historical categories of documents. Although the calculations are complex, this integrated approach resonates with a widespread understanding in literary studies of the way in which fiction and social forms relate: namely, that authors in particular social groups are likely to demonstrate certain literary tendencies. Showing that certain groups of words or topics tend to occur in women's fiction, for instance, does not mean that all women writers use these words, or that in all the women's writing that displays this characteristic the words appear with the same frequency. Rather, in indicating tendencies or inclinations in the type of literary language used by groups of authors, this integrated approach offers a way of employing quantitative methods without reducing literary meaning to them. Figure 4 shows the topic—or the most prominent 200 words in the topic—identified by this method as the most likely to characterise Australian fiction in nineteenth-century Australian newspapers.

The prominent words in this topic suggest what is commonly known as the bush tradition in Australian fiction: cattle, horses, creek, sheep, kangaroo, men. But other prominent words suggest a different bush tradition to the one we know: I am referring, here, to words such as township, veranda, buggy, homestead, station, on the one hand, and black, blacks, mob, tracks, on the other. Reading the individual stories where "Topic 80" is prominent confirms this idea. Where the bush tradition as we know it stands in opposition to domesticity—focusing on largely solitary bushmen with nonetheless intense male friendships or mateship—these stories are more likely to feature families in the bush and to be driven by emotional bonds between men, women and children. The illustration in Figure 5 is indicative of this feature of the fiction, in showing the dangers of the bush—here, as in many of these stories, a bushfire—being confronted by a man and woman together.

Topic80.txt

shepherd district homestead yards fence round kangaroo plains timber stations night blacks tea manverandah started rough sheep creek track swag shirt mob stock horses trees log dry wool horse owner camped riding plain gum country sun cattle plenty heat township tree hut bank rain huts squatter men river lot dogs dray gully coach fellow run cool tent colonial manager start buggy fiery party paddock overseer travelling tracks mate ride christmas lynch bushman grog feed range store bushrangers paddocks

Figure 4. The topic deemed by a decision tree algorithm most likely to characterise fiction by Australian authors in nineteenth-century Australian newspapers.

The timing of these stories also differs from established understandings of the bush tradition. Where that tradition is identified with the 1890s, these (computationally) characteristic Australian stories are present throughout the second half of the nineteenth century and, indeed, are slightly more common earlier in that period than later. But in terms of existing scholarship on the bush tradition, the most surprising aspect of these stories is their consistent and prominent depiction of Aboriginal characters.

Figure 5. Illustration accompanying "The Story of a Royal Pendulum" [#6966] by "Australie", published in the *Illustrated Sydney News* in 1891.

A central argument in Australian postcolonial literary studies is that, beginning in the nineteenth century, fiction replicated the legal lie of *terra nullius* by not depicting Australia's original inhabitants.[16] Yet these bush stories feature multiple Aboriginal characters. Most unambiguously affirm the colonial mission, either by depicting Aboriginal characters in harmonious and friendly relations with colonists, or by presenting them as savage or childish. But others describe complex, multi-layered interactions between colonists and Aboriginal people that lead white characters in the stories to question the colonial enterprise. Some depict such radically juxtaposed scenes of violence and purported friendship between colonial and Aboriginal characters that they must

---

16 See, for example, Ken Gelder, "Australian Gothic," in *The Routledge Companion to Gothic*, eds. Catherine Spooner and Emma McEvoy (London: Routledge, 2007), 115–23; Stephanie Trigg, "Introduction," in *Medievalism and the Gothic in Australian Culture*, ed. Stephanie Trigg (Carlton: Melbourne University Press, 2005), xi–xxiii.

surely have prompted the same thoughts in at least some of their white readers. These representations of Aboriginal characters are still profoundly racist. But they suggest that the conception of Aboriginal people as excluded from Australian fiction is an effect of subsequent publishing, editorial and critical practices, not of the type of fiction written and read by Australians throughout the nineteenth century.

These four findings demonstrate the capacity of new digital collections and methods to enable new insights into the history of publishing. In this case, they provide the basis for recognising nineteenth-century Australian newspapers—particularly provincial ones—as incredibly active and prolific fiction publishers. These periodicals were connected to global systems—cultural and economic—publishing fiction from around the world and, in the case of metropolitan newspapers, actively sourcing it from a range of British and American syndication agencies. But such publishing was also distinctively local, adaptive and independent. Australian newspapers featured an extensive amount of Australian fiction—and editors often foregrounded its presence. These newspapers, particularly provincial ones, were part of economic and cultural networks that arose in the colonies to source fiction internationally as well as to provide local opportunities for local authors. And they published stories that were distinctively Australian: of the bush, but offering a bush tradition not restricted to depicting white men.

Data Publishing in Publishing Studies

I began this chapter by discussing how digital publishing studies require us to combine existing disciplinary knowledge and expertise with new research practices relating to digital infrastructure and data provenance and construction. To end, I want to consider another—arguably more fundamental—change we need to undertake when employing digital technologies for publishing studies: data publication. My overarching claim in this final section is that grounding publishing studies on large-scale data requires that we rethink foundational issues of argumentation, sustainability and access.

These issues are fundamentally bound up together. But prior to the digital age, publishing scholars—indeed, humanities scholars in general—have typically made their arguments with reference to evidence held by cultural institutions and/or created by publishers. Thus, we have been able to delegate all but the construction of our argument to others without having to give much thought to sustainability and accessibility. When arguments are based on data, this approach is no longer sufficient. For my project, for instance, I cannot point to Trove and say there is the evidence, because the historical moment in which Carol and I interrogated Trove, and the transformations we subsequently wrought on that evidence, are constitutive of the arguments I am able to offer. Constructing literary data also involves so much labour (and often, so much public funding) and if done well, adds so much value, that we abdicate our scholarly responsibility to the collaborative accumulation of knowledge if we fail to publish—and thus to make available, sustainable and accessible—the basis of our arguments.

Data publishing, then, cannot be an optional extra. But how we perform this activity—and how we involve publishers, cultural institutions and the general public in the process—is something that we, as a field, need to give a lot more thought to moving forward. For the sustainability of my newspaper fiction project, I have lodged all the data I explore in my forthcoming book with the publishers, the University of Michigan Press. This data will appear under a creative commons license, alongside an open-access version of the monograph.[17] But not many humanities scholars can use raw

---

17 Katherine Bode, *A World of Fiction: Digital Collections and the Future of Literary History*. Open Access Version (University of Michigan Press, 2018), https://www.fulcrum.org/concern/monographs/5q47rp73f

data. The To Be Continued database attempts to solve this issue of accessibility. It publishes all of the data we collected—not just the titles I investigate in the book—with an interface that enables users to explore fiction in nineteenth- and early twentieth-century Australian newspapers by title, author, gender, nationality, newspaper, and date, and by searching full text records. To Be Continued is also linked to Trove, so that users can view stories *in situ*, on the digitised newspaper page. Data can also be exported, with users able to choose whether to download the entire database, or a subset, of bibliographical metadata and full-text records.

With these two forms of publication I feel that—in collaboration with my publisher and my institution—I have fulfilled the requirements of data sustainability and accessibility, at least into the medium term. But there is significant potential to approach data publishing in ways that not only fulfil basic requirements but extend the possibilities of what publishing in publishing studies might offer or enable. I have sought to explore these possibilities in three ways. Most basically, as well as allowing me to publish the basis of my arguments, the To Be Continued database offers a resource for future arguments. Perhaps a literary scholar is interested in Russian author Ivan Turgenev. She can use the database to explore instances where his fiction was published in the Australian colonies and how it was presented to audiences via the paratexts. To extend the example, she might investigate what other Russian authors appear in the database, and on this basis, explore whether, and if so how, the framework of Russian literature was mobilised in the Australian colonies. A periodical scholar might examine whether the publication of Russian fiction was limited to particular newspapers or widespread, and the social or political implications of this pattern; a textual scholar could investigate the translations used and the insights these offer into the sources of such fiction.

Or to give another example, this time for Australian literary studies, among many other new titles, the To Be Continued database contains two previously unknown iterations of the city mysteries genre. Begun with Eugene Sue's "The Mysteries of Paris" in 1842,[18] this genre encompasses adaptations throughout the nineteenth century for multiple cities including Amsterdam, Berlin, Boston, Lyon and more. A "Mysteries of Melbourne Life" from 1872 was known prior to our analysis of Trove's digitised newspapers; but the two Australian city mysteries thereby discovered predate this publication: by two years in the case of another Melbourne mystery ("Mysteries of Melbourne" [#14468]), and by more than two decades for "The Mysteries of Sydney" [#6498], published in *Bell's Life* in 1850. These two stories, alone, could form the basis for a rich research project. As with so much of the colonial fiction discovered in nineteenth-century Australian newspapers, these city mysteries—including the by-line of the earliest, as "Not by the author of 'The Mysteries of Paris' or 'The Mysteries of London' but by One of Ourselves"—connect to and emerge out of a transnational market, while also emphasising local authorship and distinctively colonial forms of expression.

As already noted, there are over 21,000 novels, novellas and short stories. This chapter—like my book—only explores trends in a little over 9,200 of them. For the nineteenth-century, this leaves thousands of short stories that, in the vast majority of cases, no one has considered in the Australian context, if at all. As for the thousands of short and extended stories identified in the early twentieth century, to my knowledge no previous research recognises that fiction continued to feature in newspapers at this time, let alone that its publication was so extensive. This collection of fiction, in other words, has the potential to support many more new discoveries in and understandings of the history of fiction publishing in Australia and the transnational circulation of fiction in the nineteenth and early twentieth centuries. To enable this future research, the database is editable, meaning users

---

18   Sue's novel was also serialised in an Australian newspaper, the *Geelong Advertiser and Squatters' Advocate*, four years later, in 1846.

can improve the information in existing records as well as add new instalments or entirely new stories from Trove's digitised newspapers.

A second way I have sought to extend what is possible for data publishing in publishing studies is by working with collaborators from Trove, especially Julia Hickie and Victoria Riddell, to capture these records. Trove has now harvested all the stories in the To Be Continued database, adding over 21,000 records to the NLA's online catalogue. Any stories that are subsequently added to the database will also be represented in this way. As far as I am aware, this is the first digital humanities project, internationally, to close what we might call the humanities data circle, demonstrating how a major national digital collection can both provide the basis for humanities research and draw on the results of that research to enrich its records. This approach is also another step in the sustainability of research data, in that Trove and the NLA are likely to long outlast the To Be Continued database.

I have been talking about sustainability and access for researchers. But of course, thousands of members of the public use Trove. Many spend countless hours, in particular, correcting errors in the OCR generated newspaper text. The third and final way I have sought to extend the possibilities of data publishing for publishing studies is by enabling any member of the public to use To Be Continued and Trove to read and correct fiction, where necessary to identify and add missing instalments, and to discover and add new stories to the database. These stories can be exported from the database, and published in an open-access text repository; and I am also exploring possibilities for creating publication platform to facilitate and enhance this process. There is so much—particularly Australian—fiction in To Be Continued that has never been published outside of the newspaper pages that members of the public have many opportunities to create their own first edition of a forgotten Australian work. As well as improving the quality of records and text in Trove and To

Be Continued, the crowd-sourcing features of the database present considerable opportunities for making available and curating the works of out-of-print or marginalised subjects. Alternatively, newly discovered works could be published by a print publisher, as Obiter Press has done with collections of fiction by Catherine Martin and Australian Christmas stories, previously unpublished outside the newspaper pages.[19] These are the first two in a planned series of collections of newly discovered Australian fiction, with a collection of gold mining fiction forthcoming, and future possibilities including convict stories, rural romances or cricket writing (all categories fulsomely represented in the database).

Clearly, publishing data represents a lot of additional—and different—work to that which we are accustomed to in publishing studies. And it requires that we take responsibility for demonstrating not only the foundations of our arguments, but for making those foundations sustainable and accessible to others: tasks that, as researchers, we have previously been able to relegate to publishers and cultural institutions. However, digital publishing studies can only progress—responsibly and effectively—if we take these steps. And as I hope I have shown, as well as fulfilling a basic requirement, data publication has the potential to forge new connections between publishers, publishing scholars, researchers in a range of academic disciplines, and in cultural institutions as well as members of the public. In these ways and others, digital technologies open up new possibilities for publishing studies, including new forms of exploration and understanding, and new communities with whom to share this process of discovery.

---

19 Katherine Bode and Imelda Whelehan, eds. *"Christmas Eve in a Gum Tree" and Other Lost Australian Stories* (Canberra: Obiter Press, 2018).

Works cited

Barrier Miner. "'Marjory's Mistake': Another Original Story for the 'Miner'."
   April 22, 1895, 3, nla.gov.au/nla.news-article44167084.

Bode, Katherine. *A World of Fiction: Digital Collections and the Future of Literary
   History.* Ann Arbor: University of Michigan Press, 2018.

———. *Reading by Numbers: Recalibrating the Literary Field.* London and New
   York: Anthem Press, 2012.

———, ed. *"How I Pawned My Opals" and Other Lost Stories by Catherine
   Martin.* Canberra: Obiter Press, 2017.

———, and Carol Hetherington, eds. "To Be Continued...": The Australian
   Newspaper Fiction Database. Updated 2017. http://cdhrdatasys.anu.edu.
   au/tobecontinued/.

———, and Imelda Whelehan, eds. *"Christmas Eve in a Gum Tree" and Other
   Lost Australian Stories* (Canberra: Obiter Press, 2018)

Cordell, Ryan, and David Smith. The Viral Texts Project: Mapping Networks of
   Reprinting in 19th-Century Newspapers and Magazines. n.d.
   http://viraltexts.org/.

Gelder, Ken. "Australian Gothic." In *The Routledge Companion to Gothic*, edited
   by Catherine Spooner and Emma McEvoy, 115–123. London: Routledge,
   2007.

Goldstone, Andrew, and Ted Underwood "The Quiet Transformations of
   Literary Studies: What Thirteen Thousand Scholars Could Tell Us." *New
   Literary History* 45, no. 3 (2014): 359–84.

Law, Graham "Savouring of the Australian Soil? On the Sources and
   Affiliations of Colonial Newspaper Fiction." Victorian Periodicals Review
   37, no. 4 (Winter 2004): 75–97.

Morrison, Elizabeth. *Engines of Influence: Newspapers of Country Victoria, 1840–
   1890.* Carlton: Melbourne University Press, 2005.

———, "Retrieving Colonial Literary Culture: The Case for an Index to Fiction
   in Australian (or Australasian?) Newspapers." Bibliographical Society of
   Australia and New Zealand Bulletin 13, no. 1 (1989): 27–36.

———. "Serial Fiction in Australian Colonial Newspapers." In *Literature in the
   Marketplace: Nineteenth-Century British Publishing and Reading Practices*,
   eds. John O. Jordan and Robert L. Patten, 306–24. Cambridge: Cambridge
   University Press, 1998.

National Library of Australia. Trove Newspapers. n.d. https://trove.nla.gov.au/
   newspaper/.

Nutt, Amy Ellis. "Wonder Woman Lived: Viking Warrior Skeleton Identified as Female, 128 Years After its Discovery." *Washington Post*, September 14, 2017. https://www.washingtonpost.com/news/speaking-of-science/wp/2017/09/14/wonder-woman-lives-viking-warrior-skeleton-identified-as-female-128-years-after-its-discovery/?utm_term=.f5af1b0621bc.

Smith, David A., Ryan Cordell, and Abby Mullen. "Computational Methods for Uncovering Reprinted Texts in Antebellum Newspapers." *American Literary History* 27, no. 3 (2015): E1–E15.

Stinson, Elizabeth. "Want to be a Space Archaeologist? Here's Your Chance." *Wired,* January 30, 2017. https://www.wired.com/2017/01/want-space-archaeologist-heres-chance/.

Trigg, Stephanie. "Introduction." In *Medievalism and the Gothic in Australian Culture*, edited by Stephanie Trigg, xi–xxiii. Carlton: Melbourne University Press, 2005.

Webby, Elizabeth. "Colonial Writers and Readers." In *The Cambridge Companion to Australian Literature*, edited by Elizabeth Webby, 50–73. Cambridge: Cambridge University Press, 2000.

Chapter 2

From Cultural Entrepreneurs to an Apprenticeship Practice

Examining Legacy Effects through Three Case Studies:

Arcade Publications (2007–12),
The Lifted Brow (est. 2007),
The Bowen Street Press (est. 2016)

Tracy O'Shaughnessy, Rose Michael and Ronnie Scott

Introduction

Small independent start-up presses have always been instrumental in providing a platform and offering apprenticeships for many of Australia's publishing professionals—from writers and editors to other emerged and emerging positions. The disruption of the 1970s—changes in book trade practices (the abolition of resale price maintenance and rights allowing the production of local editions of many US-originated books) and technology (the increasing affordability of offset, and ultimately offshore, printing)—paved the way for the "emergence of a swag of pacesetting independent publishers, such as Outback Press, Lonely Planet and McPhee Gribble".[1] The 'aughts' disruptors—again, changes in trade practices (self-publishing and globalisation) and technology (print-on-demand and ebooks)—created another wave of entrepreneurship and opportunity.

---

1   Jim Hart, "New Wave Seventies," in *Paper Empires: A History of the Book in Australia*, ed. Craig Munro (Brisbane: University of Queensland Press, 2006), 53.

Small independent presses are agile and experimental and, of necessity and inclination, take risks on new writers and innovative ideas. The individuals involved develop varied skill sets and learn on the job in an iterative process of experiential learning—wherein concrete experience and reflective observation are synthesised into conceptual understanding, leading, in turn, to active experimentation—that has always underpinned the publishing profession.[2] As Thompson notes, "The publishing industry—both in literary agencies and in publishing houses—remains largely an apprentice-based industry."[3] Our key point is that this process is an evolution of, and variation on, formal and informal apprenticeship practices often associated with other trades.

We are three academics from RMIT University who teach into The Bowen Street Press. Established in 2016, The Bowen Street Press is the student-led teaching imprint operating within and out of RMIT's Master of Writing and Publishing. Rose Michael (co-founder of Arcade Publications) and Ronnie Scott (founder of The Lifted Brow) teach writing, editing and research courses that support the press, while Tracy O'Shaughnessy (previously publisher at Melbourne University Press and Allen & Unwin) is publisher.

In 2017 we undertook the case studies presented here to reflect on our personal experience of skills acquisition via on-the-job learning in publishing, and document how we drew on the specific form of these apprenticeship experiences—"entrepreneurships" if you will—to create the model that underpins The Bowen Street Press. A spirit of entrepreneurial initiative is the foundation for the work-integrated-learning student experience of The Bowen Street Press. Our model emphasises independent and collaborative problem-solving, and is predicated on the principle of learning by doing. We see these as

---

2   David A. Kolb, *Experiential Learning* (New Jersey: Pearson Education, 2015).
3   John B. Thompson, *Merchants of Culture: The Publishing Business in the Twenty-First Century, 2nd ed.* (Cambridge: Polity Press, 2012), 78.

"legacy skills" insofar as they represent a valuable inheritance, not a superseded software.

Our own experience as publishers and culture entrepreneurs—including the accidents and emergencies that typify entrepreneurial publishing—enabled us to build specific skills and establish practices that we still rely on today in our work as writers, editors, publishers and teachers. This chapter explores the different approaches taken by our respective start-ups (including key drivers for forming a start-up, such as perceived opportunity, impetus and the importance of community); details the findings (articulating an apprenticeship model built on a process of iterative work and experiential learning); and summarises the benefit accrued by cultural entrepreneurship and apprenticeship practices—for individual editors and publishers, and the vitality of the publishing industry.

Case Studies

The Lifted Brow, now more than ten years old, is a literary organisation that started out as a journal and has recently expanded into book publishing as Brow Books. It is well known for its mixed focus on genre fiction, experimental and lyric forms of nonfiction, high and popular culture, visual arts, comics, and music; for a character distinctive in Australian publishing and initially influenced by mid-aughts US publishing organisations such as McSweeney's; and, initially, for its independence from government or institutional funding. In this chapter, we focus on its establishment and early growth period, from 2007–12.

Describing itself first as a "journal of letters, arts, sciences, etc." and soon after as "an attack journal"—a subtitle dropped and then reinstituted by later editors—*The Lifted Brow* originally brought out two issues a year, first a substantial saddle-stitched zine and then perfect-bound A5 journals. It moved on to a newsprint format, publishing six issues a year, and now comes out quarterly in a perfect-bound, magazine-style format on matte uncoated paper. The book publishing arm launched its first novel in 2016 and, in 2017, sold international rights to its second.

The Lifted Brow has been a significant publication/brand/presence/ platform in both Brisbane and Melbourne, the two cities it has made its home, and has been identified as a member of the renaissance of the litmag movement in Phillip Edmonds's *Tilting at Windmills: The Literary Magazine in Australia 1968–2012.*[4] According to the *Times Literary Supplement,* the organisation is "provocative, contrary, historically literate and unremittingly idealistic".[5]

Arcade Publications was a "micro" press that ran for the same period, from 2007–12. It published a dozen titles during that time, the content of which largely consisted of mini-biographies of unconventional characters from Melbourne's history—such as bookseller, publisher and builder of our well-known book arcade, E.W. Cole; brothel owner, Madame Brussels; and Fitzroy chocolatier, Macpherson Robertson—as well as broader histories such as *The Making of Modern Melbourne, Melbourne Remade, Hoax Nation,* and a collection of Oslo Davis's "Melbourne Overheard" column.

In keeping with its slogan, "small books, big stories", Arcade published practically palm-sized A6 editions. Most were mono-colour productions, printed digitally and locally. The press also experimented with early ebooks—embedding video files and distributing PDFs direct at a higher-than-usual price point—and became well known for its events, such as walking tours that ran during the Melbourne Writers Festival, in conjunction with Hidden Secrets Tours, which the press shared an office with in the famous Nicholas Building.

---

4   Phillip Edmonds, *Tilting at Windmills: The Literary Magazine in Australia 1968–2012* (Adelaide: University of Adelaide Press, 2015).

5   Houman Barekat, "Ribbons of Argument," *Times Literary Supplement,* October 25, 2017, https://www.the-tls.co.uk/articles/private/ribbons-of-argument-lifted-brow/.

According to Simon Caterson, Arcade "identified a gap in the market for short, inexpensive, carefully designed books covering aspects of Melbourne's hitherto unexplored history".[6]

Tracy O'Shaughnessy, a trade publisher with many years' experience, developed her craft through a wide-ranging apprenticeship practice across a host of small-to-medium-sized presses (John Ferguson Publishing, Lesley McKay Publishing, Susan McCulloch Publishing, Lothian Books, Reed Books, Hardie Grant Books, Melbourne University Press, and Allen & Unwin). Starting as a publisher's assistant, she worked within both the editorial and production disciplines, learning on the job and being mentored by her community (both peers and elders). She used her own apprenticeship experience to establish The Bowen Street Press, the student-led teaching press operating within and running out of RMIT's Master of Writing and Publishing, in 2016. It is a compulsory subject: an inclusive internship program. This vertically integrated "studio" is supported by complementary technical and theoretical subjects (echoing the way entry-level publishing employees learn the broader cultural context of their business from meetings and conversations—which they may participate in or simply be witness to). It is a pedagogical practice explicitly based on the on-the-job learning that Tracy recognised as having been the cornerstone of her own industry experience. First- and second-year students come together on a range of projects for a full day's work each week in a dedicated office space, and there is a stated expectation that the cohort will spend the same amount of time doing independently directed activity—such as content creation (writing and sourcing images) or book production (structural and copyediting, proofreading, collating corrections, press checks, etc.).

---

6   Simon Caterson, "From Little Ventures Small Wonders Emerge," *The Age*, January 24, 2009, https://www.theage.com.au/entertainment/books/from-little-ventures-small-wonders-emerge-20090124-ge7n2x.html.

During their time in The Bowen Street Press students work across diverse projects in a wide variety of genres, including fiction, non-fiction, journals, anthologies, poetry and digital publishing (iBooks/web-based content). They work with industry mentors, RMIT programs and not-for-profits to produce a suite of publications in various formats, from colour to black-and-white, custom publishing ventures to websites and marketing materials. They assume different roles in different publishing departments at different stages throughout their degree. By the end of its second year the press had published twenty titles, ranging from handmade zines to issues of *Rabbit* poetry journal, as well as academic research collections and trade catalogues.

The common ground between Arcade Publications and The Lifted Brow, as cultural enterprises, and then The Bowen Street Press, as both a cultural enterprise and a teaching press, is the collection of skills learned on the job, how they are passed between practitioners, and how they are used to publish books and magazines. The remainder of this chapter examines the makeup of this on-the-job learning and suggests it can collectively be called an apprenticeship practice, a model common to publishing—an industry typified by individual initiative and ad hoc opportunities.

Methodology

Key Drivers

Start-ups, as most small independent presses initially are, have always been an important part of the Australian publishing community. In the early 1970s Australian publishing experienced one of its most exciting periods with the aforementioned emergence of Hart's "pacesetting independent publishers", whose influences can still be seen today.[7] There were, among others, Outback Press (founded by Morrie Schwartz, who

---

7   Hart, "New Wave Seventies," 53.

went on to set up Black Inc.), Lonely Planet (the venture of Maureen and Jim Wheeler, patrons of The Wheeler Centre), and McPhee Gribble (the initiative of Hilary McPhee and Diana Gribble; the latter whom went on to play a key role in the establishment of Text Publishing).

These cultural entrepreneurs, fresh out of their university degrees, took advantage of the foundations laid down by their predecessors in the 1950s and 60s, and this—coupled with shifts in trade practices and copyright—created an environment ripe for experimentation and growth. According to Magner, this boom in local publishing "continued well into the 1970s with the value of Australian publishing doubling three times over the period 1961–1979".[8]

The impact of small, independent presses on the industry's ecosystem has been historically significant (think of Greenhouse, Allen & Unwin, Text, Scribe, Hardie Grant, Affirm, Spinifex, Kill Your Darlings, etc.), and this influence continues today. As The Lifted Brow has been identified as part of a resurgence of "litmags",[9] so Arcade was described by Caterson as coming at a time when the Melbourne micro-publishing scene "was very attractive. Dozens of tiny publishers are producing everything from handmade recipe books, fiction and poetry to popular nonfiction and even book-like objects that defy classification."[10]

According to *Forbes*, the American business magazine focused on finance, investing and marketing, the essential elements for a successful start-up are strategic perspective, being cash conservative, customers and commitment, integrity and transparency.[11] Translating these

---

8   Brigid Magner, "Anglo-Australian Relations in the Book Trade," in *Paper Empires: A History of the Book in Australia*, ed. Craig Munro (Brisbane: University of Queensland Press, 2006), 7.

9   Edmonds, *Tilting at Windmills*.

10   Caterson, "From Little Ventures Small Wonders Emerge."

11   Cheryl Conner, "5 Sure Signs a Start-Up Firm Will Succeed," *Forbes*, July 12, 2012, https://www.forbes.com/sites/cherylsnappconner/2012/07/12/5-sure-signs-a-startup-firm-will-succeed/#1cd949d9c1da.

elements into a publishing context, we have analysed our start-ups through the lens of perceived opportunity, impetus, and community.

Discussion

Perceived Opportunity

For Ronnie Scott and the small group of Arts students at Queensland University of Technology with whom he established *The Lifted Brow* in 2006 (to be launched in January 2007), there was a shared perception that few literary magazines were being published in Brisbane—and that there was a gap in the market nationally for non-traditional content and unconventional genres.

That same year, further south, lecturers Rose Michael and Dale Campisi started publishing from the office they shared at the University of Melbourne, similarly believing they saw a unique opportunity—in their case, for books that blurred the distinction between storytelling and history. They believed, as Allen Lane did, in the existence of a reading public (which did not need to be vast) for low-price small-format books—which, they thought, would be designed around, and appreciated for, their content rather than aesthetics.[12] The pair believed larger publishers were making unnecessarily conservative choices—in terms of authorship and format—in response to commercial pressures, such as the impending Global Financial Crisis and collapse of Borders, which would lead to its ill-conceived purchase by Pacific Equity Partners. They were convinced there was room for a different kind of quick, cheap, creative publishing.

A decade later two main factors prompted the establishment of The Bowen Street Press: the launch of the RMIT's new Master of Writing and Publishing—incorporating the university's well-respected Graduate

---

12 Anne Trubeck, "How the Paperback Novel Changed Popular Literature," *Smithsonian*, March 30, 2010, https://www.smithsonianmag.com/arts-culture/how-the-paperback-novel-changed-popular-literature-11893941/.

Diploma in Editing and Publishing, which was established in 1988 as the inaugural higher-education editorial qualification in Australia—and the diminishing capacity of the industry to offer traditional in-house editorial apprenticeships.[13] Informed by her twenty years of industry experience across a number of the independent publishers cited here as stalwarts of the trade, Tracy O'Shaughnessy developed a program based on a formal apprenticeship model—enabled by the establishment of Australia's first functional teaching press—designed to mirror industry best practice.[14]

For Ronnie and Rose, a degree of "productive" ignorance played an important part in their perception of opportunity: if they'd had more industry experience, or an awareness of prevailing market conditions, they might have been dissuaded from their enterprises at the outset. If Ronnie's peers had known where to publish revisionist historical fiction and speculative fiction in rhyming couplets, they may not have persevered with launching a platform themselves; if Rose had been able to find creative curated tales in bespoke, bookish packages, she may not have ventured into publishing.

The Impetus

But it wasn't only a (possible) gap in the market that prompted these start-ups; it was also a desire on the part of the individuals in question not just to produce something, but to be part of that production experience. While Tracy had been lucky enough to have a traditional apprenticeship, and was keen to provide that opportunity to future publishing professionals in turn, both Ronnie and Rose felt no such options were available to them at that time. Instead, they took it upon themselves to learn by doing, involving friends and partners in their

---

13 Louise Poland, "The Business, Craft and Profession of the Book Editor," in *Making Books: Contemporary Australian Publishing*, eds. David Carter and Anne Galligan (Brisbane: University of Queensland Press, 2007), 107.

14 Jean Lave and Etienne Wenger, *Situated Learning: Legitimate Peripheral Participation* (Cambridge: Cambridge University Press, 1991).

ambitious endeavours. According to Paul Carter, material thinking—thinking through doing—and collaboration between peers are natural bedfellows; indeed, collaboration "is what begins to happen whenever artists talk about what they are doing, in that simple but enigmatic step, joining hand, eye and mind in a process of material thinking".[15]

There was a strong wish on the part of all three authors to work the way they wanted to—which was not necessarily according to convention. These publishers' acts of cultural entrepreneurship sprang not only from political, personal and aesthetic convictions, but from the simple pleasure of making creative cultural artefacts with others, which was quickly followed by a wish to keep on doing and developing that. The fun of first projects kept all three publishers going, extending perceived opportunity and impetus into ongoing professional concerns.

In a 2002 interview with Eve Vincent, Gribble noted that, "Publishing in Australia was a real boys' club: they were intelligent, beer-drinking blokes. And women were editors and secretaries and publicity people, but they weren't publishers."[16] For all three of our authors there was an active desire to propagate a diversity of voices as well as provide an opportunity for those words to be read.

The Community

Authors

For The Lifted Brow the city of Brisbane offered "Goldilocks" conditions. It proved just right for the formation of a literary enterprise: it was large enough to support a venture like *The Lifted Brow* but small enough that the market was not crowded. It was possible to create

---

15 Paul Carter, *Material Thinking: The Theory and Practice of Creative Research* (Melbourne: Melbourne University Press, 2004), xiii.

16 Elizabeth Howcroft, Eric Beecher and Michael Heyward, "Gribble, Diana (Di) (1942–2011)," *Obituaries Australia*, October 22, 2011, http://oa.anu.edu.au/obituary/gribble-diana-di-16650/text28549.

and sustain a literary journal consisting of writing by non-writers (i.e. friends and acquaintances who did not aspire to write professionally), diverse visual material (including comics), and—from the second issue and in intermittent issues thereafter—music in the form of CDs, which included commissions from local bands. For those involved—the editors, illustrators, designer, regular and irregular contributors—the project formalised an established practice of hanging out and conducting literary activities—like reading nights that sometimes were and sometimes were not connected to institutions such as universities, writers festivals and bookstores.

In Melbourne, Dale and Rose had discussed publishing fiction for some time; unable to find the right manuscript they began—as The Lifted Brow had—to approach friends and acquaintances (fellow academics, generally) who they thought would have good stories that the duo could help tell. Unbeknownst to them then, this is how most publishers begin commissioning nonfiction: by approaching industry experts, frequently through personal connections. Arcade's first title would be by Lisa Lang, who was writing a novel about the author of Cole's Funny Picture Books at the time and whom Dale knew from Deakin University connections (*Utopian Man* would go on to co-win the Allen & Unwin/Vogel award). Arcade asked her to write a brief history of the man himself from the extensive research she had undertaken, and set about securing a City of Melbourne grant as an author fee. The rest, as they say, is (micro)history.

The Bowen Street Press gets its authors and projects from a broader range of sources, but they too tend to come through the publisher's personal and professional connections: there are student anthologies from RMIT's undergraduate (creative writing and professional communication) and postgraduate (communication design and communication) programs; publishing proposals passed on from smaller presses (in particular, authors whose projects are not viable in a commercial environment); and books for not-for-profits, such as the wellbeing book *Hearts in Mind,* produced for Darebin City Council's Mindful Art Project.

Readers

From the beginning The Lifted Brow's community of contributors, subscribers and one-off readers was sourced partly from a "traditional" literary community—people who found literary magazines in bookstores, at reading nights and writers festivals—and partly from a broader community of musicians, fans and visual artists. Its editors became aware that the magazine was selling outside a trade market, and began to see it as a publication that occupied a non-traditional market position, which, in turn, influenced the kind of work being produced for and published in *The Lifted Brow's* pages. As an early point of difference, the editors decided—at first informally, but it was then articulated more formally—that content would not relate to the practice of creative writing, i.e. no "writing about writing". This is one example of a creative decision that was made on the fly, which then became policy and stood the magazine in good stead with its readers.

The readership of The Bowen Street Press varies with each title, but largely falls into two categories: the creative communities of the individuals involved, who are for the most part writers and artists, and niche communities that are identified by or identify with a particular publication—such as *Silver Linings: True Stories of Resilience from a General Practitioner,* which has sold over two thousand copies (a respectable print run for a small press with no formal distribution network) through targeted bookshop and local community sales.

As with the other presses, Arcade Publications' readers were also its contributors—writers and illustrators etc.—and their friends. Unusually, for a book publisher, these individuals made it clear they were committed to the imprint, rather than specific titles or even authors—they asked whether they couldn't subscribe to the press, as they might to a literary magazine like *The Lifted Brow*, saying they trusted the publishers to create and curate a list. Basically, they were offering to crowdfund future titles by pre-ordering sight unseen. That brand loyalty showed the imprint's popularity and possible significance for the community it came from and published into.

In retrospect, the Arcade venture was most successful where it challenged extant processes and changed the conventional economic model by moving from a traditional sale-or-return deal with an established distributor, through individual firm-sale arrangements with non-traditional book outlets, towards direct-to-consumer sales at events (where the buy-before-publication idea was mooted). By the time their "business" model had evolved in this way, Dale and Rose had learnt that they were not that interested in distribution or sales—let alone chasing payments. As well as teaching what you want to do, and how to do it, an apprenticeship is an effective way of learning what you don't want to do. It became clear to the pair that they were drawn to the conception and creation side of bookmaking: writing, editing, design and production.

The diverse, yet not so dissimilar, audiences of these three publishers evidence what Emmett Stinson has described as "prosumer" culture: "contemporary literary audiences are increasingly made up of prosumers who are themselves engaged in the creation or mediation of literary works".[17] The communities reached by smaller—and especially the very smallest—publications are, to a considerable degree, composed of readers who already have some connection to the literary sphere: as writers, editors and publishers, or those who aspire to such positions (such as students in creative writing programs, members of writers' centres and the like). The participatory audiences of the presses we have been investigating play(ed) a key part in the success of each.

---

17   Emmett Stinson, "Small Publishers and the Emerging Network of Australian Literary Prosumption," *Australian Humanities Review* 59 (April/May 2016): 33.

Findings

Apprenticeships

Neither The Lifted Brow nor Arcade Publishing was established as a learning opportunity for its staff, and they never evolved into "proper" apprenticeships for Ronnie or Rose. Few if any of the key players in these start-ups had any formal training in editing and publishing; running the organisations constituted that training. In this way these presses satisfy Lave and Wenger's definition of an apprenticeship model—providing an opportunity to learn "through interactions between individuals, cultural tools and social communities"[18]—and this chapter argues for their recognition as an incidental amalgam of apprenticeship practices: collections of activities that constitute a range of experience, which, when recognised and recorded, can be passed on.

Early editions of *The Lifted Brow* were produced and edited primarily by undergraduate creative writing students. There was no formal process. The editing of each piece constituted a form of peer-to-peer mentorship, with an inexperienced editor (or sometimes more than one) negotiating the final form of a work through various versions with an often more experienced writer. These editorial practices were effectively on-the-job training, some of which built on skills formally acquired via a degree program—such as a second-year subject focused on the writer–editor relationship at Queensland University of Technology—but most of which evolved through a process of trial and error, where the process was a key part of what was learnt, as much as any final expertise.

Only the designer, who also worked part-time in-house for a non-publishing business, had relevant specialist tertiary training (interestingly, this was the same for Arcade).

---

18 Lave and Wenger, *Situated Learning*.

Between the fourth and fifth issues of *The Lifted Brow*, the staff was reduced to one and the magazine began to take on volunteers in specific roles—as publicists, proofreaders, guest editors, special project officers and interns. From that time on more traditional mentorship structures began to emerge, generally clustered around a small group of tasks, a specific day of the week, and a limited span of time. Slowly The Lifted Brow developed the larger, clearer structure that it has today, where many editors work within different arms of the organisation.

The editors at Arcade developed hard and soft skills through the same organic, responsive process: developing author contracts (with the help of the brother of one of the founders, who was a barrister) and researching territorial rights (when an advertisement in *Think Australian* unexpectedly produced interest) as the need arose. As at The Lifted Brow, there were many mistakes that proved extremely educational: those involved learnt that books were printed in sixteen-page sections when an edition came back from the printer with blank pages at the end, and discovered the long lead time for selling-in to traditional channels when their distributor demanded marketing materials in advance of manuscripts.

These relationships with career printers and distributors—combined with the way Arcade's two editors and two designers (who now constituted its four directors) shared knowledge and resources—provided a contemporary, collaborative, peer-networking version of an old-school, top-down traditional apprenticeship.

The Bowen Street Press, in contrast, was consciously established according to an apprenticeship model in order to provide students with an opportunity to learn-by-interning. Mirroring Tracy's own career—from assistant (first to a managing director and then to the production department) to editor, and ultimately a publishing role—The Bowen Street Press studio cycles individuals through different projects each semester and, over the course of their degree, typical publishing departments. Students acquire technical skills and practical experience in the same way that she did: by receiving mentoring from more experienced editors (whether second-years, already-employed peers or tutors). They learn what can go wrong, and how to make things right—a large part of publishing is, after all, problem-solving—via an iterative process of continual making.

For every hard skill—such as copyediting, proofreading, laying out pages or seeking copyright permissions—there is an equally important soft skill that future producers need to master: from basic professional communication to diplomacy, persuasiveness, resourcefulness and time management. Academic understanding is not necessarily the only or, indeed, most effective way to develop such subtle but essential attributes for a career in our industry, which is so fundamentally based on relationships.

By contrast with The Lifted Brow and Arcade Publications, The Bowen Street Press is intentionally structured as an apprenticeship practice, conceived and communicated to students as such by Tracy—as providing an opportunity to learn "through interactions between individuals, cultural tools and social communities".[19] The pedagogical approach that underpins The Bowen Street Press's iterative process—where skills are acquired on a case-by-case basis—reflects Kolb's "Cycle of Experiential Learning":[20] experiences suit the learner and are supported by reflection, critical analysis and synthesis; experiences are structured for the learner to take initiative, make decisions and be accountable. At every stage, the learner is actively engaged in posing questions, investigating, experimenting, being curious, solving problems, assuming responsibility, being creative and constructing meaning.

Learning that progresses in line with Kolb's cycle (from concrete experience to reflective observation to abstract conceptualisation to

---

19   Ibid.
20   Kolb, *Experiential Learning*.

active experimentation) both reflects the way our industry works—as producers move from project to project—and is well suited to the current challenging publishing context.

The cycle of experiential learning can be seen in action through an itemisation of the task of checking corrections in The Bowen Street Press—a seemingly simple activity that in fact involves a mix of hard and soft skills:

1. First, the junior editor is given the task of checking corrections (a concrete experience).

2. Then, the junior editor sees corrections made by someone with more experience, studies both the type of editorial corrections and the technical proofreading mark-up (the learner makes observations and reflections based on that concrete experience).

3. Then, the junior editor starts to develop a list of editing, proofreading, and typesetting principles or best practice, as well as mark-up language (i.e. the learner synthesises observations and reflections into a new conceptual understanding and interpretation of experience).

4. Finally, following more iterations, the junior editor is able to edit and proofread other texts as well as understanding mark-up and undertaking their own (in other words, they apply their conceptual understanding and use it to guide new and purposeful experiences).

Legacy Skills

Although neither Arcade Publications nor The Lifted Brow were formal apprenticeships—they were not recognised as such in advance, regardless of whether they might be co-opted as such retrospectively—the individuals involved built up a substantial bank of experience, much of which quickly moved into the area of tacit knowledge and was thereafter only visible upon reflection and, in the case of this chapter, comparison between individual experiences.

Regardless of the kind of knowledge acquired, and how they came by it, in the case of both Arcade Publications and The Lifted Brow, the final skill sets were such that their respective editors were able to secure new situations in paying workplaces, proving their hard and soft skills were robust and relevant.

From Arcade, Dale continued in the direction in which the business had been evolving, going on to create a range of distinct titles for New South Publishing that he and partner (in life and business) Michael Brady continue to develop and promote today. Rose took up a position in-house at Hardie Grant Books, where she project-managed a diverse range of titles and wide variety of authors—some of which would have fitted well with Arcade's list (most obviously, *Cole's Funny Little Picture Book*, a best-of collection curated by Dale and Michael, and a reprint of the press's original guide to parenthood: *Sh*t on My Hands*).

While working at The Lifted Brow may have left Ronnie with distinct gaps in his editorial experience—when first freelancing for a trade publisher, he had to hunt for a guide to standard proofreading marks—the ranging responsibilities of a publishing start-up (from conceiving issues and reading submissions to commissioning content and artwork, from copyediting to managing budgets and promoting content on social media) has allowed him to pursue a varied career. Like Rose, he is a published fiction and nonfiction writer, has copy-edited for trade and commercial clients, and now lectures in creative writing and publishing, as well as conducting academic research in these areas.

It is perhaps no surprise that both Rose and Ronnie have found themselves particularly interested in the intersection of writing and publishing—teaching writers how to edit, editors how to write, and both groups how to be effective "prosumers"—frequently finding themselves drawn to or hired for those jobs that exist somewhere between the categories of commissioning, copywriting, rewriting, ghostwriting and copyediting: the type of work that requires "legacy" skills to be used in an intuitive and responsive way.

According to Tony Gleason of the Australian Institute of Management, where graduates were once mentored into more well-rounded workers "companies now want job-ready individuals".[21] Apprenticeship practices train workers to adapt to contemporary conditions and to be continually adaptable; to learn on the job; and to expect nothing less than to keep learning—on one job or via a range of jobs.

Conclusion

This chapter shows how cultural entrepreneurship can constitute an informal apprenticeship practice that may be purposed towards a communication and dissemination of on-the-job skills—perhaps chief among them being the ethos that skills *are* learned on the job, i.e. through models of apprenticeship, as well as via complementary theoretical courses. Although editors and publishers may develop a range of hard and soft skills via an ad hoc mix of mentoring, experimentation and serendipity, each pathway takes the individuals involved to the same place, resulting in a publishing-specific skill set—see the list of legacy skills and specific knowledge acquired through the authors' apprenticeships in Appendix 1—particularly relevant in today's fast-changing and challenging times.

Through their apprenticeships the authors have developed a range of legacy skills and acquired specific knowledge (encompassing research, making books, marketing and promotion, event management, social media, advertising, sales, distribution and business management—in

---

21 John Elder, "The Rise of Soft Skills: Why Top Marks No Longer Get the Top Jobs," *Sydney Morning Herald,* March 15, 2015, http://www.smh.com.au/national/the-rise-of-soft-skills-why-top-marks-no-longer-get-the-best-jobs-20150314-1440ds.html.

other words, cultural entrepreneurship skills, which are listed in Appendix 1) that they are passing on to others through their Bowen Street Press teaching, and continuing to develop via their own now-habitual creative and professional practice.

The aim of any apprenticeship is to learn enough to advance to the next stage. According to Richard Sennet, "All craftsmanship is founded on skill developed to a high degree... As skill progresses it becomes more problem-attuned".[22] The skills attained through an apprenticeship predicated on case-by-case vicissitudes are beyond rote learning; they allow editors and publishers to engage deeply with the fundamentals of our trade—problem-solving and people skills.

Apprenticeship practices, which may move between formal models and ad hoc practices, are particularly well suited to the writing and publishing industry—an industry of novel ventures and original personalities. From gentleman publishers to collaborative presses, publishing has always been a close community, and cultural entrepreneurs, apprentices (including via informal, possibly unintended peer-to-peer networks), teaching presses and start-ups all stand to benefit from this history, built from valued relationships within established networks. As our industry comes under increasing financial pressure—needing to produce different outputs, and more quickly—outsourcing has become the norm. Yet the quality of our industry depends on small, independent cultural entrepreneurs that offer not only new, diverse voices, but a proving ground for future professionals and leaders. The Bowen Street Press now provides students with what Arcade and The Lifted Brow once offered their founders: an apprenticeship with in-built mentoring (by industry professionals), experimentation (with university peers), and an opportunity to glean legacy skills and relevant knowledge by working on iterative projects. These skills are crucial for the ongoing development and professionalism of our industry. Passing them on is critical.

---

22 Richard Sennet, *The Craftsman* (New Haven: Yale University Press, 2008), 20.

Appendix 1

A non-exhaustive list of legacy skills and specific knowledge acquired through the authors' apprenticeships

commissioning fiction, nonfiction, interviews, poetry, experimental works, and illustrations; conceiving themes and ideas; submission call-outs; reading and evaluating submissions; giving feedback on submissions; undertaking research to identify story ideas; approaching fiction writers, journalists, experts and academics; liaising with existing authors and readers about potential future titles; production; image sourcing; contacting libraries, newspapers and individuals; briefing designers and typesetters on covers, images and text; checking pages; fact-checking; taking in changes in InDesign; checking printers' proofs; scheduling; developing and posting AIs and press releases; managing a marketing database; writing irregular newsletters and promotional copy; designing counter packs, posters and business cards; sending out media and review copies; following up to confirm receipt; confirming print promotional opportunities (ads and reviews); booking media events for authors (radio, TV, walking tours and launches); supplying programming for writers' festivals; preparing and delivering guest lectures and industry panels; booking venues for events; hiring bands and associated artists; designing and distributing invites; decorating venues and sound-checking; booking interstate flights for artists; designing, developing and maintaining a website; creating social media profiles; updating social media; developing press packs and media kits; developing advertiser packs; cold-calling prospective advertisers; invoicing advertisers; negotiating distributor arrangements; liaising with readers and subscribers; physically stocking bookstores; physically collecting stock from bookstores; researching and engaging distributors; cold-calling prospective firm-sale outlets; invoicing stockists and following up on outstanding payments; registering a company; establishing partnership agreements; opening and managing bank accounts and company cheque books; purchasing domain names, ISPs and email servers; buying ISBNs; generating barcodes; securing office space; managing a lease; drafting author contracts; paying royalties; lodging books with library services such as the National Library of Australia, the State Library of Victoria and Trove; registering for ELR and PLR; purchasing, addressing, packing and posting envelopes; applying for and acquitting grants; and fixing printer jams.

Works cited

Barekat, Houman. "Ribbons of Argument." *Times Literary Supplement*, October 25, 2017. https://www.the-tls.co.uk/articles/private/ribbons-of-argument-lifted-brow/.

Carter, Paul. *Material Thinking: The Theory and Practice of Creative Research*. Melbourne: Melbourne University Press, 2004.

Poland, Louise. "The Business, Craft and Profession of the Book Editor." In *Making Books: Contemporary Australian Publishing*, edited by David Carter and Anne Galligan, 96–115. Brisbane: University of Queensland Press, 2000.

Caterson, Simon. "From Little Ventures Small Wonders Emerge." *The Age*, January 24, 2009. https://www.theage.com.au/entertainment/books/from-little-ventures-small-wonders-emerge-20090124-ge7n2x.html.

Conner, Cheryl. "5 Sure Signs a Startup Firm Will Succeed," *Forbes*, July 12, 2012. https://www.forbes.com/sites/cherylsnappconner/2012/07/12/5-sure-signs-a-startup-firm-will-succeed/#1cd949d9c1da.

Edmonds, Phillip. 2015. *Tilting at Windmills: The Literary Magazine in Australia 1968–2012*. Adelaide: University of Adelaide Press.

Elder, John. "The Rise of Soft Skills: Why Top Marks No Longer Get the Best Jobs." *Sydney Morning Herald*, March 15, 2015. http://www.smh.com.au/national/the-rise-of-soft-skills-why-top-marks-no-longer-get-the-best-jobs-20150314-1440ds.html.

Epstein, Jason. "Publishing: The Revolutionary Future." *New York Review of Books*, March 11, 2010. https://www.nybooks.com/articles/2010/03/11/publishing-the-revolutionary-future/.

Hart, Jim. "New Wave Seventies." In *Paper Empires: A History of the Book in Australia*, edited by Craig Munro, 53–7. Brisbane: University of Queensland Press, 2006.

Howcroft, Elizabeth, Eric Beecher, Michael Heyward, "Gribble, Diana (Di) (1942–2011)", Obituaries Australia, October 22, 2011. http://oa.anu.edu. au/obituary/gribble-diana-di-16650/text28549.

Kolb, David A. *Experiential Learning.* New Jersey: Pearson Education, 2015.

Lave, Jean, and Etienne Wenger. *Situated Learning: Legitimate Peripheral Participation.* Cambridge: Cambridge University Press, 1991.

Magner, Brigid. "Anglo–Australian Relations in the Book Trade." In *Paper Empires: A History of the Book in Australia,* edited by Craig Munro, 7–10. Brisbane: University of Queensland Press, 2006.

Sennet, Richard. *The Craftsman.* New Haven: Yale University Press, 2008.

Stinson, Emmett. "Small Publishers and the Emerging Network of Australian Literary Prosumption." *Australian Humanities Review,* 59 (April/May 2016): 23–43.

Thompson, John B. *Merchants of Culture: The Publishing Business in the Twenty-First Century,* 2nd ed. Cambridge: Polity, 2012.

Trubek, Anne. "How the Paperback Novel Changed Popular Literature." *Smithsonian,* March 30, 2010. https://www.smithsonianmag.com/arts-culture/how-the-paperback-novel-changed-popular-literature-11893941/.

CHAPTER 3

Crowdfunding and Small Publishers

SOPHIE MASSON

Introduction

The word "crowdfunding" might have a modern origin—it is credited to pioneer online audio/video distributor Michael Sullivan in 2006[1]—but the idea of people donating or pledging funds to bankroll a creative or other project has roots going back far into the past. When it comes to literature, you could claim, for instance, that it is thanks to a version of crowdfunding that Shakespeare occupies his central place in our culture. The First Folio, which was the first complete published edition of Shakespeare's plays, was "crowdfunded" after his death by his friends and associates. It is a matter of record of course that the publication of the First Folio made a big difference to the endurance of Shakespeare's work. Of the plays published in it, eighteen had never been published before, and some of the plays most famous today, such as *Macbeth*, *The Tempest* and *Twelfth Night*, might have disappeared altogether if they hadn't been published in the First Folio.[2] An even closer example of early crowdfunding can also be seen in Alexander Pope's six-volume translation of Homer's *Iliad*, whose publication from 1713 to 1720

---

1 Daniela Castrataro, "A Social History of Crowdfunding, Social Media Week," December 12, 2011, https://socialmediaweek.org/blog/2011/12/a-social-history-of-crowdfunding/.

2 State Library of NSW, "Shakespeare's First Folio," https://www.sl.nsw.gov.au/stories/shakespeare-library/shakespeares-first-folio.

was funded by subscribers, who paid one guinea per volume and as a reward had their names inscribed in the front of the book.[3] It wouldn't be the last time a creative work saw the light of day because of the generosity of donors. But the first recorded instance of artists using the huge reach of the internet to fund their project was in 1997, when British rock band Marillion successfully funded both a new album and a North American tour with online donations from thousands of fans.[4] Inspired by their example, the world's first crowdfunding platform, ArtistShare, started up in 2001. Crowdfunding slowly gained momentum. In 2008, Indiegogo was launched. Other major platforms soon followed: Kickstarter (2009) and Australia's own Pozible (2010). These new platforms made creating a crowdfunding campaign accessible to thousands of creative people in all kinds of fields, including, of course, publishing. Crowdfunding platforms offer either a fixed model (such as Kickstarter), where you must reach your goal; or a flexible model (as with Indiegogo), where you obtain whatever funding you have managed to raise, even if you do not reach your goal. Rewards or "perks" are very much a part of the crowdfunding experience for supporters: these can include anything from names inscribed in the published work (just as in Pope's day!), to copies of a book, product, prints or original artwork, to invitations to events and launches. Platforms such as Kickstarter, Pozible and Indiegogo have hosted many book-production campaigns, but there is also a crowdfunding site specifically for publishing projects, UK-based Unbound, which was launched in 2011. Based on the fixed model, it has enabled the production of publishing projects from over 185 countries. It differs from the other crowdfunding sites in offering a curated experience, with the Unbound team choosing around ten to

---

3   Francesca Tondi, "Alternative Publishing Models in a Changing Cultural Landscape," *Logos* 28, no. 4 (March 2017): 32–7, doi: https://doi.org/10.1163/1878-4712-11112139.

4   Castrataro, "A Social History," 2011.

fifteen projects from more than five hundred submissions per month. In a 2015 interview published in *The Guardian*, Dan Kieran of Unbound noted that reader-supporters enjoy the experience of crowdfunding in part because it's about much more than just buying a book, and that they enjoyed "seeing under the bonnet of publishing".[5]

Credibility, Endorsement and Preparedness

The appeal of crowdfunding to businesses as well as individuals in terms of publishing projects is obvious. With crowdfunding, publishers get immediate support for their project from their target market: their readership. The value is not just the direct financial support, but also the pre-orders and promotional word-of-mouth buzz generated by these campaigns. Other benefits, as reported by publishers in a recent paper on crowdfunding and the market, include discoverability and audience reachability for riskier titles.[6] But there are other appealing aspects. In "Swept Away by the Crowd? Crowdfunding, Venture Capital, and the Selection of Entrepreneurs", Ethan Mollick proposed that crowdfunding can eliminate in-built biases, such as those based on geography and gender, which venture capital initiatives may struggle to overcome.[7] He goes on to describe four ways in which crowdfunding differs markedly from venture capital as a source of funding: 1) it is democratic rather than oligopolistic; 2) it is loosely organised rather than tight-knit; 3) access occurs in open

5   Alison Flood, "Literary Launches: how Crowdfunding Is Fuelling the Avant-Garde," *The Guardian*, September 12, 2015. https://www.theguardian.com/books/2015/sep/11/literary-launches-how-crowdfunding-is-fuelling-the-avant-garde.

6   Alan Scott Holley, "We'll Want It When We Say We Want It: How the Market Speaks to the Publishing Industry via Crowdfunding, and Why Publishers Should Listen," Book Publishing Final Research Paper, Portland State University, 2016. https://pdxscholar.library.pdx.edu/eng_bookpubpaper/15.

7   Ethan Mollick, "Swept Away by the Crowd? Crowdfunding, Venture Capital, and the Selection of Entrepreneurs," *SSRN's eLibrary*, March 25, 2013. https://repository.upenn.edu/mgmt_papers/263.

online communities rather than closed networks; and 4) backers receive no equity or monitoring rights.[8] Most still hold true in 2019—though, as I address later in this chapter, the last point has become more complicated.

Despite the differences between crowdfunding and venture capital, Mollick identifies several factors that he argues successful crowdfunding and venture capital entrepreneurs both share, factors which can predict whether their projects will attract funding. These are the credibility of the project creators (both their background and track record), the endorsement of the project by third parties, and the demonstrated preparedness of the entrepreneurs in terms of their project campaign.[9] These three factors may be expected also to apply to crowdfunded publishing ventures, including those engaged in by small presses as well as individual writers and illustrators.

In an interview published in *Books+Publishing* in 2012, Zoe Dattner, then general manager of SPUNC (now known as the Small Press Network), expressed doubts about the feasibility of crowdfunding for small publishers. She commented that there was a danger books funded in this way, especially by start-up publishers, could be "undervalued". She worried that publishers might be seen as "needy" and dissipate their efforts trying too hard to get money up front, while neglecting production and distribution.[10] Dattner's comments sound a necessary note of caution about not seeing crowdfunding as a "money tree",[11] but publishers who have successfully used crowdfunding do not lose sight of the risks or indeed the need for high standards. In the seven years since Dattner's observations, crowdfunding has come of age as highly regarded small presses around

---

8 Mollick, "Swept Away."

9 Ibid.

10 Zoe Dattner, quoted in Lucy Stewart, "Following the Crowd: Crowdfunding Books," *Books+Publishing*, October 16, 2012. https://www.booksandpublishing.com.au/articles/2012/10/16/25249/following-the-crowd-crowdfunding-books/.

11 Ibid.

the world and individual creators have made very good use of these platforms, raising, in some cases, substantial funds. For instance, in 2015 alone, new US-based independent press Restless Books ran a successful crowdfunding campaign to publish an illustrated 400th anniversary edition of *Don Quixote*, and literary magazines such as *McSweeney's* (US) and *The White Review* (UK) also funded a host of publishing projects in this way.

In Australia, too, crowdfunding campaigns have successfully been used by small-press publishers and literary magazines. In this chapter, a small-scale close-up examination of the crowdfunding experience as it pertains to small press book publishers, I survey three Australian presses who within the last five years have successfully used crowd-funding for specific projects. The three small presses are: Dirt Lane Press, which publishes illustrated narrative books; Gumbootspearlz Press, founded initially to publish a poetry collection for children but with a goal to set up a broader list; and my own Christmas Press, which produces a wide range of juvenile literature, from picture books to novels, chapter books to anthologies, poetry and plays. Though given the small sample size it is not possible to generalise, it is interesting to note in light of Mollick's observations on crowdfunding's capacity to eliminate biases such as geography and gender that all three presses are based in regional areas—Dirt Lane Press and Christmas Press in regional NSW, Gumbootspearlz Press in regional Queensland—and all three have women as either sole or co-directors.[12] Two other aspects are of interest: all three presses publish primarily for children and young people, though Dirt Lane Press sees its brief as "illustrated narratives for all ages"; and for each publisher, their first crowdfunding campaign was focused around a launch title that was at least partly the creation of one of the publishing team, but which was intended

---

12 The quotes from Anna Maguire, Margrete Lamond, June Perkins and Chris Pash are all from email interviews I conducted with them in early March 2018. All have given their consent to be quoted in full.

to provide a launch pad for a much wider list featuring other authors and illustrators.

Before turning to those individual experiences, however, it is worth reporting the words of Anna Maguire, author of the popular crowdfunding guide *Crowdfund It!*, who has presented many talks and workshops on successful approaches to crowdfunding. I asked her for her thoughts on two questions: does crowdfunding offer a viable funding alternative for small publishers for book publication? And if so, what projects might most benefit? Her response considered crowdfunding to be:

> Just one possible business model—no surety, but worth considering. While crowdfunding is no longer the 'shiny new thing' to use, it has evolved into an accepted possible business model for small publishers to consider, to launch new titles or imprints. There is a lot of work involved in running a campaign and publishers have to weigh up the financial and marketing benefits versus the time drain. Another significant consideration is how often they can use crowdfunding—is it a one-off form of funding or are their supporters willing to continue to be involved?[13]

Maguire's observations, as well as Mollick's list of factors for success, were echoed in the individual crowdfunding campaign experiences of all three publishers.

Fresh and Different: The Experience of Dirt Lane Press

In early 2017, Dirt Lane Press, a new not-for-profit publisher, launched a Kickstarter campaign to fund production of its first title, *The Sorry Tale of Fox and Bear*, written by Margrete Lamond and illustrated by

---

13 Anna Maguire, email interview, March 9, 2018.

Heather Vallance. Margrete Lamond is well-known nationally in Australian children's literature, both as an author and a publisher. She worked previously as the publisher at Little Hare (Hardie Grant) and Scholastic Australia before founding Dirt Lane Press with academic and former publisher Mark McLeod. She has also written several books for children herself. Meanwhile, Heather Vallance is new to book illustration but has exhibited frequently as an artist and has strong regional support. The Dirt Lane Press campaign, based on Kickstarter's fixed funding model, was fully funded, and the subsequent publication of the book has seen even more success, with a Notable Books citation in the 2018 CBCA Book of the Year Awards, a shortlisting in the 2018 NSW Premier's Literary Awards, and UK rights sold to independent publisher Old Barn Books. It has been a great validation for Dirt Lane, who from the beginning have adopted a bold approach to illustrated narratives. Coupling their industry knowledge with a non-profit structure has given them the opportunity to successfully publish books that might be deemed "uncommercial" but have high literary and artistic value.

Dirt Lane's crowdfunding campaign was simple but effective, easily achieving its aim of creating a fund to produce the book. Yet it presented several challenges, as Margrete Lamond describes:

> Our main challenges were putting together the video, to be honest. That took quite some time, and some redoing. We had trouble getting a good clear voice-over, our illustrations weren't ready and I spent three hours creating a one-minute video-clip of myself speaking as author. Other challenges were delivering the 'rewards', which was hard work and time consuming. What I learnt was that it was hard work![14]

All the hard learning has not put them off. They are doing it again for another title with a different author and illustrator:

---

14   Margrete Lamond email interview, March 2018.

We are in fact working on another campaign now, but it is specifically tailored for a very different target audience, and the book has social and cultural importance for public and mental health, so we're going about it very differently in terms of who we send it out to. The author and illustrator's contacts for this one will be largely different from the Fox and Bear mailing list (though there will of course be overlap), and we will engage the author and illustrator quite heavily in promoting the campaign. So long as we have clear new angles, we will continue to crowd-fund until we are better established.[15]

Generally, Dirt Lane believes that crowdfunding is indeed a viable funding alternative for small publishers:

If we see backers as being people who are pre-ordering the book (which is what in effect they are doing), then it seems a logical and fair way to gain funding, and isn't all that different to any other pre-ordering of a book that is yet to be published. The main challenge would be to make each campaign fresh and different, with a new specific reason for existing, and ideally targeting a largely new audience (for example, the author's contacts, or the contacts/mailing lists of partner organisations). Asking the same group of people to contribute to every campaign would not be successful in the long run, as the group is likely to experience donation fatigue, even if one markets the campaign as "pre-ordering".[16]

---

15 Lamond email interview.
16 Ibid.

Creating Something of Value: The *Magic Fish Dreaming* Project

Another successful Kickstarter publishing project was Gumboots-pearlz Press's campaign for the publication of *Magic Fish Dreaming*, a collection of poems for children with an environmental/nature focus, written by June Perkins and illustrated by Helene Magisson. The campaign was initiated in early 2016 by June Perkins, who had been involved in several other publications in her home region of Far North Queensland in the past. This book, however, would be more personal, focused on her passion: bringing the joy of poetry to children, in the context of a publishing climate that she felt did not favour the availability of poetry. As she put it in her Kickstarter pitch:

> The situation in publishing is that poetry books are not taken on by most commercial publishers and yet it remains a loved art form supported by independent small presses and literary presses, and taught in the school curriculum.[17]

Her gamble that supporters might agree was validated by the fact not only that the book production was fully funded, but that it has since won awards and been acclaimed by reviewers around the country. Reflecting on the successful campaign, she observed that:

> I chose a project I felt people might love that I was passionate about, but that a bank or grant would be unlikely to fund. The challenge then was to make this project as attractive to backers as I could through letting them know enough about the product, in my case an illustrated poetry book for children with a focus on nature.[18]

---

17 June Perkins' email interview, March 2018.
18 Ibid.

She emphasised the importance of a professional approach not only in terms of the book production, but also in the look of the crowdfunding campaign: "I commissioned the illustrator I was booking to create work for the Kickstarter campaign and saw this as an investment to show how serious I was about my product."[19]

She noted that a key initial challenge was producing multiple budgets, from a "shoe-string" budget to a more generous one that would have enabled her to do more. She commented that although the funding was achieved and the campaign successful, "It was only just above shoestring level that was achieved. But still that enabled me to get it off the ground."[20]

As with Lamond and Dirt Lane Press, Perkins's established presence as a successful book creator gave wide validity to her crowdfunding project, as she noted:

> The more background and credibility you have with previous successful projects the more likely I feel you are to receive support from others. I did smaller projects of publishing before attempting a larger one.[21]

Illustrator Helene Magisson's connections also helped, as she has illustrated several books for other publishers. Perkins observed:

> The challenge with a Kickstarter is to have more than just immediate family and friends keen about your vision, and to attract a large enough community of interest to make your project possible. If you can create that buzz, through radio, television, personal contacts, all can be possible. I was lucky enough to get some radio and newspaper coverage, others I know have also managed to get television coverage.[22]

---

19 Ibid.
20 Ibid.
21 Ibid.
22 Ibid.

But it wasn't just about literary or media connections: the right approach to research and marketing plays a big part, she stressed, illustrating Mollick's "success factor" of preparedness:

> You have to do this with a focus on creating something others want, not just something you feel passionate about. It is about understanding marketing. A balance of keeping it in people's minds and engaging them and not sending them crazy with asking for support is crucial. Crowd funding success will be enhanced by studying other successful campaigns in the same field. Look at them carefully, and also look at ones that didn't happen. This can teach you a great deal. Importantly, I did not run my Kickstarter without training and mentoring in principles of how to do it well, and I did have a background in project design and community development.[23]

She also emphasised the necessity for publishers to "follow through" on all the preparation and organisation by making sure that, at the end, all supporters received everything they had pledged for, in a timely fashion. Finally, she noted that she believes crowdfunding works for very specific book projects:

> It's a way of making risky book projects possible, because you create a pre-publishing buzz. You can use crowd funding to test the waters and if your campaign succeeds you have shown there is an audience for such a book. However, I say that with caution, because you need to still create a project that is attractive and has viability and an audience that are keen to have that book. It is all about offering something of value to the world of publishing and explaining why a book like yours isn't possible except through crowd funding and yet is adding value to the world of literature.[24]

23 Ibid.
24 Ibid.

A Natural Extension: The Experience of Christmas Press

Like many other people in the creative industries, I'd been interested in how crowdfunding offered new ways that arts projects and start-up enterprises could be funded, and I had contributed, as a supporter, to several book production projects by individual authors and illustrators. Then, in early 2013, with two illustrator friends, David Allan and Fiona McDonald, I sat at my dining-room table, covered with notes and layouts for *Two Trickster Tales from Russia*, which was to be the launch title of Christmas Press, the boutique children's publishing house we had started just a few weeks previously. We'd decided on this first title, written by me and illustrated by co-director David Allan, as a way of dipping our toes into the publishing waters, not wanting to risk other people's creative labour on something that might not work. But if, as we hoped and planned, it did work, we always intended that Christmas Press would not be a self-publishing enterprise, but a fully fledged small press, primarily concerned with publishing other creators' work.

The creative idea was well in place; but how would we fund our first print run? Our financial capital was low; our skills and talent capital high. We might not have had a lot of money but, jointly, we knew quite a bit not only about the creative but also the technical part of book design. As someone who'd been in the literary world a long time, I also had a large network of contacts with creators, publishers and media. I also had extensive experience with strategy, marketing and organisation through my service on the boards of literary organisations. Crowdfunding our launch title seemed a natural extension of our assets and our own nimble connected small-scale approach. We researched the process extensively before launching into it, and unlike the other two small press publishers interviewed for this survey, chose the Indiegogo flexible funding model because we had committed to our project going ahead regardless. We had already started work on it, and had negotiated with the printer. We felt that, even if we didn't reach our target, the funds raised would help to defray the costs, and the goodwill generated too would be valuable.

We concentrated on an eye-catching but simple campaign: a nice little video, imaginative perks, personal thank you messages (not just generic Indiegogo ones), and regular but not annoyingly frequent updates. Creating an effective video—always one of the most important parts of the pitch—was made easier and cheaper by the fact that I could call on my close family for skills in both video and music. The availability of "perks" such as prints and original artwork was facilitated by the fact that my two co-directors are both professional artists and illustrators. Keeping the campaign professional yet friendly and direct was an important focus for us. From experience as contributors, we knew that backers were likely to come, at least initially, from our own circles—families, friends, fellow creators and industry professionals—but we knew also that it must not seem like a private club, and it must attract people who had no idea who we were, but who loved beautiful books and wanted to be part of an exciting project.

We made mistakes of course—everyone does—but we must have done something right, because that first campaign raised over two-thirds of the cost of the first print run of *Two Trickster Tales from Russia*. Better still, it generated a great buzz, which meant that even after supporters received their books and perks, the first print run sold out within six weeks. And by then we had enough income from those sales to reprint without the need for extra funding. We had increased confidence in what we were doing. Bookshops responded very positively to the quality of the book, and the distributor we approached after selling the first print run directly took us on at once. Furthermore, well-known authors approached us expressing interest in submitting work to us in the genre of our first title (retold traditional tales from around the world) so we quickly signed up a wonderful list of some of Australia's most acclaimed children's writers. We also obtained the support of Australian Standing Orders for two of our next titles. In summary, this first campaign was an excellent launching pad for our press, and its effects are still being felt today.

Our next crowdfunding campaign, in 2015, was also for a launch title—for our adventure fiction imprint, Eagle Books—but for a very different kind of book, and it attracted a very different kind of audience. *Jules Verne's Mikhail Strogoff* is a new translation—the first in over a hundred years—of a classic nineteenth-century French adventure novel, instead of a new original text as was the case with our first campaign. Translated by Stephanie Smee and illustrated by David Allan, it was produced as a limited-edition book designed to evoke the luxury editions of Verne's own time: a fine-grain hardback with gilded cover and page edges, satin bookmark, fine creamy internal paper, and coloured end-papers. Just as the production was designed to mark an important literary event, so the crowdfunding campaign had to be framed differently to that first one.

It had to emphasise the book's cultural importance as well as its creative appeal. The video had even higher standards of production than the first one, the perks were substantial and we targeted the campaign internationally as well as nationally, for Verne's work is known globally. As the book is very highly regarded in France, we also approached Australian-based French cultural services such as the Alliance Française and the French Embassy, both of whom promoted it enthusiastically. There was mention of the campaign and the book in national newspapers as well as industry magazines. It was also noted internationally in *Publishers' Weekly* (US) and the newsletter of the French Embassy in New York (neither of whom we had approached directly). We soon had backers not only from across the country but all over the world, some of whom chose to support it at high levels. There was some crossover of backers from our first campaign, but most of the people who contributed had not done so in 2013 and knew very little if anything about our press. They came into the project for other reasons: because they knew the translator, because they were Verne aficionados, because they were Francophiles, because they loved limited editions, or simply because they had come across the project and were intrigued by it. At the same time as the campaign was going on, we also targeted selected independent bookshops around Australia, offering them pre-order copies at an attractive discount but on firm sale only, an initiative which succeeded in attracting support from a wide range of independent bookshops in every state. (For the first year, we had decided not to offer the book through our distributor, but to concentrate on direct sales only; three years later, the book is now available through our distributor.)

Proportionally speaking, the *Mikhail Strogoff* campaign did not raise as much as the *Trickster Tales* one, although the actual amount raised was substantially higher (the discrepancy of course was to do with the much higher cost of production of *Mikhail Strogoff*). Yet it too was successful in defraying a substantial part of the high cost of printing—the success of our independent bookshop initiative reduced the risk to us further. The campaign succeeded in drawing significant media attention to the book even after the book's release: for instance, we received the accolade of a long and very positive review by Geordie Williamson, chief literary reviewer for the *Weekend Australian*. And it also achieved the specific cultural goals we had hoped for: it ensured that this very special book now has its place in the history of Verne editions, and that the book that I and many other French-language people consider to be this popular author's masterpiece now has an English translation that is every bit as sparkling and gripping as the original French, unlike the previous translations, which had dulled its impact and caused it to fall out of the sight of English-language readers.

These two campaigns were each targeted to different markets: original picture books and luxury limited editions of classics suitable for both adults and children. Yet they each had similar challenges: dedicating the time required to create and maintain the campaign, on top of all the other things you have to do, as a small publisher; and publicising the campaign to our networks in the most effective yet least intrusive way. But they also worked for similar reasons. They were both about clearly articulated "firsts"—the first picture book title for Christmas Press, the first English translation in over a hundred years of Verne's novel. Both had high production values, which brought high levels of support from creative and professional book industry people but also had appeal beyond that. For us as a press, they also functioned as an invaluable market research tool. So, from us, the answer to whether crowdfunding works as a viable funding alternative for small publishers would have to be yes, as long as it is for the right kind of project, as these two clearly were. Even if it does not provide the full funding for a project, it will help significantly with costs. And as to what kinds of projects most benefit, from our experience and that of the two other publishers profiled here, the answer would have to be that they must have a distinctive quality. The books in question must stand out in some way, and those distinctive qualities must be front and centre of your campaign. As a publisher, you will of course feel that all the books on your list are individually special—but there has to be something more than that for a book project to be successfully crowdfunded. People need to feel, as June Perkins observed, that you are adding value to the world of literature, or you run the risk, as Margrete Lamond put it, of donor fatigue.

Equity Crowdfunding: The Next Step?

Traditionally (if such a term can be used of such a recent phenomenon) crowdfunding has meant, as Mollick noted, that campaign contributors do not have equity in the business whose product they are supporting, but this is now changing with the rise of what is known as "equity crowdfunding" in which start-up companies and businesses offer equity to small and medium investors well before any public listing, through campaigns run on specialised crowdfunding platforms. In the UK and the US, innovative regulation on equity crowdfunding has enabled many start-ups and small and medium companies to fund projects. Australia is now set to join the trend: ASIC, early in 2018, licensed several equity crowdfunding platforms, including Equitise, OnMarket, Birchal, and others.[25] According to new regulation, Australians are now able to invest as little as $50 or as much as $10,000 in a business through equity crowdfunding with eligible companies able to raise up to $5 million in any twelve-month period in this way.

Most equity crowdfunding ventures in Australia so far appear to be in the technology and financial sectors, but there's no reason why it couldn't become appealing to publishers, especially small press publishers. As Chris Pash, author, journalist and former business editor of *Business Insider Australia*, commented:

> I think there's good potential in equity crowdfunding for small projects, especially those that have widespread appeal. Perhaps a biography of a popular person? Or fiction done differently, perhaps a hybrid graphic novel. So, it would be worthwhile I think to try such a project, offering shares in a literary project. It would have to be the right one, but it could work.[26]

Conclusion

Though crowdfunding should not be regarded as a principal or major business model, it remains a viable alternative for small publishers as well as individual creators wanting to raise money to fund book

---

25   Anthony Keane, "Equity Crowd-Funding Is Off and Running as ASIC Licenses Platforms," *News.com.au*, February 10, 2018. https://www.news.com.au/finance/money/equity-crowdfunding-is-off-and-running-as-asic-licenses-platforms/news-story/e7c068d910d2e53c0e678fa447477da1.

26   Chris Pash, email interview, March 7, 2018.

projects—especially launch titles or those that might be seen as either "risky" or highly distinctive. It is clear that a high degree of professionalism is required for a campaign to work. Preparedness, research and careful planning are all important predictors of a campaign's success, as are the publisher's/creator's standing in the industry, their access to a connected community, and their ability to reach a wider audience. Challenges include the substantial investment of time required to create and run a professional campaign, and the work required to craft an effective video pitch. Publishers also need to be aware of the inherent risks of running more than one crowdfunding campaign to avoid "donation fatigue". In the future, publishers may choose to investigate equity crowdfunding opportunities too, but it remains to be seen if these broader, more regulated options will work as well for the small press sector as standard crowdfunding for specific projects has done.

Works cited

Castrataro, Daniela. "A Social History of Crowdfunding, Social Media Week." December 12, 2011, https://socialmediaweek.org/blog/2011/12/a-socialhistory-of-crowdfunding/.

Dattner, Zoe, quoted in Stewart, Lucy. "Following the Crowd: crowdfunding books." *Books+Publishing*, October 16, 2012. https://www.booksandpublishing.com.au/articles/2012/10/16/25249/following-the-crowd-crowdfunding-books/.

Flood, Alison. "Literary Launches: how Crowdfunding Is Fuelling the Avant-Garde." *The Guardian*, September 12, 2015. https://www.theguardian.com/books/2015/sep/11/literary-launches-how-crowdfunding-is-fuelling-the-avant-garde.

Holley, Alan Scott. "We'll Want It When We Say We Want It: How the market speaks to the publishing industry via crowdfunding, and why publishers should listen." Book Publishing Final Research Paper, Portland State University, 2016. https://pdxscholar.library.pdx.edu/eng_bookpubpaper/15.

Keane, Anthony. "Equity Crowd-Funding Is Off and Running as ASIC Licenses Platforms." *News.com.au*, February 10, 2018. https://www.news.com.au/finance/money/equity-crowdfunding-is-off-and-running-as-asic-licenses-platforms/news-story/e7c068d910d2e53c0e678fa447477da1.

Maguire, Anna. *Crowdfund It!* Canberra: Editia, 2014.

Mollick, Ethan. "Swept Away by the Crowd? Crowdfunding, Venture Capital, and the Selection of Entrepreneurs." *SSRN's eLibrary* (March 25, 2013). https://repository.upenn.edu/mgmt_papers/263.

State Library of NSW. "Shakespeare's First Folio." Retrieved 2018, https://www.sl.nsw.gov.au/stories/shakespeare-library/shakespeares-first-folio

Tondi, Francesca. "Alternative Publishing Models in a Changing Cultural Landscape." *Logos* 28, no. 4 (March 2017): 32–37, doi: https://doi.org/10.1163/1878-4712-11112139.

CHAPTER 4

The Publishing Contract

A Complicated Inheritance

KATHERINE DAY

Introduction

A contract is a private agreement between two parties and can be used for many purposes in business and personal relations. In book publishing, contracts tend to be, prima facie, highly negotiable.[1] The degree of negotiability, however, has proven problematic, particularly when balancing financial and legal interests within the highly subjective territory of cultural production—the result of an inheritance of laws seemingly unable to resolve all interests. Publishers have, because of their economic power and their crucial role in traditional book production, tended to dictate the contract's terms and tailor it towards the pecuniary rights of the author, from which they also inevitably benefit.[2] Recent industry developments, however, have forced existing publishers to reassess their position in the publishing field and approach this legally binding transaction anew. Likewise, a changing landscape for writers has potentially shifted archaic perceptions of what it means to be an author and what the contract represents.

This chapter explores how our inherited copyright law has impacted publishers' and authors' interests in Australia, and then views the

---

1 Melvin Simensky et al, *Entertainment Law*, 3rd ed (New York: LexisNexis, 2003), 152.

2 Isabella Alexander, *Copyright and the Public Interest in the Nineteenth-Century* (Oregon: Hart Publishing, 2010), 23.

contract from two specific perspectives: as an ideological artefact and as an instrument that sanctions the negotiating parties' economic and legal directives. In doing so, it asks if there is scope for further research in the area of book publishing contract negotiations.

The Romanticised Author—a Legacy

Copyright has always driven the business of making books and the ensuing negotiations between all vested parties.

The first codified forms of copyright legislation attempted to balance authors' and publishers' rights and were enacted in Europe and England in the eighteenth-century.[3] These laws and principles were formed as a result of negotiations dating back to the late-1400s, after the emergence of printing allowed texts to be preserved, reproduced economically and disseminated to the public, resulting in the emergence of the business of book publishing.[4] Thus, consideration for an author's pecuniary rights has long been established, alongside the publishers' economic rights, too. But by the time copyright was codified in the Statute of Anne (1710), and directly after the Statute's implementation, a shift in favour of protecting the author, specifically, and their works, had emerged. The author as genius and creator became the basis for an ideology that has continued to penetrate copyright law and influence decisions regarding intellectual ownership in contemporary culture, economics and law.

Literature on the history of book publishing practice provides an in-depth historical commentary on how authorship has been balanced with the public interest; how this has impacted copyright law; and

---

3   Fernando Zapata López, "The Right of Reproduction, Publishing Contracts and Technological Protection Measures in the Digital Environment," in *Copyright Bulletin* 36, no. 3 (July–September 2002), 3; refer also to the English Statute of Anne (1710), the French Council of State (1761) (that authors derived rights for their work), and in Spain in 1763 when Charles III decreed exclusive privileges to authors.

4   Ibid.

how authors' and publishers' rights are now defined as a consequence of particular developments in the British legal system. In analysing the impact of this legacy, Alexander's *Copyright Law and the Public Interest in the Nineteenth-Century* "highlights the central role of competition and the demands of the market in the law's development".[5] Alexander explains that "[o]ne of the main strategies employed by those with a stake in the copyright industries was the use of the rhetoric of Romantic authorship, emphasising the natural rights of authors, often in combination with a Lockean labour-based theory of property",[6] which was championed by the stakeholders in the creation and dissemination of books of the time, and "enshrined the booksellers' tactic of linking their trade interests to more general social interests in encouraging learning… with consequences that would emerge again and again over the next few centuries".[7] In asserting that the author be rewarded for their efforts so that they continue to produce works, the booksellers of the time conceived of the author as a "meaning-maker"[8] and "originator".[9] However, it was not until the mid-nineteenth century that this ideology became entrenched in the interpretation of the law.

Donaldson v Becket and the Common Law Right

Donaldson v Becket was a defining legal case that questioned the intention of the Statute of Anne—whether it was a statute made to break the monopoly of the London booksellers, by assigning authors power over their own copyright—as well as robustly interrogating

---

5 Alexander, *Copyright and the Public Interest*, 295.

6 Ibid., 292.

7 Ibid., 23.

8 Carys J. Craig, *Copyright, Communication and Culture* (Massachusetts: Edward Elgar, 2011), 16.

9 Michel Foucault, "What is an Author?" in *Language, Counter-memory, Practice*, ed. D. F. Bouchard et al. (New York: Cornell University Press, 1997), 124.

authors' alienable and inalienable rights, the results of which "became established and institutionalised in legal discourse".[10]

In *Becket*, bookseller Becket argued that Donaldson's publication of *The Seasons* (a collection of James Thomson's poetry) infringed upon his exclusive rights. Donaldson's view was that the statute's wording, which gave a 28-year maximum term for exclusive rights, meant that the copyright had expired. Becket claimed that copyright was a common law right, and, therefore, perpetual.[11] In asserting this right, Becket argued from the basis of possessive individualism—based on John Locke's theory of natural law—that the author should enjoy the fruits of their labour via the ownership of their work as property.[12] The counter-argument was that the work was, rather, the result of an assembly of ideas, similar to the creation of a machine, which would have a limited patent, after which it should be available to everyone. This particular view stressed a public interest consideration from which a second justification arose from Becket's counsel:

> They argued that although ideas could be common and shared widely, the same was not true of the form in which the irreducible singularity of style and sentiment was expressed. The legitimation of literary property was thus based on a new aesthetic perception designating the work

---

10 Mark Rose, "The Author as Proprietor: *Donaldson v Becket* and the Genealogy of Modern Authorship," in *Of Authors and Origins: Essays on Copyright Law*, ed. B. Sherman et al (Oxford: Oxford University Press, 1994), 29.

11 Ibid., 24.

12 John Locke, *Two Treatises on Government* (London: Thomas Tegg, 1823), 123. John Locke claimed that: "Though the Earth, and all inferior Creatures be common to all Men, yet every Man has a *Property* in his own *Person*. This no body has any Right to but himself. The *Labour* of his Body, and the Work of his Hands, we may say, are properly his. Whatsoever then he removes out of the State that Nature hath provided, and left it in, he hath mixed his *Labour* with, and joined to it something that is his own, and thereby makes it his *Property*."

as an original creation recognizable by the specificity of its expression.[13]

The importance of this legal argument, in terms of positioning the author in the publishing field, cannot be underestimated. The author possessed alienable rights in terms of their attachment to the physical property, the book; but their inalienable rights with regard to their individual cultural contribution was also "invested with an aesthetic of originality... immediately referable to the subjectivity of its author".[14]

Although the outcome for Becket was, ultimately, not favourable, the seed was planted for an author-centric focus at a time when the printing press had resulted in an "enormously increased" reading public,[15] allowing authors to leverage negotiations via their work being a "commodity endowed with a *valeur commerciale*... which enabled it to become the object of contract and to be evaluated in monetary terms".[16]

Mark Rose reminds us that the judges presiding over *Becket* had focused on what would happen if the author's perpetuity were permitted—that is, preventing the publishers' monopoly by giving the author unlimited ownership of their work. If the author were to license that work to a publisher, this transaction would give the publisher a continued degree of power. And while Rose also acknowledges the ideological shift towards author as creator of "original" works, he also cautiously submits that "if the sense of 'original' is simply a work that has not been copied, then every composition actually produced by the writer will be distinct"; but that distinction may be further defined by the publisher—a distinction "between an 'original genius' and a mere hack writer".[17] Rose describes this power play, in its historical

---

13 Roger Chartier, "Figures of the Author," in *Of Authors and Origins: Essays on Copyright Law*, ed. B. Sherman et al. (Oxford: Oxford University Press, 1994), 14.

14 Ibid.

15 Rose, "The Author as Proprietor," 26.

16 Chartier, *Figures of the Author*, 16.

17 Ibid., 45, 50.

context, as "a significant vagueness, one that very precisely preserves the blindnesses, the strategic indecision, of the culture of eighteenth-century possessive individualism".[18]

It has, therefore, become difficult to separate the author from their work, and also difficult to separate the work from its perceived legitimacy in the social sphere, as defined by the publisher, who manifests this value in the physical product: the book. How, exactly, does this power play translate in a modern context?

The Modern Author: Pecuniary or Moral Interest?

Book publishing, now, appears far more democratised, with authors taking on board the risk of self-publishing, as well as creating their own social media platforms to reach their readers.[19] Decisions about what to publish are driven by readers' tastes, as publishers defer more and more to "their [audience's] reception of genres in terms of sales".[20] In addition, the increase in adaptations and transformative works, which have gathered content from a wealth of online sources, has also cast a new light on the traditional meaning of "author".[21] Particularly in the digital era, the author has proven very adaptable, sometimes bypassing traditional publishing avenues and self-publishing on their own terms, and the publisher is perhaps more vulnerable than ever. An author, now, has the means, via online communities and digital technology, to publish their work on their own; the publisher, however, who relies on the author for list building, may not.

---

18   Ibid.

19   John B. Thompson, *Merchants of Culture: The Publishing Business in the Twenty-First Century*, 2nd ed. (Cambridge: Polity Press, 2012).

20   David Carter, "General Fiction, Genre Fiction and Literary Fiction Publishing 2000–13," in *The Return of Print? Contemporary Australian Publishing*, eds. Aaron Mannion and Emmett Stinson (Melbourne: Monash University Publishing, 2016), 2.

21   Craig, *Copyright, Communication and Culture*, 23.

In asserting control over how and when their work is communicated, authors are perhaps permitted a stronger sense of ownership of their writing and how it is exploited. In addition, attention to moral rights—a relatively new development in Australian copyright law—has granted authors more bargaining power over how publishers attribute and amend their work. But have authors taken charge of this renewed playing field? Or are they still beholden to publishers' entrenched control?

Cantatore's *Authors, Copyright, and Publishing in the Digital Era* complicates the scholarship about authorship as an ideology, observing that contemporary authors consider their moral rights as more important than economic reward.[22] While Alexander examines this tension from a historical perspective, Cantatore's contemporary viewpoint unveils a distinct position of the author assuming a sense of fairness—that they will be rewarded for their hard work, as well as the right to be attributed to the work as they conceive of it. This appears contradictory to the publisher's perspective, which *must* consider the commercial in order to remain viable.

We might assume that these interests would be asserted in the contract—consecrating the author's possession over their property as well as their personality inherent within it. According to Cantatore's research, however, authors generally do not take steps to ensure this fairness is actuated, in monetary terms or in the publisher's appraisal of the work.[23] Instead, misunderstandings about the work's value and the author's attachment to it are more likely.

In reiterating this gap between the publisher's economic focus and the author's moral concerns, Cantatore's study quotes writer Frank

---

22 Francina Cantatore, *Authors, Copyright, and Publishing in the Digital Era (Hershey:* IGI Global Publishing, 2014).

23 Francina Cantatore, "Negotiating a Changing Landscape: Authors, Copyright and the Digital Evolution" (PhD Thesis, Bond University, 2011), 4, https://research. bond.edu.au/files/18265714/negotiating_a_changing_landscape_authors_ copyright_and_the.pdf.

Moorhouse, who claims: "Most young writers do not think too much about how they will live and what the economics of their art form is... For the publisher it is a speculative venture. For the writer as well, it is, unconsciously, also a speculative investment."[24]

Ginsburg also explores the link between authorship and moral rights and proposes that it allows for and encourages creation because: "[a] writer who feels secure that she will receive some credit for her work... may find this background knowledge more conducive to creative activity."[25] Ginsburg states that moral rights may be "more important than material gain" for the author.[26] This position, based on her analysis of the French translation of *dommage moral*, from which moral rights emerged, and which translates as "non-material damage", includes "encroachments upon the personality, such as emotional distress, loss of amenities, injury to honor or diminution of a person's reputation".[27] The most interesting aspect of this definition, in Ginsburg's view, focuses again on the author subject, whereby the:

> ... work incorporates the personality of the author because the authorial persona permeates and invades the work. Therefore, when something happens to the work—such as deformation or mutilation—that constitutes an attack on the person or personality of the author herself.[28]

But with respect to the law, is it even necessary for authors to assert their rights? How are authors' moral rights reflected in copyright law, and contracts in particular?

---

24 Ibid.
25 Jane C. Ginsberg, "Moral Rights in a Common Law System," *Entertainment Law Review* 1, no. 4 (1990): 3.
26 Ibid.
27 Ibid.
28 Ibid.

Moral Rights in Practice

In Australia (unlike the UK), moral rights are assumed, and are viewed as independent of economic rights.[29] The genesis of this law can be traced back to Article 6*bis* of the Berne Convention (to which Australia is signatory). Although this international treaty has informed how moral rights have been managed in Australian copyright law generally, moral rights weren't actually codified in Australia until 2010.

The Copyright Amendment (Moral Rights) Act 2010 contains no specific clause to allow authors to waive their moral rights, but there is nothing to prevent a publisher inserting a clause prescribing a waiver in the publishing contract. An example of this might be the serialisation of the work, abridged versions and film scripts.[30] But Ginsburg affirms that "any waiver, to be effective, must be stated with considerable specificity".[31] This might suggest that the waiver is a negotiable aspect of the contract, which the author must agree to, or even instigate themselves, for it to be effective. To what extent might negotiations influence an author's decisions to waive their rights, and what other cultural influences might impact on an author's decision to do this? For example, in the case of derivative works, would an author's objection to different editions and variations of their writing affect the publisher's ability to exploit the work?

In addressing these current concerns, Ginsburg inadvertently reiterates the problematic structure of the publishing contract and admits that "defacto waivers are likely to occur".[32] She suggests, however, that: "The artist is protected under a regime requiring specificity of waivers better than under one where an ideologically pure no-waiver law is in fact rarely observed."[33]

29 "Arts Law Info Sheet 'Moral Rights,'" Australian Society of Authors, http//www.artslaw.com.au.

30 Ibid.

31 Ginsberg, *Moral Rights in a Common Law System*, 10.

32 Ibid., 11.

33 Ibid.

It appears that a "highly individualistic model" asserting the "authorial persona"[34] continues to exist and does not factor in derivative, borrowed and adapted works (as mentioned above), which Ginsburg describes as "the erosion of the paradigm of single authorship".[35] This muddy area in the contemporary landscape also broaches the question of originality, in the copyright sense of the term.[36] Ginsburg states: "If the author's persona cannot be 'found' in the work, then neither can the author be harmed by third party alterations made to the work."[37] What evidence is there of development towards a new paradigm? And how does this renewed field of cultural production intersect with book contracts and legal theory?

Framing the Field in a Contemporary Context

In *The Rules of Art*, Bourdieu describes the interplay between the publisher and the writer as a field of "power" in which there is a "space of relations of force between agents or between institutions having in common the possession of the capital necessary to occupy the dominant positions in different fields (notably economic or cultural)".[38]

Bourdieu suggests that the field is "characterized... by a weak degree of codification... by the extreme permeability of [its] boundaries and the extreme diversity of the diffusion of *posts* [it] offer[s] and the principle of legitimacy which confront each other there".[39] This, he explains, results in a dynamic "illusio", which is invested in, but also challenged, by the players in the field.[40] Each player either accepts or provokes the illusio, in their attempts to define the "distinctions" in their art and in their "position-taking" challenging the "problematic"

---

34 Ibid.
35 Ibid., 13.
36 Commonwealth of Australia, *Copyright Act* 1968, § 32(1) and § 10.
37 Ginsberg, *Moral Rights in a Common Law System*, 13.
38 Pierre Bourdieu, *The Rules of Art* (Cambridge: Polity Press, 1996), 210.
39 Ibid., 220.
40 Ibid., 221.

to become a "space of possibles", "the struggle itself".[41] It is, therefore, impossible to extract a fixed and dependable set of rules from the field, which the law invariably sets out to do. Bourdieu reveals: "Each position is objectively defined by its objective relationship with other positions",[42] and in defining the value of the work: "The producer of the *value of the work of art* is not the artist but the field of production as a universe of belief which produces the value of the work of art as a *fetish* by producing the belief in the creative power of the artist."[43] This statement would affirm the publisher's investment in the work and their influence in how the work is received by its audience. Bourdieu maintains that the work must be recognised by the dominant players in the field, who have the credibility to invest "not only [in] the material production of the work but also the production of the value of the work or what amounts to the same thing, of the belief in the value of the work".[44] But, as discussed, publishers, as agents in the game, are decidedly impacted by economics, too. Bourdieu refers to this as an economic illusio, which impacts on the artistic illusio and which publishers must renegotiate and challenge in order to inform their own habitus and position in the field. In "impos[ing] the boundaries of the field most favourable to their own interests" (whether economic or cultural),[45] Bourdieu suggests that publishers have contributed to the creation of two poles of literature—"autonomous" (or prestigious) publishing, and "heteronomous" (or middlebrow) publishing[46]—and the "monopoly of the power to say with authority who is authorised to call himself a writer... or, if you prefer, the monopoly of *power of consecration* of producers and products".[47]

---

41 Ibid., 221, 226, 228, 226.
42 Ibid., 224.
43 Ibid., 222.
44 Ibid., 223.
45 Ibid., 217.
46 Ibid., 228.
47 Ibid., 218.

Bourdieu posits that this monopoly is bound to be challenged—the "ensemble of probable constraints" giving way to a set of "possible uses".[48] In other words, proof of what has gone before allows for the possibility of change—and existing structures must be acknowledged before a "space of possibles" can be realised. Bourdieu uses the example of younger generations "asserting their identity… by imposing new modes of thought and hence are destined to disconcert by their 'obscurity' and their 'gratuitousness'".[49]

In *Copyright, Communication and Culture*, Craig provides a convincing example, which can be applied to how the illusio of the literary field is ruptured in the contemporary landscape. He claims that "the moral divide between… origination and imitation… captures and hypostasises a moment in the evolution of authorship; and that moment has passed".[50] He suggests that greater access to copyrighted works via the internet, for example, has exposed us to vast stores of ideas and their expressions. Thus, it is difficult for anything to be unique any more. Almost every new creation can be attributed to an influencing source. Indeed, "appropriation, adaptation and reinterpretation of existing texts is an established mode of cultural meaning-making".[51] Appropriative works can be openly resistant to the concept of copyright; instead, the sharing of ideas and expression is becoming "communitarian", and valuable to our ongoing "cultural dialogue".[52] In other words, rather than become attached to the idea of an author-focused original creation, emerging authors are less likely to adopt the positions in the field as Bourdieu describes them. In effect, authors create a "space of possibles" simply by way of navigating the literary field from a whole new perspective—a perspective impacted by globalisation. For publishers, this greater access to sources can help them ascertain the position of

---

48 Ibid., 229.
49 Ibid., 233.
50 Craig, *Copyright, Communication and Culture*, 16.
51 Ibid., 174.
52 Ibid., 25.

works, in the field, more effectively. In many cases, the author's belief in the degree of originality in their work may be disproportionate to their expectations of its commercial value.[53] What they perceive as a literary masterpiece may be a commercial burden in the eyes of a publisher and therefore rejected. As a result, authors may choose to abandon pursuing a contract with a typical trade publisher.

In *Entertainment Law: Legal Concepts and Business Practices*, Simensky et al. discuss how emerging writers are using this communitarian landscape to enable them to circumnavigate traditional publishing models, by engaging with online communities "through a shared appreciation of a writer, a piece of art, a game, an idea, or… more".[54] In *Merchants of Culture*, Thompson suggests that *established* writers are self-publishing more, now, and using their "platforms" to influence existing relationships with commercial publishers.[55] Mark Davis observes that astute writers are taking this platform further and using the publishers' own "cross-platform convergence strategies"[56] to renegotiate the terms of their contracts, including controlling their digital rights.[57] Observing how this phenomenon transpires in the contemporary field, Davis also suggests that destabilisation of a top-down vertical business model, and the threat of deregulation, have forced publishers to reposition themselves in a widespread market and find new ways to remain profitable, including embracing the phenomenon of "[c]elebrity-driven titles [which] offer a… sense of certainty".[58] Magner explores the emergence of Nielsen Bookscan, which allows publishers to effectively publish by numbers,

---

53   Paul L.C. Torremans, ed., *Copyright and Human Rights (New York:* Kluwer Law International, 2004), 99.

54   Melvin Simensky et al., *Entertainment Law* (New York: LexisNexis, 2003), 152.

55   Thompson, *Merchants of Culture*, 87.

56   Mark Davis, "The Decline of the Literary Paradigm in Australian Publishing," in *Making Books: Contemporary Australian Publishing*, eds. David Carter et al (Brisbane: University of Queensland Press, 2007), 116.

57   Meredith Nelson, "The Blog Phenomenon and the Book Publishing Industry," *Publishing Research Quarterly 22, no. 2*, (Summer 2006): 3.

58   Davis, "The Decline of the Literary Paradigm," 116.

using previous sales figures to ascertain potential success, and Carter proposes a new, dynamic literary field in which economics has shifted the poles of reading towards more heteronomous works.[59] Stinson and Mannion describe the impact of these pressures as resulting in an industry "in a constant state of flux, shifting between old and new media practices in paradoxical ways that simultaneously reinforce and undermine aspects of traditional print culture".[60] In *The New Literary Middlebrow: Tastemakers and Reading in the Twenty-First Century*, Beth Driscoll argues that Bourdieu's definitions of different forms of capital are too rigid and fail to adapt to the changing literary field.[61] She proposes that the incidence of literary (autonomous) authors seeking broader markets, for example, tends to amalgamate Bourdieu's strict categories because "market-oriented behaviour works together with an attraction towards elite culture."[62] Questions arise about what is considered literary, in the changing field; perceptions of what constitutes "highbrow" works are being challenged; the "illusio" of the literary field, breached. This new landscape has shown that the democratisation of the industry has placed the author, potentially, in an unprecedented, powerful position.[63]

All of these positions would indicate a reimagined illusio. Indeed, Bourdieu suggests that "The 'profession' of the writer… is, in effect, one of the least codified there is; one of the least capable, too, of completely defining (and nourishing) those who claim it."[64] This statement avows

---

59 Brigid Magner, "Behind the Bookscan Bestseller Lists: Technology and Cultural Anxieties in Early Twenty-First-Century Australia," *Script and Print* 36 (2012): 243.

60 Emmett Stinson, and Aaron Mannion, "Post-Digital Publishing: An Introduction," in *The Return of Print? Contemporary Australian Publishing, eds.* Aaron Mannion and Emmett Stinson (Melbourne: Monash University Publishing, 2016), viii.

61 Beth Driscoll, *The New Literary Middlebrow: Tastemakers and Reading in the Twenty-First Century* (London: Palgrave Macmillan, 2014), 17.

62 Ibid.

63 "Lawrence Lessig on the Google Book Search Settlement—'Static Goods, Dynamic Bads,'" lecture by Lawrence Lessig, The Berkman Klein Center for Internet & Society, August 2009, https://youtu.be/Svytkew5qPI.

64 Bordieu, *The Rules of Art*, 221.

the identified conflict between the writer and the publisher, which is "constantly being negotiated, rather than consecrated in law" and encapsulates the illusio in a way that allows a platform upon which to interrogate its re-creation in publishing agreements.[65] In essence, the new terrain embodies Bourdieu's literary field theory post-publisher, where the space of possibles has allowed the authors' and publishers' positions to evolve. In many ways, this could be seen to expose their vulnerabilities further. On the other hand, the renewed space of possibles, by virtue of its challenging the status quo, allows both authors and publishers to take advantage of the new ways in which works are created, adapted and distributed in publishing today.

Why, then, would authors still seek a commercial publisher's contract, which appears quite a rigid document in its current form? What level of flexibility might the contract offer in order to incorporate these changes? One reason may be found in the "capital" that individual publishers possess. This capital can be identified as economic or symbolic, and determines how the author might be supported in their endeavour.[66] Furthermore, the traditional publisher is still seen as a "gatekeeper" of quality; the commercial publishers' expertise in the areas of editing and production, and rights exploitation and distribution, continue to attract authors.[67] This is certainly so for commercial publishers, who have the ability to achieve the complex network of licensing arrangements, which fundamentally characterise the universal success of prominent titles. Thompson says (of symbolic capital) that publishers "are also cultural mediators and arbitrators of quality and taste... and want to be seen by others as organisations that publish works of 'quality' however that might be defined (and there are many

65 Ibid., 220.

66 Ibid., 210.

67 Monica Seeber and Richard Balkwill, *Managing Intellectual Property in the Book Publishing Industry.* World International Property Organisation, 2007. https://www.wipo.int/edocs/pubdocs/en/copyright/868/wipo_pub_868.pdf.

ways that it can be)".[68] As has been noted, however, what constitutes quality and originality is subject to the views of the vested parties, and can differ drastically according to how each party positions the work in terms of its audience. From the publisher's perspective, this might entail degrees of literary genius based on the style of the prose and its reception in relation to the publisher's own position in the literary field. But the ideology of the literary genius in its historical meaning cannot survive in a global industry. For this reason, commercial recognition of an author's platform is, perhaps, as paramount to the title's success as its actual content. For this reason, works that might otherwise be considered "good" will not necessarily translate to the work being contracted. This commercial consideration is one the author, not having access to the internal processes of the publishing house's selection criteria, might be oblivious to, or disagree with.

Interestingly, though, the terms of the contract still assert the author as having created an "original" work by way of its "Warranties and Indemnities" section. But while the author must warrant that the work is original, the author must also indemnify the publisher should the work infringe copyright. Both would seem to question the genius of the author as original creator. Yet, the "Copyright Infringement" section permits the publisher to defend the copyright in the work should it be infringed by a third party. This, it seems, would be an economic concern—one that asserts the publisher's monopoly, and that reflects the persistent author ideology for the benefit of the publisher.

The Contract as a Legacy

Craig argues that the Romantic ideology of the author continues to permeate the "current construction of copyright and the policies that inform its development".[69] This, he maintains, is because it "supports

---

68 Thompson, *Merchants of Culture*, 8.
69 Craig, *Copyright, Communication and Culture*, 21.

calls for wide protection and generates complacency around the expanding domain of intellectual property and the corporate ownership that dominates the intellectual realm".[70]

Likewise, Saunders suggests that if it has always been the intention, both historically and culturally, to treat the author in a Romanticised way—"a remarkable, ethical artefact"—then the aims of copyright law could never be achieved.[71] Deazley proposes that if it is the law's responsibility, primarily, to the interests of society, the law would not, as a result, develop in a way inclined to consider the interests of the individual author. He says:

> In allocating the right to exclusively publish a given literary
> work, the eighteenth-century parliamentarians were not
> concerned primarily with the rights of the individual, but
> acted in the furtherance of these much broader social goals.
> The pre-eminence of the common good as the organising
> principle upon which to found a system of copyright regulation
> is revealed.[72]

This is precisely because copyright law has proceeded in a positivist, as opposed to subjective, manner,[73] which has exposed it as "a publisher's proprietary instrument inappropriately applied to interests and rights that were authorial and therefore both pecuniary and personal".[74]

In order to understand how legal positivism has influenced the development of the law, it is necessary to note how it differs from natural law and what impact it has had on constructing a standard publishing contract.

---

70 Ibid., 22.

71 David Saunders, "Dropping the Subject: An Argument for a Positive History of Authorship and the Law of Copyright," in *Of Authors and Origins: Essays on Copyright Law* (Oxford: Clarendon Press, 1994), 95.

72 Ronan Deazley, *On the Origin of the Right to Copy: Charting the Movement of Copyright Law in the Eighteenth-century (1695–1775)* (Oxford: Hart Publishing, 2004), 226.

73 Saunders, *Dropping the Subject*, 94.

74 Ibid., 95.

Legal Positivism or Natural Law?

Legal positivism focuses on the law as a codified set of rules that do not assume any specific moral values. Rather, legal positivism is a socially constructed framework not based on any inherent and divine rights. It evolved in contrast to Locke's theory of natural law, which assumed a sense of right and wrong—a sense of what is moral. The theory of legal positivism is, rather, based on three principles:

1. separation thesis—that the law is imposed by a sovereign;
2. command theory of law—that the people must abide by the law as imposed by the sovereign; and
3. sanctions—that the people will be punished if they do not obey the sovereign.[75]

Legal positivism, because of its moral neutrality, focuses on a clear-cut right and wrong, which is not flexible or subjective. As a result, it has attracted much criticism in democratic societies, where it is more likely to converge with natural law to produce a body of rules aligning the code with the 'right thing to do'. In creating this alignment in democracies, "the ultimate political authority and the power to coerce behaviour seem to reside in different entities".[76] Hart describes these entities as forming a secondary legal framework, which allows individuals to "create, modify, and extinguish rights and obligations"[77] of the primary structure, in order to: 1) encompass the views forming the basis of new laws; and 2) create flexibility in the new laws.

Hart suggests that the law of contract is an example of this secondary structure, acting as a mediating set of rules between what the law of copyright (as codified law) may have intended (author's rights), with

---

75   John Austin, *Lectures on Jurisprudence* (St. Claire Shores: Scholarly Press, 1997), 166.
76   Kenneth E. Himma, "Legal Positivism," in *Internet Encyclopedia of Philosophy*, https://www.iep.utm.edu/legalpos/.
77   H. L. A. Hart, *The Concept of Law, 2nd ed.* (Oxford: Clarendon Press, 1994), 92.

what actually transpires. The contract, therefore, has the potential to empower individuals to create a more sophisticated, nuanced arrangement within a larger, primary legal framework (codified, positive law).[78] But does the contract, as a secondary structure, fulfil this function? Or does the contract still struggle to align the competing interests of law, commerce and culture?[79]

The contract's focus on pecuniary interests signifies a preference, still, towards the publisher's rights, yet the author, as has been established, still appears to seek the contract to legitimise their work. Thompson maintains that a publisher's investment in the editing, production, rights exploitation and distribution of a manuscript is assurance of their enthusiasm and endorsement, which plays to the author's own sense of value in their work.[80] As this investment unfolds, however, the author's and publisher's perception of the value of the work may differ, resulting in potentially conflicting ideas about the positioning of the work and its respective market, to which the author still appears at the mercy of the publisher.[81]

Does the Romantic ideology of the author still impede the publishing contract as a tool for negotiation within copyright legislation? Do the mediating qualities of the contract as a secondary legal structure work against the author, by allowing the publisher to impose degrees of literary genius and genre, as well as an active distinction between literary hierarchies? In other words, is the contract simply an amalgam of the same complex struggle that our inherited copyright law framework has seemingly failed to reconcile, despite the contract's promise as a flexible platform made to "ascertain, introduce and eliminate" the primary structure?[82]

---

78 Ibid.
79 Ibid.
80 Thompson, *Merchants of Culture*, 43.
81 Bourdieu, *The Rules of Art*, 5.
82 Hart, *The Concept of Law*, 92.

Contract as the Key to Understanding Author–Publisher Relations

In his influential book *Contract As Promise*, Fried describes the contract as a private agreement between two parties, which elaborates upon a criterion of consent, with enforceable conditions, and requires a "meeting of minds" on the "reasonable" interpretation of its terms.[83] Fried's highly regarded theory of "contract as promise" discusses and reflects upon the various aims of the parties—in particular on the "will" of each, entering the contract.[84] Fried reimagined "will" as "promise", whereby "persons may impose on themselves obligations where none existed before".[85] He describes this concept of "will" as: "An individual [being] morally bound to keep his promise because he has intentionally invoked a convention whose function it is to give grounds—moral grounds—for another to expect the promised performance."[86] This theory bridges the particularities of book publishing contracts with a more fundamental philosophy underpinning legal agreements, which allows us to observe the possible inherent tensions between them.

The negotiable aspects of publishing contracts converge around the specific areas of assignment of copyright and licences. But, in signing the contract, the parties also show a general intention "to create legal relations", which commits them to their individual understandings of the agreement.[87] Of contracts in cultural production, Fried says they are "an interdependent, distinct part of the structure of value" but, also, "if the legal foundation is to support the whole, then the ideals

---

83 Charles Fried, *The Convergence of Contract As Promise* (Oxford: Oxford University Press, 1981), 2, 16, 61.

84 Ibid., 4.

85 Ibid., 16.

86 Ibid.

87 Des Butler and Geoff Holland, *Entertainment Law* (Annandale: Federation Press, 2017), 182.

and values must constrain, limit, inform and inspire the foundation—
but no more", essentially affirming the conflict between negotiating
cultural products and enforcing legal obligations.[88]

In "Contract Is Not Promise; Contract Is Consent", Barnett argues
that Fried's "moral" principle is problematic. This is because it must
support the terms of the contract; and the desire of the promisor to
perform these terms is "freely assumed".[89] Barnett says that the promisor understands these terms subjectively, which means, in essence,
that the sanction is imposed, not chosen. Barnett suggests that the
"promise" cannot be sustained, as a result; rather, the contract is one
of "consent". However, Barnett also affirms that the contract signifies
a "manifested intention to create a legal relation".[90]

In this sense, the contract has ideological meaning, as an indicator
of the author as genius and creator, as well as sanctioning properties,
via its legal parameters as a reflection of copyright law. These contrast-
ing arms are enmeshed with the "industrial"[91] considerations of the
publisher and the "aspirational"[92] ideals of the author, exacerbating
contract negotiations and defining two camps of thought: the publishing contract as *ideology*, and the publishing contract as *sanction*. For
the author, the contract represents validation in the cultural "space";[93]
for the publisher (and the author), it presents a level of protection
from "misunderstandings, broken promises, or the ability of a party
to extricate itself from a project in which it is no longer interested".[94]

In exploring the legacy of the traditional publishing contract,
and considering the juxtaposition of the authors' and publishers'

---

88 Fried, *The Convergence of Contract and Promise*, 17.

89 Randy E. Barnett, "Contract Is Not Promise; Contract Is Consent," *Suffolk University Law Review* 45, no. 3 (2012): 650.

90 Ibid., 655.

91 Carter, *General Fiction, Genre Fiction and Literary Fiction Publishing 2000–13*, 10.

92 Barnett citing Fried, "Contract is Not Promise," 20.

93 Pierre Bourdieu, *Distinction* (New York: Routledge, 1984), 95.

94 Simensky et al., *Entertainment Law*, 152.

understandings of contract negotiations and how their respective positions are consecrated in law, this chapter asks the following questions:

1. How are the utilitarian and ideological spaces in book publishing contracts negotiated?
2. What can the negotiation process tell us about new developments in the contemporary publishing industry?

Despite the democratised landscape, authors' new platforms to self-publish, and an emphasis (if somewhat vague) on authors' moral rights, a tension still clearly exists in contract negotiations. I believe that the contract's ideological focus juxtaposed against its sanctioning properties has not been fully identified and, therefore, not resolved between the author and publisher. While current literature reiterates this strain, existing agreements have not been explored sufficiently to ascertain why the tension persists, and what it reveals about the industry in a global and digital realm.

The Australian Society of Authors' publication *Australian Book Contracts* provides an outline and analysis of the terms of publishing contracts, which identifies specific areas where development in negotiations may have occurred recently. In particular, the areas of "Moral Rights" and "Licensing and Territories" in the standard contract may shed some light on how the contract is evolving.[95] But this information fails to offer a nuanced voice to the current players in the field—their involvement and particular expressions about negotiations in the contemporary field. A more extensive analysis of standard contracts and new contracts could also highlight any movement in these areas. In addition, authors', agents' and publishing professionals' responses to these potentially negotiable areas can be examined via in-depth interviews.

---

95 Australian Society of Authors, *Australian Book Contracts* (Strawberry Hills: Keesing Press, 2001), 16.

Conclusion

The utilitarian underpinnings of Australian copyright law, an inheritance from eighteenth-century British book publishing practice, appear to have left us with a complicated legacy implicit in the book contract—a tension between the industrial aspects of publishing contracts (their *sanctioning* properties) and the aspirational aspects (*ideological*). Most Australian publishing contracts appear quite rigid and unable to bridge the legal, economic and cultural divide—a difficulty compounded by the nature of the industry as a dynamic field adapting to new practices and external pressures. It is clear that the contract's legal underpinnings contribute greatly to its inflexibility, but this cannot be the sole reason for potentially stymied negotiations. The contract is not concrete until it is agreed upon.

In the interstices between the positions of the author and the publisher in this transformative landscape, we witness renewed distinctions, positions and investments in the field of power. But while these developments and innovations provide inspiration, the changing dialogue between the players in the field also produces ramifications for existing structures—one being the book contract.

Bourdieu suggests that the literary field is one of the least codified, yet the standard publishing contract prescribes fairly rigid parameters. This framework, however, is also unarticulated and unbound—evidenced by its gaps, which are open to misinterpretation.

The existing principles of contract law also point to other fundamental flaws in the contract's framework, which also highlight a potential ideological conflict in the categorisation of works, as well as in the understanding of the contract as one of promise or consent. With this knowledge, some theories arise:

1. The expression of copyright law within publishing contracts is beholden to significant historical influences and mostly dominated by publishers' needs.

2. These influences create conflicting perceptions of contract negotiations for authors and publishers.

3. Globalisation and digitalisation have given authors greater flexibility and power to publish their works on their own terms.

4 Despite this new power, authors still see the publishing contract as the ultimate endorsement of their work.

5. Authors are not fully satisfied with the terms of their contracts.

What, then, are the parties agreeing to? And why do authors still seek the contract as an endorsement of their work, even in its convoluted format? What does the book-publishing contract represent for the contemporary author, and publisher? Does it have ideological, legal or economic significance?

There is a clear need for research in this area, in order to understand how our inherited institutions—and form and use of the contract as an instrument for the ultimate agreement between these parties—are applied in the new publishing landscape. Is there a distinction between how publishers and authors perceive the terms of publishing contracts, and which particular areas of the contract have been shown to convey commercial publishing's shifting landscape, and how?

Works cited

Alexander, Isabella. *Copyright and the Public Interest in the Nineteenth-Century.* Oregon: Hart Publishing, 2010.

Austin, John. *Lectures on Jurisprudence.* St. Clair Shores: Scholarly Press, 1997.

Australian Society of Authors. *Australian Book Contracts.* Strawberry Hills: Keesing Press, 2001.

———. "Arts Law Info Sheet 'Moral Rights.'" Accessed August 2018, http//www.artslaw.com.au.

Barnett, Randy E. "Contract Is Not Promise; Contract Is Consent." *Suffolk University Law Review* 45, no. 3 (2012) 627–46.

Bourdieu, Pierre. *Distinction*. London: Routledge, 1984.

———. *The Rules of Art*. Cambridge: Polity Press, 1996.

Butler, Des and Geoff Holland. *Entertainment Law*. Annandale: Federation Press, 2017.

Cantatore, Francina. *Authors, Copyright, and Publishing in the Digital Era*. Hershey: IGI Global Publishing, 2014.

———. "Negotiating a Changing Landscape: Authors, Copyright and the Digital Evolution." PhD Thesis, Bond University, 2011. https://research. bond.edu.au/files/18265714/negotiating_a_changing_landscape_authors_ copyright_and_the.pdf.

Carter, David. "General Fiction, Genre Fiction and Literary Fiction Publishing 2000–13." In *The Return of Print? Contemporary Australian Publishing*, edited by Aaron Mannion and Emmett Stinson. Melbourne: Monash University Publishing, 2016.

Chartier, Roger. "Figures of the Author." In *Of Authors and Origins: Essays on Copyright Law*, edited by B. Sherman et al. Oxford: Oxford University Press, 1994.

Craig, Carys J. *Copyright, Communication and Culture*. Massachusetts: Edward Elgar, 2011.

Davis, Mark. "The Decline of the Literary Paradigm in Australian Publishing." In *Making Books: Contemporary Australian Publishing*, edited by D. Carter et al. Brisbane: University of Queensland Press, 2007.

Day, Katherine. "Introduction." In *Publishing Means Business*, edited by Aaron Mannion, Millicent Weber, and Katherine Day. Melbourne: Monash University Publishing, 2017.

Deazley, Ronan. *On the Origin of the Right to Copy: Charting the Movement of Copyright Law in the Eighteenth-century (1695–1775)*. Oxford: Hart Publishing, 2004.

Driscoll, Beth. *The New Literary Middlebrow: Tastemakers and Reading in the Twenty-First Century*. London: Palgrave Macmillan, 2014.

Foucault, Michel. "What is an Author?" In *Language, Counter-memory, Practice*, edited by D. F. Bouchard et al. Cornell University Press: New York (1997): 113–38.

Fried, Charles. *Contract as Promise*. Oxford: Oxford University Press, 1981.

Ginsburg, Jane C. "Moral Rights in a Common Law System." *Entertainment Law Review* 1, no. 4 (1990).

Hart, H. L. A. *The Concept of Law*. 2nd ed. Oxford: Clarendon Press, 1994.

Himma, Kenneth. E. "Legal positivism." *Internet Encyclopedia of Philosophy*. Accessed August 2018, https://www.iep.utm.edu/legalpos/.

Lessig, Lawrence. "Lawrence Lessig on the Google Book Search Settlement—'Static Goods, Dynamic Bads'." Lecture by Lawrence Lessig. The Berkman Klein Center for Internet & Society, Harvard University, August 2009. https://youtu.be/Svytkew5qPI.

Locke, John. "Property." In *Two Treatises on Government* (Second Treatise). London: Thomas Tegg, 1823.

Magner, Brigid. "Behind the Bookscan Bestseller Lists: Technology and Cultural Anxieties in Early Twenty-First-Century Australia." *Script and Print* 36, no. 4 (2012): 243–58.

Nelson, Meredith. "The Blog Phenomenon and the Book Publishing Industry." *Publishing Research Quarterly* 22, no. 2 (Summer 2006): 3–26.

Rose, Mark. "The Author as Proprietor: Donaldson v Becket and the Genealogy of Modern Authorship." In *Of Authors and Origins: Essays on Copyright Law*, edited by B. Sherman et al. Oxford: Oxford University Press, 1994.

Saunders, David. "Dropping the Subject: An Argument for a Positive History of Authorship and the Law of Copyright," in *Of Authors and Origins: Essays on Copyright Law*. Oxford: Clarendon Press, 1994: 94–110.

Seeber, Monica and Richard Balkwill. *Managing Intellectual Property in the Book Publishing Industry. Creative Industries – Booklet 1.* World International Property Organisation, 2007. Accessed February 2018, https://www.wipo.int/edocs/pubdocs/en/copyright/868/wipo_pub_868.pdf.

Simensky, Melvin, Thomas Selz, Robert C. Lind, Barbara Burnett, Charles A. Palmer, and F. Jay Dougherty. *Entertainment Law.* 3rd ed. New York: LexisNexis, 2003.

Stinson, Emmett and Aaron Mannion. "Post-Digital Publishing: An Introduction." In *The Return of Print? Contemporary Australian Publishing*, edited by Aaron Mannion and Emmett Stinson. Melbourne: Monash University Publishing, 2016.

Thompson, John B. *Merchants of Culture: The Publishing Business in the Twenty-First Century*, 2nd ed. Cambridge: Polity Press, 2012.

Torremans, Paul L. C. Editor. *Copyright and Human Rights.* Kluwer Law International: New York, 2004.

Zapata López, Fernando. "The Right of Reproduction, Publishing Contracts and Technological Protection Measures in the Digital Environment." *Copyright Bulletin* 36, no. 3 (July–September 2002): 2–23.

CHAPTER 5

On the Road to the Standardisation of the Printed Page

The Legacies of John Degotardi and Benjamin Fryer

JOCELYN HARGRAVE

The process leading up to and including printing is a collaborative experience in which all stakeholders—editors, designers, typesetters, publishers and printers, to name a few—are accountable not just for the page but for the final printed product. These stakeholders typically consult style manuals for instruction on how to produce the printed page. Presently, the style manual to which stakeholders in the Australian book publishing industry generally refer is *The Style Manual for Authors, Editors and Printers*, first published in 1966 by the Commonwealth Government Printing Office and now in its sixth edition, published by John Wiley & Sons Australia in 2002. A natural question that arises from this observation is: which resources did stakeholders use before the well-known *Style Manual*? Australia's first book on printing, John Degotardi's *The Art of Printing in Its Various Branches*, was published in 1861; only one other industry manual appeared before the *Style Manual*: Benjamin Fryer's *A Book and Its Elements* in 1930.

Scant research has been conducted into the standardisation of print production in nineteenth-century Australia and, specifically in this case, how this standardisation was documented, such as by contemporary style manuals. Notably, in regard to Degotardi, Jürgen Wegner produced a facsimile edition of *The Art of Printing* in 1982, with an accompanying commentary; John Fletcher published a preliminary article on Degotardi in *Biblionews* in 1981, which culminated in his biography in 1984; and Dennis Bryans included a minor study of Degotardi and his *Art of Printing* in his doctoral thesis in 2000. No scholarly research has been discovered to date on Fryer. The objective of this chapter therefore is to resume this enquiry, uncovering the legacies of Degotardi and Fryer to the Australian book publishing industry by building their historical biographies and undertaking textual analyses of their manuals. Synthesising both secondary sources and primary materials, such as nineteenth-century newspaper articles, assisted with building the historical biographies.

According to the *Macquarie Dictionary*, Australia's national dictionary, style relates to "the rules of spelling, punctuation, capitalisation, etc., observed by a publishing house, newspaper, etc."[1] Furthermore, while not specifically utilising the term "editorial style", but a publishing house's "house style", the *Style Manual* further supplies that editorial guidelines address "hyphenation, the use of shortened forms, the treatment of numbers, the method of citation" and so on.[2] That is, editorial style relates to rules designed to ensure not only consistency within and across all titles produced by a publishing company, but also the consistency and effectiveness of authors' meaning.

Style guides outline the rules pertaining to grammar, punctuation, spelling, hyphenation, capitalisation and italicisation, for example; explain the parts of a book, such as the preliminaries, headings, body text and end matter, their typography and typesetting; and include proofreading symbols that are used to mark authorial and editorial corrections, either interlineally or in margins, on manuscript and typeset page proofs. These corrections are then incorporated by typesetters before proceeding to print. Such mark-up represents the communication

---

1   Macmillan Publishers. *Macquarie Dictionary Online*. 2003.
2   Snooks & Co. *Style Manual for Authors, Editors and Printers*, 6th ed. (Milton, Qld: John Wiley & Sons, 2002): 258.

channel, or metalanguage, necessary for these stakeholders to share the same working space, regardless of where or in what manner they complete their individual daily tasks.

As mentioned, Australia's first book on printing was John Degotardi's *The Art of Printing in Its Various Branches*. A question that arises from this is: how then did late eighteenth- and nineteenth-century stakeholders obtain practical instruction before 1861? Many of the printing and publishing professionals working in Sydney and Melbourne, for example, were migrants who brought their experience with them, obtained primarily on the job, but on occasion through family. Notable examples include George Howe (1769–1821) and Ferdinand François (F. F.) Baillière (1838–81). Acknowledged to be "the Father of Australian printing",[3] George Howe, son of printer Thomas Howe, worked as his father's apprentice in the British West Indies, where he was born, before moving to London in 1790 to find employment, such as at *The Times*. However, owing to a "period of uneven prosperity"[4] and unemployment, Howe was arrested for theft in 1799 and sentenced to death, though this sentence was commuted to transportation for life. He arrived with his family in Sydney Cove on the *Royal Admiral* in November 1800 and was employed as the governor's printer in 1802. And, born in London but descended from a French bookselling and publishing family, F. F. Baillière migrated to Melbourne in 1860 and established his bookselling business that year in Collins Street; he would later undertake publishing work as well.[5] For those stakeholders beginning their training in the colonies, according to Hauser, it would be "many decades... before schools for

---

3   Don Hauser, *Printers on the Streets and Lanes of Melbourne (1837–1975)* (Melbourne: Nondescript Press, 2006), 13; Victor Crittenden, "Pioneers of Publishing: Book Publishing in the Australian Colonies, 1788–1860," *Publishing Studies* 1 (1995): 5.

4   Sandy Blair, "George Howe and Early Printing in New South Wales," *The Australian Printing Historical Society Journal* 1 (1986): 4.

5   Laurel Clark, "F.F. Baillière: Book Seller to the University of Melbourne," *The University of Melbourne Library Journal* 6, no. 2 (2000).

apprenticeship training began in Australia"; that "apart from internal training provided by government printers and large commercial firms, young trainees entering the print trade mostly learned their skills from senior 'gratuitous' journeymen, who... kept their 'trade secrets to themselves'".[6]

Christened Johann Nepomuk Degotardi, John Degotardi (1823–82) was born in Laibach, now Ljubljana, the capital of Slovenia. Similar to Baillière, Degotardi's immediate and extended families worked in the print trade. A "peripatetic" printer, Degotardi's father, Johann, moved in 1824 to Graz, Styria, when Degotardi was nine months old.[7] Johann was presumed by Fletcher to be related to Anton Degotardi, who owned a printing house in Laibach.[8] Degotardi's own professional experience began in September 1836, with a five-year apprenticeship as a compositor at Andreas Leykam, in Graz, where his father also worked as a printer. Demonstrating an equally peripatetic nature as his father, Degotardi decided in 1843 that he would "perfect his trade" in Europe, in particular Germany.[9] Degotardi moved first to Tübingen and worked for the printing house of L. F. Fues and then to Stuttgart at the printing house of J. G. Cotta. From there, Degotardi travelled in September 1844 to Itzehoe, where, besides eight months' employment with C. H. Anderson in Tönning from July 1845 to February 1846, he worked as a compositor until August 1848. Motivated not only by his ambition to "spend some time in one of Europe's leading cities", as he related in his diary, but also by the beginnings of the German–Danish War in 1848, Degotardi travelled to London in August of that year

---

6 Hauser, *Printers on the Streets*, 17.

7 Jürgen Wegner and Johann Nepomuk Degotardi, *The Art of Printing: Text* (Boronia: Brandywine Press, 1982), 1.

8 John Fletcher, "John Degotardi: Printer, Publisher and Photographer." *Studies in Australian Bibliography*, no. 25. (Sydney: Book Collectors' Society of Australia, 1984), 3.

9 Dennis Bryans, "A Seed of Consequence: Indirect Image Transfer and Chemical Printing: the Role Played by Lithography in the Development of Printing Technology," (PhD diss., Swinburne University of Technology, 2000), 21.

and was employed at John Wertheim and Co. for the next five years.[10] Degotardi also acted as London correspondent for German newspaper *Grazer Zeitung* from 1849 to 1850. On January 23, 1853, Degotardi departed with his wife, Minna, for Sydney on the *Panthea* and arrived in Port Jackson on May 8.

Degotardi is thought to have worked for a short time as a compositor at the *Sydney Morning Herald* before establishing in June 1853 his printing company, John Degotardi and Co., Engravers, Lithographers and General Printers, at 481 George Street;[11] though, more recently, Neidorf reported that Degotardi had been employed briefly at Allan & Wigley before establishing his printery.[12] Neidorf neither confirmed Degotardi's employment at the *Sydney Morning Herald* nor elaborated on Degotardi's responsibilities at Allan & Wigley, besides noting that he worked as a "pressman".[13]

John Degotardi and Co. printed diverse titles for equally diverse publishers: the company "printed maps, plans, prints, pamphlets, magazines, a newspaper (German), circulars, labels and sheet music" for J. H. Anderson, D. Buist & Son, Woolcott & Clarke and Smith & Gordon, to name a few.[14] The first publication to be printed in 1853 was an eight-page bilingual pamphlet, *Rules of the German Club in Sydney*, where the German text appeared on the verso and English on the recto. The following year, Degotardi moved his business to 20 York Street, where he printed, for example, ephemera "traditional to the jobbing

---

10 John Fletcher, "John Degotardi: Printer, Publisher and Photographer," *Studies in Australian Bibliography*, no. 25), 9. Jürgen Wegner and Johann Nepomuk Degotardi, *The Art of Printing: Reprint* (Boronia: Brandywine Press, 1982), 4.

11 Fletcher, "John Degotardi: Printer, Publisher and Photographer"; Keast Burke, "Degotardi, John (1823–1882)," in *Australian Dictionary of Biography* (Canberra: National Centre of Biography, Australian National University, 1972), http://adb. anu.edu.au/biography/degotardi-john-3387/text5129; W. D. Thorn, "Use of Galley Proofs in Australia in 1860", *The Library* 5, no. 2 (June 1, 1977), 161–2.

12 Prue Neidorf, "A Guide to Dating Music Publishing in Sydney and Melbourne, 1800–1899," (MA thesis, University of Wollongong, 1999), 15.

13 Ibid.

14 Ibid., 154.

printer", such as the maps 'Plan No. 2. Sydenham Farms. Illawarra and Cooks River New Road' for auctioneers Bowden and Threlkeld;[15] as well as sheet music, such as the *Australian Presentation Album* for Woolcott & Clarke.[16] Degotardi's next sizeable publication was a thirty-page booklet, including a fold-out plate of twelve diagrams, entitled *On the Construction and Management of Chronometers, Watches and Clocks*, which he printed in 1855 for Edwin Beckmann, a chronometer and watchmaker who, according to Hawkins, was "Degotardi's business associate, former landlord and next door neighbor in Balmain".[17]

Degotardi's first publishing endeavour was the thirty-two-page, monthly-issued *The Spirit of the Age*, which started in June 1855, had a circulation of 2000 copies and cost one shilling and six pence for a single copy and twelve shillings for an annual subscription; rural subscription cost 14 shillings per annum.[18] *The Spirit of the Age* contained "carefully selected articles from all the best works and periodicals of the day published in Europe and America" and were "a carefully weighted balance between history, travel and science".[19] Despite the magazine's publicised selling point of being "the cheapest Monthly Magazine published", healthy subscription list and revenue from advertisers, it ceased publication after eight issues in January 1856.[20] The reason for its demise has not yet been explained;[21] however, Fletcher has surmised that "Degotardi's hand of German pragmatism lay too weightily

---

15 Fletcher, "John Degotardi: Printer, Publisher and Photographer," 25.

16 Neidorf, "A Guide to Dating Music," 154.

17 John Hawkins, "Julius Hogart, Behind the Shop Front: Part 2," *Australiana* (August 2000): 74.

18 Fletcher, "John Degotardi: Printer, Publisher and Photographer," 27, 110; and Wegner and Degotardi, *The Art of Printing: Text*, 6.

19 Fletcher, "John Degotardi: Printer, Publisher and Photographer," 27.

20 Wegner and Degotardi, *The Art of Printing: Text*, 6.

21 For instance, see Michael Richards, *People, Print & Paper: A Catalogue of a Travelling Exhibition Celebrating the Books of Australia, 1788–1988* (Canberra: National Library of Australia, 1988); and Bryans, "A Seed of Consequence."

on the reading matter too carefully selected",[22] which suggests that Degotardi's editorial imperative failed to sufficiently cater to the reading needs of his audience. Degotardi also published the four-page German weekly newspaper *Australische Deutsche Zeitung* at his new premises of 313 George Street. Subscription cost four shillings per quarter. This was a short-lived publication, however: it ceased in 1859.[23] One final notable title is the sheet music edition by George Peck of Henry Kendall's poem "Silent Tears", which Degotardi printed in late 1859.[24] Its noteworthiness derives from the numerous typographical errors in the text—Fletcher noted that "Degotardi or his engraver [treated] with abandon"[25]—which did not reflect well on a compositor and printer known for his meticulous practice. According to Burke, "the poet's letter of correction was printed in the *Empire* [on December 8], but the words were engraved on copper and could not be changed".[26] *The Art of Printing* was published in 1861 at a third premises at Robin Hood Lane, off George Street.

The Art of Printing was a singular production with "irregular dimensions", measuring 216–21 millimetres in height and 140 millimetres in width[27] and side sewn, with a bright-green paper jacket with the letters of the short title set in uppercase and printed in gold.[28] Besides the title page, the book comprised two signatures: one unsigned signature of sixteen pages, which included the preface, introduction, contents and illustrations lists on the same page, and fourteen pages of body text, starting on page 3 and ending on page 16; and the other signed 'B' of eight pages, which comprised pages 17–24 of the remaining body

22 Fletcher, "John Degotardi: Printer, Publisher and Photographer," 30.
23 Wegner and Degotardi, *The Art of Printing: Text*, 6; see also Richards, *People, Print & Paper*.
24 Wegner and Degotardi, *The Art of Printing: Text*; and Bryans, "A Seed of Consequence."
25 Fletcher, "John Degotardi: Printer, Publisher and Photographer," 47.
26 Burke, "Degotardi, John (1823–1882)," para. 1.
27 Wegner and Degotardi, *The Art of Printing: Text*, 14.
28 Fletcher, "John Degotardi: Printer, Publisher and Photographer," 54.

text. It also featured end matter of nine leaves of plates, or printing specimens, one of which was folded; all appeared on recto pages only, with verso pages left blank. These specimens included a copper engraving of a bill-head, an engraved music score, photolithographic map printing, photolithographic printing from stone and nature printing (of a fern frond).

Degotardi's *The Art of Printing* is an extremely rare book: Richards has observed that only three copies exist, though without identifying where these copies reside.[29] Wegner has confirmed that one incomplete copy is at the Mitchell Library, in Sydney; the second is at the National Library of Australia (NLA), in Canberra; and the third is a private copy.[30] The incomplete copy at the Mitchell Library comprises, according to Wegner, "the front wrapper and text pages only. The important pages of specimens are lacking." However, the catalogue of the State Library of New South Wales (SLNSW) has not substantiated this, only that their copy is "bound with other pamphlets, some of which are signed 'G. F. Rusden'". Wegner has also mentioned that the copy at the NLA was "missing at the time of writing but which has reported... as being complete with both specimens of printing and the wrappers bound in"; however, the NLA's catalogue verifies that a copy can indeed be viewed there. Wegner produced a limited-edition facsimile reprint in 1982 from the private copy, copies of which can be accessed on-site such as at the NLA, the SLNSW and the State Library of Queensland. In the introduction to his biography of Degotardi, Fletcher recounts how he was "introduced [in the early 1970s] by Wallace Kirsop of Monash University to Mrs Edith Degotardi of Newport, NSW, and to the John Degotardi papers in her possession" and how these papers were "left behind in Sydney in [his] care" after she relocated to South Australia in 1976; Fletcher reprinted these papers in his appendices.[31]

---

29 Richards, *People, Print & Paper*.
30 Wegner and Degotardi, *The Art of Printing: Text*, 12.
31 Fletcher, "John Degotardi: Printer, Publisher and Photographer," vi.

He also states that Wegner requested that he "write a brief note on John Degotardi" for Wegner's facsimile edition; Fletcher never identifies in whose possession this private copy resides, nor does Wegner in the commentary accompanying his facsimile reprint.

In his preface to *The Art of Printing*, Degotardi explained clearly his dual objectives for publishing his manual: first, "to make known the extraordinary progress that is daily being made in the Art of Printing, and which entitles this to be placed in the foremost ranks of scientific arts"; and second, "to supply the deficiency", to fill "the absence of a descriptive work explanatory of the subject", by publishing the first book on printing in Australia that could be "comprehended by every class of readers".[32] Directly afterwards, Degotardi emphasised proudly, and strategically in a commercial sense, his manual's entirely Australian production: "All the specimens and illustrations... have been executed at his establishment, and that the entire pamphlet is an Australian production, the type having been cast in Sydney". After completing an examination of colonial type specimens, Bryans confirms this local production when he identifies that the "slightly wider colonial modern face roman employed by John Degotardi... may have come from the Davies Brothers foundry", which has been located at that time in Chippendale, Sydney.[33]

Degotardi demonstrated in *The Art of Printing* a thorough, dedicated attention to his task. First, he provided twenty definitions of key printing terms, such as typography, lithography and nature printing. These definitions were featured in the footnotes of pages 4–6, accompanying his brief survey of the early progress of printing, from Johannes Gutenberg, Johann Fust and Peter Schöffer to William Caxton. Next, Degotardi comprehensively explained the four branches

---

32 Wegner and Degotardi, *The Art of Printing: Reprint*, i.
33 Dennis Bryans, "Nineteenth-Century Australian Type Foundries," *BSANZ Bulletin* 23, no. 3 (1999): 171; see also Bryans, "The Beginnings of Type Founding in Sydney: Alexander Thompson's Type, His Foundry, and His Exports to Inter-Colonial Printers," *Journal of Design History* 9, no. 2 (1996): 75–6, 81–2.

of the Art of Printing, which were impressions in haut-relief, such as typography, or letter-press printing; impressions in bas-relief, such as engraving; chemical impressions, such as lithography; and natural impressions, such as photolithography. He then supplied an account of the Imperial Printing Institute in Vienna and a description of Alois von Auer's self-feeding steam press—von Auer (1813–69) was at that time director of the Imperial and Royal Court and State Printery in Vienna, with whom Degotardi frequently corresponded from 1859 to 1864.[34]

Degotardi separated letter-press printing into two distinct groups: composition and press-work.[35] For the purposes of this chapter and its focus on the printed page, composition is considered only. Similar to contemporary nineteenth-century English printer's manuals, such as C. H. Timperley's *The Printer's Manual*, which was published in 1838, Degotardi related in detail for the Australian print trade how each book page was specifically produced. Simply put, the "compositor [made] himself acquainted with the different sorts of type possessed by the office in which he [was] working". The principal or overseer, not the compositor, arranged the specific "measure (or size of the page) and the description of type". "After receiving his manuscript or printed copy", the compositor then proceeded to fill his composing stick with type from "a pair of type-cases before him". Once filled, the compositor emptied it on "a brass or wooden galley" and repeated this procedure until his section of copy was finished—that is, if more than one compositor was involved in the task of typesetting an entire publication. All pieces of copy were brought together, the required length of a page measured off, the head line attached, and a string finally tied around each page. The proof-sheet of a specific number of pages was next taken. The proofreader then compared the proof-sheet with the original manuscript or printed

---

34 Fletcher, "John Degotardi: Printer, Publisher and Photographer," 42–5.
35 Wegner and Degotardi, *The Art of Printing: Reprint*, 13–5.

page, marking any corrections in the margin. The compositor revised the proof-sheet according to the proofreader's instructions, and the entire "form" was then sent to press. An accompanying footnote briefly outlines the role of editors and proofreaders, specifically in relation to the newspaper presses. Degotardi stated that "[when] the 'copy' has been selected and arranged by the editor or sub-editor of the day, it is handed over to the manager of the printing department... a galley is soon filled; a proof of this is immediately pulled on a small galley-press, at once given to the proof-readers, and then corrected whilst the next 'slip' is in the course of progress". In this way, Degotardi delineated—and initiated standardising progress towards—not only the composition of the Australian printed page, but also the production process of a publication.

A search of the NLA's Trove online database of nineteenth-century newspapers provided evidence of Degotardi's success in instructing not only the Australian print trade but also the general community— hence, "every class of readers".[36] For example, an article regarding photolithography in the *Sydney Morning Herald*, dated July 7, 1862, advised that a recently published map of New South Wales by Reuss and Brown represented the first use of photolithography in the colony; Degotardi's printery had been responsible for its production. The article then explained how photolithography was carried out, "as furnished... by Mr Degotardi": "Photolithography is the art of reproducing the original drawing by means of the lithographic stone; the subject being first photographed in the ordinary way and then transferred to the stone, from which any copies may be obtained." The article also identified its numerous commercial advantages: for example, "it diminishes the cost of production", "supplies copies of plans, maps, pictures, or any subject with astonishing accuracy" and "[preserves] plates for future printing". The furnishing of this instruction by Degotardi presumably resulted from an interview, evinced at the article's conclusion by a personal

36 Ibid., i.

invitation to readers by Degotardi to inspect "specimens at his establishment"; however, the instruction not surprisingly mirrored that in *The Art of Printing*, which was published one year prior to this article.

Regrettably, Degotardi's *The Art of Printing* did not address how each feature of a page, such as headings and footnotes, was typeset. Such instruction was supplied approximately seventy years later in 1930 by Benjamin Fryer in his limited-edition publication *A Book and Its Elements*—its final page enumerates that the print run for this title was two hundred copies. To date, no scholarly examination of Fryer has been uncovered. A search of Trove has yielded a letter to the editor of the *Sydney Morning Herald* on May 19, 1928 by F. Neville Barnett, Honorary Secretary of the Ex Libris (Bookplate) Society, in which he identified Fryer as "of the Printing Industry Craftsman of Australia". Barnett also related that Fryer gave regular lectures on books and printing to the society. This was confirmed in a later piece, published in the *North Western Courier* and dated April 28, 1930. This piece further revealed that Fryer's specific position was president and that he was travelling to Los Angeles in August of that year to attend the Printing Craftsmen Convention. To promote Australia and Australian printing while in the United States, Fryer took "some samples of Australian printing for distribution". Moreover, Fryer was identified as being part "of Carmichael and Co. Ltd". Evidence so far points to this company being an importer of printing materials. An advertisement in the November 1936 issue of the journal *Art in Australia* revealed that Fryer also held the position of secretary for the Australian Limited Editions Society.

A further search of Trove is building a picture of Fryer as a regular, often passionate, writer and commentator regarding typography, in particular, and the Australian print trade, in general. Between 1930 and 1953, Fryer published nine print-related titles, such as *Mass Craftsmanship* in 1934, *New System Linotype Operating Handbook* in 1940, *Newspaper Handbook: Typographical Practices for Australian*

Offices in 1942, and *A Book is Built* in 1952. Fryer wrote two articles for trade journals in 1936 and 1941: the first, "A Note of Australian Typography" in *Art in Australia*; and the second, "A New Typeface in The Home" in *The Home: An Australian Quarterly*. He also wrote more than twenty-five articles or letters to various New South Wales newspapers between 1925 and 1938 relating to such matters as the establishment of university presses, trade education and the American printing trade. For example, appearing in the *Sydney Morning Herald* were Fryer's articles "Not a Golden Age of Book Production" on March 21, 1925 and "A New Order. A Mass Craftsmanship" on November 24, 1933; his piece on "William Caxton: The Father of Printing" was printed in *Manilla Express* on April 12, 1935.

From the first line of the preface to *A Book and Its Elements*, Fryer offers an eloquent analogy to express his philosophy of book production, or "bookwork": "Bookwork is the riverbed of thought carved through history by the sentiments and emotions of humanity."[37] From this, he declared that printers "[worked] in a plastic medium that enshrines the spirit of his craft, and the craftsman knows without vigorous outpouring in the making of books, a people makes no real progress". These ruminations could be interpreted in diverse ways; however, for the purposes of this discussion, the following appears pertinent: first, the print trade is integral to social formation and the creation of communities of knowledge;[38] and second, "bookwork" is a fluid craft that adapts to institutional and intellectual changes to ensure both the successful publication of books, or any other printed matter such as newspapers, and the building of a literary canon. This becomes clear when Fryer writes the following: "Native expression lies as much in the printing of a book as in literary form. We therefore submit this

---

37　Benjamin Fryer, *A Book and Its Elements* (Sydney: Printing Industry Craftsman of Australia, 1930), 7.

38　Benedict Anderson, *Imagined Communities: Reflections on the Origin and Spread of Nationalism* (London: Verso, 1983).

short treatise in the hope of furthering the growing interest in the book as an expressional of national taste and culture."[39] In addition to this, in a more practical sense, Fryer presented in his preface an expertise, confidence and pride in the Australian print trade that is reminiscent of Degotardi, writing that, "Hints for good usage are what are here suggested, and the work itself practice of preachment. It fares forth as a bit of Australian workmanship, in the hope that there will be much emulation."[40] These "hints" amount to comprehensive instruction on not only the physical materials used to make books, namely typefaces, paper and ink; but also specific features of a page from header to footer, including the body text between them, and from preliminaries to end matter, such as imprint pages and bibliographies. Each feature—running heads, footers, body text, imprint pages and bibliographies—are addressed below to demonstrate how Fryer contributed to the standardisation of the Australian printed page.

For running heads, Fryer advised that running heads improve the appearance of pages; however, repeating the same heading from verso to recto produced monotony. Therefore, to ensure that "every piece of type in a forme should be doing useful work", Fryer recommended that the verso running heads should relate to the book's chapter, while those on the recto should refer to the subject on the page.[41] Though, with poetry, Fryer stated that the poem's title be placed on the recto and verso. For footnotes, Fryer instructed that they be typeset two or three sizes smaller than the body text. Footnotes at that time, according to Fryer, were usually set in double-column format, though a single-column layout was acceptable as well. The reference marks were typically superior figures; traditional symbols, such as the asterisk and dagger, were to be used for period works. For body

39 Fryer, *A Book and Its Elements*, 7.
40 Ibid., 18.
41 Ibid., 18.

text between the header and footer, Fryer counselled that fewer than thirty and more than fifty letters on a line would be "difficult for the eye"; that forty to the line were sufficient.[42] In terms of spacing, close spacing was considered to be "best typography" as long as readers did not experience difficulty distinguishing one word from the next. And em quad spaces, which were equal to one em, were no longer required after full points.

Typesetting preliminaries and end matter, such as imprints and bibliographies respectively, requires not just a substantive perspective, as shown by Fryer's instruction here. For example, as is commonly known today, imprint pages are usually placed on the verso directly after the recto title page. More particularly though, Fryer recommended that small capitals be used to ensure that the text appeared "presentable", though lower case was acceptable if the "book is in lower case style".[43] Fryer noted that most typographers were opposed to mixing italics and small capitals on imprint pages for aesthetic reasons. It is important to recognise here that Fryer's awareness of printers' opposition to the intermixing of italics and small capitals points to his knowledge of typographic practice dating back to eighteenth-century England. As Barker has observed, "sobriety was the new style" of the eighteenth-century.[44] Before this, italic, for example, was liberally employed to the extent that two-thirds of a book could be typeset in italic. Printer John Smith, in his manual *The Printer's Grammar*, was the first to advise the English print trade against the overuse of italic: "The mixing of said two species of Letter... ought to be avoided."[45] Moving on, identical

---

42 Ibid., 24.

43 Ibid., 21.

44 Nicholas Barker, "Typography and the Meaning of Words: The Revolution in the Layout of Books in the Eighteenth-century," in *The Book and the Book Trade in Eighteenth-Century Europe*, ed. Giles Barber and Bernard Fabian (Hamburg: Dr Ernest Hauswedell & Co, 1981), 131.

45 John Smith, *The Printer's Grammar* (London: printed for the editor; and sold by W. Owen, near Temple Bar; and by M. Cooper, at the Globe in Pater-Noster Row, 1755), 13.

to their modern counterparts, bibliographies preceded indexes, similar to appendices and glossaries; and Fryer advised that these sections be typeset a size smaller than the body text, though following the latter's style, and begin on a recto page.

From this, it is evident that bookwork relies on its inherent fluidity to accommodate, and complement, each of the features on the printed page, from header to footer and from preliminaries to end matter. Furthermore, proceeding from the minutiae to the substantive, each feature combines to form the architecture of not only the page but also the book in its entirety. As Fryer stated in his introduction: "A book should be regarded as a complete work to be done, in the same sense that an architect should visualize his building before he lays foundation. Before the typographer sets a single line of type, he should have traversed the book from subject to binding, and have planned to have the whole in keeping."[46]

While Fryer explains further on that this "principle of unity in bookwork is one descended from William Morris, whose teachings, now in general practice with good printers, brought about the revival of bookmaking as an art", such architectural unity relating to bookwork manifested in the late seventeenth-century, with English printer Joseph Moxon and his printer's manual, *Mechanick Exercises, or the Doctrine of Handy-works Applied to the Art of Printing*, which was printed in 1683. Moxon includes "architect" to assist with defining, and conceptualising the omniscience of, the "typographer" in bookwork:

> *By a* Typographer, *I do not mean a* Printer, *as he is Vulgarly accounted, any more than Dr. Dee*[47] *means a* Carpenter *or* Mason *to be an* Architect: *But by a* Typographer, *I mean such a one, who by his own Judgement, from solid reasoning with himself, can either*

---

46 Fryer, *A Book and Its Elements*, 11.

47 Moxon refers to John Dee (1527–1608), English mathematician and astronomer.

perform, or direct others to perform from the beginning to the end, all the Handy-works and Physical Operations relating to Typographie.[48]

In conclusion, the purpose of this chapter was to resume research earlier conducted by, notably, Wegner, Fletcher and Bryans to uncover the legacies of John Degotardi and Benjamin Fryer to the Australian book industry, notably through building their historical biographies and undertaking textual analyses of their respective manuals, *The Art of Printing* and *A Book and Its Elements*. Both Degotardi and Fryer manifested strong ties with the industry, either familially and/or professionally, and exploited their practical knowledge to provide instruction when either no material, in the case of Degotardi, or very little, for Fryer, was on offer for the Australian context. Degotardi's focus was principally substantive: outlining the different forms of printing, and how the printed page was typeset by compositors and corrected by proofreaders. Through this, the production cycle of a book was demarcated. Fryer similarly concentrated on substantive matters, considering the physical materials used to make books and explaining all the parts of a book, from preliminaries to end matter, though he also examined the minutiae, the specifics on the page, from header to footer. Fryer extended this standardisation with the publication of *A Book Is Built* in 1952. While *The Style Manual for Authors, Editors and Printers* has been the leading style guide for the Australian book trade since 1966 and both Degotardi and Fryer are sadly little known, their legacies are clear: they provided the practical means to guide the Australian print trade and the wider community and, through this, as Fryer expressed, support the "growing interest in the book as an expression of national taste and culture."[49]

---

48 Joseph Moxon, *Mechanick Exercises, or the Doctrine of Handy-works Applied to the Art of Printing* (London: Printed for Joseph Moxon on the West-side of Fleet-ditch, at the Sign of Atlas, 1683), 81–82, author's italics retained.

49 Fryer, *A Book and Its Elements*, 7.

Works cited

Anderson, Benedict. *Imagined Communities: Reflections on the Origin and Spread of Nationalism*. London: Verso, 1983.

Barker, Nicolas. "Typography and the Meaning of Words: The Revolution in the Layout of Books in the Eighteenth-century." In *The Book and the Book Trade in Eighteenth-Century Europe*, edited by Giles Barber and Bernard Fabian, 127–65. Hamburg: Dr Ernst Hauswedell & Co, 1981.

Barnett, F. Neville. "Ex libris: To the Editor of the Herald." *Sydney Morning Herald*, May 19, 1928. Accessed August 1, 2017, http://nla.gov.au/nla. news-article16465896.

Blair, Sandy. "George Howe and Early Printing in New South Wales." *The Australian Printing Historical Society Journal* 1 (1986): 1–15.

Bryans, Dennis. "The Beginnings of Type Founding in Sydney: Alexander Thompson's Type, His Foundry, and His Exports to Inter-Colonial Printers." *Journal of Design History* 9, no. 2 (1996): 75–86.

———. "Nineteenth-Century Australian Type Foundries." *BSANZ Bulletin* 23, no. 3 (1999): 164–179.

———. "A Seed of Consequence: Indirect Image Transfer and Chemical Printing: The Role Played by Lithography in the Development of Printing Technology." PhD diss., Swinburne University of Technology, Melbourne, 2000.

Burke, Keast. "Degotardi, John (1823–1882)." [Electronic Resource]. *Australian Dictionary of Biography*. Canberra: National Centre of Biography, Australian National University, 1972. Accessed March 22, 2018, http://adb. anu.edu.au/biography/degotardi-john-3387/text5129.

Clark, Laurel. "F. F. Bailliere: Book Seller to the University of Melbourne." *The University of Melbourne Library Journal* 6, no. 2 (2000): 13–26.

Crittenden, Victor. "Pioneers of Publishing: Book Publishing in the Australian Colonies, 1788–1860." *Publishing Studies* 1 (1995): 5–11.

Fletcher, John. "J.N. Degotardi, Author of 'The Art of Printing.'" *Biblionews*, no. 248–9 (1981): 30–44.

———. "John Degotardi: Printer, Publisher and Photographer." *Studies in Australian Bibliography*, no. 25. Sydney: Book Collectors' Society of Australia, 1984.

Fryer, Benjamin. *A Book and Its Elements*. Sydney: Printing Industry Craftsman of Australia, 1930.

"Gathered News." *North Western Courier*, April 28, 1930. Accessed August 1, 2018, http://nla.gov.au/nla.news-article138427098.

Hawkins, John. "Julius Hogarth, Behind the Shop Front: Part 2." *Australiana* (August 2000): 68–79.

Hauser, Don. *Printers on the Streets and Lanes of Melbourne* (1837–1975). Melbourne: Nondescript Press, 2006.

Macmillan Publishers. *Macquarie Dictionary Online*. 2003.

Moxon, Joseph. *Mechanick Exercises: Or, the Doctrine of Handy-works Applied to the Art of Printing. The second Volume*. London: Printed for Joseph Moxon on the West-side of Fleet-ditch, at the Sign of Atlas, 1683.

Neidorf, Prue. "A Guide to Dating Music Published in Sydney and Melbourne, 1800–1899." MA thesis, University of Wollongong, 1999.

"Photo-lithography." *Sydney Morning Herald*, July 7, 1862. Accessed August 1, 2018, http://nla.gov.au/nla.news-article28622697.

Richards, Michael. *People, Print & Paper: A Catalogue of a Travelling Exhibition Celebrating the Books of Australia, 1788–1988*. Canberra: National Library of Australia, 1988.

Smith, John. *The Printer's Grammar*. London: Printed for the editor; and sold by W. Owen, near Temple Bar; and by M. Cooper, at the Globe in Pater-Noster Row, 1755.

Snooks & Co. *Style Manual for Authors, Editors and Printers*. 6th ed. Milton, Qld: John Wiley & Sons, 2002.

Thorn, W. D. "Use of Galley Proofs in Australia in 1860." *The Library* 5, no. 2 (June 1977): 161–2.

Wegner, Jürgen, and Johann Nepomuk Degotardi. *The Art of Printing: Text*. Boronia: Brandywine Press, 1982.

———. *The Art of Printing: Reprint*. Boronia: Brandywine Press, 1982.

CHAPTER 6

Scholarly Feminist Presses

Germaine Greer and Stump Cross Books

MILLICENT WEBER

Book publishing and feminist politics are categorically intertwined. Publishing as an industry is primarily female, and yet a disproportionate number of leadership roles in the industry are occupied by men.[1] As a field of cultural production, literary culture demands significant cultural knowledge of its participants, it has clear commercial and populist imperatives, and it has historically published and promoted certain types of stories while pushing others to the sidelines. The entrenched and gendered power structures of publishing-as-industry are revealed by important industry research like the surveys conducted by *Books+Publishing* and *The Bookseller* into sexism and sexual harassment of publishing professionals, and is also being investigated by cutting-edge scholarly research.[2] Gender imbalances within the literary field—such as the unequal numbers

---

1 Sarah Couper, "Bookish Girls: Gender and Leadership in Australian Trade Publishing," in *The Return of Print? Contemporary Australian Publishing*, eds. Aaron Mannion and Emmett Stinson (Melbourne: Monash University Publishing, 2016), 43.

2 *Books+Publishing*, "Over Half of Book-Industry Survey Respondents Report Sexual Harassment," December 12, 2017, https://www.booksandpublishing.com. au/articles/2017/12/12/99463/over-half-of-book-industry-survey-respondents-report-sexual-harassment/; *The Bookseller*, "Sexual Harassment Reported by over Half in Trade Survey." November 10, 2017, https://www.thebookseller.com/ news/sexual-harassment-reported-over-half-trade-survey-671276; Claire Squires and Beth Driscoll, "The Sleaze-O-Meter: Sexual Harassment in the Publishing Industry," *Interscript*, 2018, https://www.interscriptjournal.com/online-magazine/ sleaze-o-meter.

of men and women being published, reviewed, programmed to speak and discussed by other writers—have likewise garnered recent attention as a result of surveys like the VIDA or the Stella Count, which tally gender disparity in publications and reviews.[3] Similar disparities between the gender of authors published and cited also exist within academic publishing.[4]

Publishing holds political power as a communicative act, and particularly as a form of mass-communication consecrated as authoritative through long tradition. In Simone Murray's words, "the act of publishing is, because of its role in determining the parameters of public debate, an inherently political act [...] women, recognising this fact, must intervene in the processes of literary production to ensure that women's voices are made audible".[5] Against this backdrop, how do we understand the efforts of feminists to intervene in the publishing industry and through it in the literary field, and against what criteria—political, aesthetic, commercial, or otherwise—can we evaluate their success? This chapter explores these questions in relation to the work of Germaine Greer in setting up and running independent publisher Stump Cross Books in the 1990s and 2000s.[6]

Feminist Presses

A number of independent presses subscribing to this vision of the enormous political potential of publishing and writing grew out of the

3   VIDA: Women in Literary Arts, "About the VIDA Count," 2012,
    https://www.vidaweb.org/the-count/; The Stella Prize, "2016 Stella Count," 2016,
    http://thestellaprize.com.au/the-count/2016-stella-count/; cf. also Harvey &
    Lamond's chapter in this volume.

4   Danica Savonick and Cathy N. Davidson, "Gender Bias in Academe: An
    Annotated Bibliography of Important Recent Studies," *LSE Impact Blog*, 2017,
    http://blogs.lse.ac.uk/impactofsocialsciences/2016/03/08/gender-bias-in-
    academe-an-annotated-bibliography/.

5   Simone Murray, *Mixed Media: Feminist Presses and Publishing Politics* (London:
    Pluto Press, 2004), 2.

6   Stump Cross Books, "Welcome to Stump Cross Books," http://www.sxbxsx.com/.

second-wave feminist movement, becoming increasingly prominent in the late 1970s and 1980s. Publishers like Virago, Spinifex Press and, more recently, Persephone Books offer successful examples of the viability of politically self-aware publishing, and also operate as useful contrasts to enable us to triangulate Greer's political and aesthetic efforts with Stump Cross Books.[7]

Virago styles itself "the international publisher of books by women for all readers, everywhere", and has been publishing books by women writers since its inception in 1973.[8] As well as contemporary literary writers—their list includes Sarah Waters, Linda Grant, Marilynne Robinson, Sarah Dunant, Maya Angelou and Margaret Atwood—Virago publishes literary non-fiction, and since 1978 has also been running an imprint, Virago Modern Classics, dedicated to republishing lost literary works.[9] Australia-based Spinifex describes itself as "publishing innovative and controversial feminist books with an optimistic edge", and has been publishing politically motivated feminist non-fiction, as well as some fiction and poetry, since 1991.[10] Persephone, which has been operating since 1998, "reprints neglected fiction and non-fiction by mid-twentieth-century (mostly) women writers".[11] Described by Rachel Cooke in an article for *The Guardian* as "the nearest thing British publishing has to a cult", Persephone started as a passion project, and has grown from a readership comprised of founder Nicola Beauman's own friendship circle into a subscription-like model

---

7   Virago, "About Virago," https://www.virago.co.uk/about/; Spinifex Press, "About Us," http://www.spinifexpress.com.au/About_Us/; Persephone Books, "Home," http://www.persephonebooks.co.uk/.

8   Virago, "About Virago."

9   Virago, "About Virago"; Rachel Cooke, "Taking Women off the Shelf," *The Guardian*, April 6, 2008, https://www.theguardian.com/books/2008/apr/06/fiction.features1.

10 Spinifex Press, "About Us."

11 Persephone Books, "Home."

whereby twenty-five thousand people are mailed and purchase from a biannual catalogue.[12]

Like other independent publishers and booksellers, feminist presses and bookstores in the late 1990s and into the new millennium struggled to keep abreast of rapid technological change, suffered from the online migration of the book-buying public, and operated in a publishing landscape increasingly dominated by multinational corporations. Spinifex touts itself as operating "at the forefront of technological change" (at least by the standards of the 1990s and early 2000s), with their early adoption of ebooks and online catalogues.[13] Virago and Persephone, by contrast, make a prominent feature of the tactile nature of the high quality of their print publications. In 2018 Virago released "a baker's dozen of stunning, deluxe paperbacks and a hardback anthology, designed by Hannah Wood and featuring artwork by the incredible illustrator, Yehrin Tong",[14] while each Persephone title "has an elegant grey jacket, a 'fabric' endpaper with matching bookmark, and a preface by writers such as Jilly Cooper, David Kynaston and Elaine Showalter".[15]

While the lists of Virago and Spinifex link them closely to mainstream and grassroots gender politics, Persephone's list is not overtly feminist, and its aesthetics, priorities, and business model align it more closely with middlebrow reading practices.[16] This is evident in the trajectory of Persephone's development, from friendship circle to subscriber in-group; in the description of their titles, eschewing both the overtly literary and the populist, as "chosen to appeal to busy people

---

12 Rachel Cooke, "One Shade of Grey: How Nicola Beauman Made an Unlikely Success of Persephone Books," *The Guardian*, November 25, 2012, https://www.theguardian.com/books/2012/nov/25/nicola-beauman-persephone-books-founder-interview.

13 Spinifex Press, "About Us."

14 Virago, "About Virago."

15 Persephone Books, "Home."

16 Cf. Beth Driscoll, *The New Literary Middlebrow: Tastemakers and Reading in the Twenty-First Century* (Basingstoke: Palgrave Macmillan, 2014).

wanting titles that are neither too literary nor too commercial";[17] and in the domestic setting evoked by the matching "elegant jacket[s]" and "'fabric' endpaper".[18] The success—vis-à-vis the introduction—of Virago and Spinifex might be measured against criteria relating to the political visibility of their titles and authors or the breadth of their circulation. Persephone's success, by contrast, is in its creation of a sustainable and vibrant reading community, evidenced by the cultish devotion of Persephone's readers and supporters.

The case study that is the focus of this chapter—Stump Cross Books—was both a scholarly and a political project, and one which was ultimately commercially unsuccessful in managing the shift to twenty-first century ways of doing business. It was started and run by Germaine Greer: ubiquitous feminist, journalist, writer, public speaker, and professional controversialist. Stump Cross was intermittently active during the late 1980s through the early 2000s and, under its auspices, Greer and other co-editors produced several collections of the poetry of seventeenth- and eighteenth-century women writers. It was a revisionist exercise, seeking to reinsert early women writers into the predominantly male tradition of English literature. It was also a project that revelled in the trimmings and trappings of print materiality—evidence of which is retained in Greer's archive held at the University of Melbourne Archives (discussed in more depth below). Building on research undertaken using this archive, this chapter situates the Stump Cross Books venture within the context of Greer's literary, scholarly and feminist work.

---

17 Persephone Books, "Home."
18 This domesticity is also playfully evoked by the publisher's well-known tradition of stopping daily for afternoon tea. From their website FAQs (Persephone Books, "Frequently Asked Questions," https://www.persephonebooks.co.uk/faq): "Do you really all stop for tea and cake every day at 4 o'clock? Yes, certainly."

Stump Cross Books and Greer's Politics

As I've discussed elsewhere, Germaine Greer's cultural and political commentary has been both influential and extremely problematic.[19] A major player in the second-wave feminist movement in Australia and the UK in particular, Greer completed a PhD on Shakespeare's comedies at the University of Cambridge in 1969, and has worked in English literature departments in the UK and US.[20] Her best-known work, feminist treatise *The Female Eunuch*, was followed by other titles variously feminist, literary, critical and environmental.[21] Her journalism, political and environmental—including a stint writing a gardening column under the pseudonym "Rose Blight"—was primarily aimed at a politically aware general audience, appearing in, for example, *The Guardian*, *The Daily Telegraph* and *The Independent*. Other publications Greer was involved in in the late 1960s and early 1970s are underground exemplars of the sexual libertarian movement; these include *Oz* magazine, for which she wrote, and *Suck* magazine, which she helped establish in 1969.[22]

Greer's influence as a feminist remains widely recognised—she still writes regular opinion pieces, is programmed to speak at events and festivals,[23] and in 2018 was awarded Australian of the Year in the UK.[24] Greer is also widely recognised as holding increasingly problematic political views associated with the second-wave movement, in particular

19 Millicent Weber, *Literary Festivals and Contemporary Book Culture* (London: Palgrave Macmillan, 2018), 211–212.

20 Christine Wallace, *Germaine Greer: Untamed Shrew* (Sydney: Pan Macmillan Australia, 2013).

21 Germaine Greer, *The Female Eunuch* (London: MacGibbon & Kee, 1970).

22 Kate Gleeson, "From Suck Magazine to Corporate Paedophilia. Feminism and Pornography—Remembering the Australian Way," *Women's Studies International Forum* 38 (2013).

23 Cf. Weber, 2018, 211.

24 Alison Flood, "Germaine Greer Criticises 'Whingeing' #MeToo Movement," *The Guardian*, January 23, 2018, http://www.theguardian.com/books/2018/jan/23/germaine-greer-criticises-whingeing-metoo-movement.

in relation to gender essentialism. As a Fellow of all-women Newnham College at the University of Cambridge, Greer campaigned unsuccessfully in 1997 to have transgender physicist Rachel Padman thrown out.[25] In *The Whole Woman*, the sequel to *The Female Eunuch*, Greer characterised transgender women as "pantomime dames", and she has been vocal in her refusal to accept transgender women as women, recently and prominently in relation to Caitlyn Jenner.[26] These views have led to Greer's labelling as a trans-exclusionary radical feminist, or TERF, alongside other prominent second-wave feminists like Sheila Jeffreys.[27] Greer has also expressed highly problematic views about sexual assault and consent.[28]

Greer's second-wave politics dovetail with the work of Spinifex Press. Spinifex's list includes determinedly anti–sex work titles—recent and prominent ones include edited collections *Prostitution Narratives: Stories of Survival in the Sex Trade* and *Big Porn Inc: Exposing the Harms of the Global Porn Industry*, and the Australian edition of Julie Bindel's *The Pimping of Prostitution: Abolishing the Sex Work Myth*.[29] Like TERFs, sex

---

25 Clare Garner, "Fellows Divided over Don Who Breached Last Bastion," *The Independent*, June 25, 1997.

26 Germaine Greer, *The Whole Woman* (New York: Doubleday, 1999), 64.
    Germaine Greer, "Trans Women 'Not women'," interview by Kirsty Wark, *BBC Newsnight*, October 24, 2015, http://www.bbc.com/news/av/uk-34625512/germaine-greer-transgender-women-are-not-women.

27 Alex Schede and Anna Theris, "Controversy in the Classroom," *Farrago*, May 26, 2014. https://umsu.unimelb.edu.au/farrago/controversy-in-the-classroom/.

28 E.g. Broede Carmody, "Germaine Greer Announces New Book in Wake of #MeToo Backlash," *The Sydney Morning Herald*, March 28, 2018, https://www.smh.com.au/entertainment/books/germaine-greer-announces-new-book-in-wake-of-metoo-backlash-20180328-p4z6mk.html; Amanda Erickson, "Feminist Germaine Greer Says Most Rape Is Just 'Bad Sex,'" *Washington Post*, May 31, 2018, https://www.washingtonpost.com/news/worldviews/wp/2018/05/31/feminist-germaine-greer-says-most-rape-is-just-bad-sex/; Flood, "Germaine Greer Criticises."

29 Julie Bindel, *The Pimping of Prostitution: Abolishing the Sex Work Myth* (Melbourne: Spinifex Press, 2017); Caroline Norma and Melinda Tankard Reist, eds., *Prostitution Narratives: Stories of Survival in the Sex Trade* (Melbourne: Spinifex Press, 2016); Abigail Bray, and Melinda Tankard Reist, eds., *Big Porn Inc: Exposing the Harms of the Global Pornography Industry* (Melbourne: Spinifex Press, 2011).

work exclusionary radical feminists, or SWERFs, are closely associated with the second-wave movement, one of the most prominent being Andrea Dworkin, whose criticism of pornography suggested close links between the industry and violence against women.[30] Despite historical contrast between Greer's sexual libertarianism and the anti-pornographic forerunners of the SWERF movement—in 1974, for example, Dworkin notably condemned *Suck* as "a typical counterculture sex paper" in which "the sexism is all-pervasive, expressed primarily as sadomasochism..."—both of these radical feminist subcultures come increasingly under fire from the contemporary feminist mainstream as outdated.[31]

Despite Greer's politics having their roots in similar movements to publishers like Spinifex, Greer's own work as a publisher, specifically in setting up and running Stump Cross Books, is scholarly and historical in its outlook. Without the broad, mainstream appeal of contemporary controversy to leverage its visibility, it is far less widely known than Greer's other work. Despite this limited publicity, and the publisher's ultimate failure as both commercial and technological enterprise, Stump Cross makes intellectual and literary contributions to the feminist movement—and it is against these criteria that we can most productively understand its success.

The Greer Archive

Research into Stump Cross Books leading to this chapter was primarily undertaken using Greer's archive of personal and professional papers,

---

30 Andrea Dworkin, *Pornography: Men Possessing Women* (New York: Perigee Books, 1981).

31 Andrea Dworkin, *Woman Hating* (New York: Dutton, 1974), 78; cf. protests against the launch of *Prostitution Narratives* discussed in Millicent Weber, "At the Intersection of Writers Festivals and Literary Communities," *Overland Literary Journal*, 2017, https://overland.org.au/2017/09/at-the-intersection-of-writers-festival-and-literary-communities/.

which was bought by the University of Melbourne Archives in 2013.[32] The archive is a work in progress, with Greer continuing to deposit material sequentially. At the time of writing it comprises 487 archive boxes, which between them occupy over eighty-two metres of shelf space. It documents Greer's activities between 1959 and 2010: her work as an academic including teaching literature at the universities of Warwick, Tulsa and Newnham College, Cambridge; her activities as a performer for film, television and theatre; her journalistic and political writing; her passions, including her environmental projects, notably the purchase of Cave Creek rainforest in Queensland; and, of course, her numerous personal and professional relationships.

The archive is made up of a number of series, covering Greer's work as a print journalist (series 2014.0046); her correspondence (2014.0042); her early professional work, including writing *The Female Eunuch* (2014.0044); her major works post-*Eunuch* (2014.0045); audio recordings of interviews, lectures and personal reflections (2014.0040); video, including television and film appearances and home video footage (2014.0041); photographs (2014.0054); ephemeral material (2017.0010); and copies of all publications that Greer either wrote or contributed to (2014.0056). It also includes the Women and Literature series (2014.0047), which combines research notes on women writers, and documentation of Greer's activities as researcher and publisher in this area.

From a feminist publishing history perspective, some of the archive's highlights include French, German and Arabic translations and British and American first editions of *The Female Eunuch*; forty-nine fanzines created and distributed by young women in the mid-1990s; and correspondence between Greer and Marsha Rowe, co-founder of feminist magazine *Spare Rib*.

---

32 University of Melbourne Archives, 2018.

Women and Literature

The Women and Literature series, like other series in Greer's archive, juxtaposes material of serious research interest with other more whimsical records. A file of religious sheet music also contains a handwritten transcript of the lyrics to Lucille Bogan's 1930s dirty blues song "Shave 'Em Dry" (2014.0047.00632). The blank backs of meeting minutes showcase sketches and shopping lists that, like the example here, are a kind of found poetry.

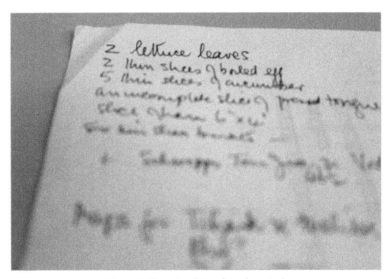

Figure 1: Shopping list or found poetry?
From Germaine Greer's Women and Literature series,
University of Melbourne Archives, 2014.0047.00042.

These touches of whimsy sit within a series that documents Greer's serious and self-consciously feminist work as a researcher and publisher of early women writers. Chief among this work is her setup of university programs and centres—like the Tulsa Centre for the Study of Women's Literature—that research and teach women's writing. The series holds extensive evidence of Greer's research practice:

painstakingly annotated photocopies of rare manuscripts, handwritten research notes and index cards, an abundance of drafts and redrafts of critical work. It also offers a record of the establishment and operation of Stump Cross Books.

Stump Cross began operation in the late 1980s. It was a platform for the careful republication of works by neglected and pioneer women poets. Under this imprint, Greer and her collaborators and assistants assembled, edited and published *The Uncollected Verse of Aphra Behn* (1989); *The Collected Works of Katherine Philips, the Matchless Orinda*, published in three volumes between 1990 and 1993: *Volume I – The Poems* (1990), *Volume II – The Letters* (1992), and *Volume III – The Translations* (1993); and *The Surviving Works of Anne Wharton* (1997).[33] Copies of each of these volumes are held with the Greer Archive, alongside Greer's other published works.

Addressing the lack of recognition traditionally accorded women writers is undoubtedly a feminist cause, but Greer's work goes beyond this. Her activities with university programs and centres like Tulsa, and those with Stump Cross Books, mesh together as both research and research-supporting work. They both place a determined and consistent emphasis on combining scholarship and publishing to recover and reconstruct a lost historical tradition of women's writing. The original words and intentions of each of the writers published through Stump Cross were, as Greer's research archive demonstrates, often elided by zealous editorial revisions, or lost due to a lack of surviving original

---

33 Aphra Behn, *The Uncollected Verse of Aphra Behn*, ed. Germaine Greer (Stump Cross, Essex: Stump Cross Books, 1989). Katherine Philips, *The Collected Works of Katherine Philips, the Matchless Orinda: Volume 1 – The Poems*, ed. Patrick Thomas (Stump Cross, Essex: Stump Cross Books, 1990). Katherine Philips, *The Collected Works of Katherine Philips, the Matchless Orinda: Volume 2 – The Letters*, ed. Patrick Thomas (Stump Cross, Essex: Stump Cross Books, 1992). Katherine Philips, *The Collected Works of Katherine Philips, the Matchless Orinda: Volume 3 – The Translations*, ed. Germaine Greer and Ruth Little (Stump Cross, Essex: Stump Cross Books, 1993). Anne Wharton, *The Surviving Works of Anne Wharton*, ed. Germaine Greer and Susan Hastings (Stump Cross, Essex: Stump Cross Books. 1997).

editions. Overlooked among their male peers in traditional canon-based renderings of English literature, each of the writers Stump Cross published were at the time out of print, and were indeed deliberately chosen by Greer on this basis. Greer and her co-editors and assistants recovered their bodies of work through the careful piecing together of fragmentary manuscript and scarce or partial early published editions. Photocopies and transcripts of these manuscripts—together with analysis, correspondence, and related research notes—can be found throughout the Women and Literature series. The following quote from Greer encapsulates the ethos that informed this:

> Scholars who struggle to get women poets admitted to the "canon"… have been stymied in the past by a lack of reliable texts… In the case of Emily Dickinson, the world was happy to have a highly edited text, which had been completely repunctuated, until a body of scholars produced an edition based on the poet's autograph, which transformed our understanding of how Dickinson wrote and how she should be read. If we try to use the same procedures of bibliographical and textual investigation on poets like Katherine Philips, the "Matchless Orinda", the texts that we have begin to fall apart in our hands. For most women poets we do not have copies of works in their own hand-writing, let alone examples of work in progress, with corrections and emendations. For Aphra Behn, a figure of overriding importance, we have not a single literary text of her own hand. We cannot establish her actual authorship of any poem or play… Scholarly ethics require that we try a great deal harder to get at the truth about them. Only when we understand their circumstances can we arrive at a correct assessment of their achievement.[34]

---

34 Germaine Greer, *Slip-Shod Sibyls: Recognition, Rejection and the Woman Poet* (New York: Viking, 1995), xvii.

Greer's work—her research, and particularly her public facing efforts with Stump Cross—responds directly to this call-to-arms. This passage is from the prologue to *Slip-Shod Sybils: Recognition, Rejection and the Woman Poet*, in which Greer presents a difficult, ambivalent argument for the re-evaluation of historical poetry. The references in this passage to the paucity of manuscripts created by Philips and Behn, and the scholarship that Greer has published on each, are particularly interesting when considered in conjunction with Stump Cross, and with the story told by Greer's manuscripts about her own careful and critical work on these writers.

There is an important critique buried in this call-to-arms. Controversially, as contemporary reviews of *Slip-Shod Sybils* show, Greer is not arguing that these writers' poems have the literary quality of other poetry of the same era commonly considered canonical. Rather, she is saying that these writers—these "figures of overriding importance"—themselves need to be acknowledged, and acknowledged alongside a recognition that the production and publication of their works were consistently halted by barriers put in place by social, educational and financial structures. In other words, the concept of a 'canon' of literature structured around concepts like literary quality, however subjective, would necessarily exclude those who had been debarred from a literary cultural tradition due to social, political and financial constraints traditionally tied up with gender. This was an argument that reviewers and other literary scholars found troubling, and even deliberately provocative, in its dismissal of the literary merits of the women poets scarce in a male-dominated literary canon. Margaret Anne Doody described *Slip-Shod Sybils* as "an interesting, infuriating, brilliant, maddening book", and one in which Greer "can see no art in her artists".[35] In Norma Clarke's words, "Greer's project

---

35 Doody, Margaret Anne Doody, "Poxy Doxies," *London Review of Books*, December 14, 1995, https://www.lrb.co.uk/v17/n24/margaret-anne-doody/poxy-doxies.

is to dash us with cold water, tear down our false goddesses, and rub our noses in reality. You would think, from her impassioned tone, that the world had been jabbering about women poets (and getting them wrong) for decades, when the truth is that most literary academics wouldn't know a Charlotte Smith sonnet if it reached out and bit them".[36] Greer's argument is carefully contextual, but it also has occasional meritocratic hints:

> The more we know about women who wrote poetry in
> English before 1900, the more we must realise that it is not
> a question of women poets having been ignored or obscured
> but of women's poetry remaining unwritten [and unpublished]
> because women were disabled and deflected by the great
> tradition itself, while a select band of arbitrarily chosen token
> women, all young, beautiful and virtuous, were rewarded for
> their failures. Second-rate, dishonest, fake poetry is worse
> than no poetry at all. To insist on equal representation or
> positive discrimination so that She-poetry appears on our
> syllabuses... is to continue the system of false accounting that
> produced the double standard in the first place. This is not to
> say that we should not work at reclaiming women's work, but
> simply that we should be aware that we are more likely to find
> heroines than poets.[37]

In a review for *The Independent*, Michele Roberts described *Slip-Shod Sybils* as "three books in one"; the first an intervention into the dismantling of a gendered literary canon, the second, "a series of essays providing close readings of the works of these women poets", and the third "a discussion of the moral and ideological climate in which

---

36 Norma Clarke, "Review: Slip-Shod Musing. Germaine Greer. *Slip-Shod Sybils: Recognition, Rejection and the Woman Poet*," *History Workshop Journal* 41, no. 1 (March 1996): 263.

37 Greer, *Slip-Shod Sibyls*, xxiv.

women tried to write".[38] Stump Cross Books represents an extension of each of these projects. It is inarguably a revisionist exercise, a project by which Greer seeks to reinsert neglected women writers into a male-dominated conception of English literature. Crucially, however, it is not only a textual but also a contextual revision of literary canonicity that Greer seeks to achieve. Her efforts with Stump Cross intend to make these works accessible and known, but the process of knowing them and reading them involves knowing and reading the social and industrial constraints within which they were produced—and recognising the bastard, partial state in which they commonly circulate, and which can only be restored by the kinds of careful manuscript research Greer undertook.

Print Materiality

Material print culture is a prominent feature, both literally and conceptually, in Greer's archive. Like social and industrial constraints, print contextualises—in a very real, very material way—the reading, interpretation and valuing of literary texts.

Greer recognises the importance of a published edition's material qualities in the choices she makes as a publisher. Correspondence held in the Women and Literature series discusses printing and binding processes for the Anne Wharton and Katherine Philips volumes. Alongside this correspondence sit brochures and promotional catalogues of typefaces and paper samples. The metal stamp used to emboss the spine of the Stump Cross hardback edition of Anne Wharton's works is held with samples of the edition's cover boards, and sits alongside files of correspondence investigating and evaluating printing and binding processes.

---

38 Michele Roberts, "Books: Why Did Sappho Leap?" *The Independent*, September 16, 1995, http://www.independent.co.uk/arts-entertainment/books-why-did-sappho-leap-1601572.html.

Figure 2: Cover board and embossing stamp for *Anne Wharton: Surviving Works*. From Germaine Greer's Women and Literature series, University of Melbourne Archives, 2014.0047.00461.

The Wharton edition was the only Stump Cross volume produced in both hard and soft covers. Each of the soft-cover books the publisher produced were bound, in Greer's words, "like French ones, in off-white paper",[39] a prioritisation that echoes the emphasis on tactility and high-quality printing expressed by Persephone and Virago.

Other collocated files hold designs for the publisher's phoenix emblem (2014.0047.00471). As well as the original drawings and designs, reproductions of the emblem reappear in the corners of Stump Cross Books letterhead and form correspondence slipped inside other files. Other earlier designs for the publisher's device are also sketched on the backs of documents in the Print series (2014.0046.00197).

---

39 Comment published in a journalistic piece; see 2014.0046.00914.

Figure 3: Documents featuring the Stump Cross Books phoenix emblem.
From Germaine Greer's Women and Literature series,
University of Melbourne Archives,
2014.0047.00471.

The Stump Cross Books phoenix appears prominently in the archive. An invoice from the company Talking T's attests to the creation of custom Stump Cross Books t-shirts in December, 1992 (2014.0047.00472). A fax sent by Greer's assistant in March, 1992 (held at 2017.0026.00009, part of the Contraceptives, Cars and Gardens series) discusses painting it on a car:

> I spoke to you on the telephone regarding the artwork for a car. The car is a black Ford Fiesta Popular 950 and the emblem would be put on the driver's door and the front passenger's door.
>
> I am enclosing the basic outline of the design we would like but it needs to be re-drawn in 17th century fashion.

Greer's making and wearing of these t-shirts, and customisation of her Ford Fiesta, are celebratory juxtapositions of very different cultural practices. The t-shirts in particular are a commercial, promotional exercise out of keeping with the image of the painstaking, serious, high cultural, and unprofitable project that is Stump Cross Books. Greer accords great care and attention to each element of the process of physically creating the book-as-codex, as well as to the other material trappings of her publishing activities. Both the care and this occasional irreverence show her commitment to publishing traditions, and to the books' material quality. This commitment is a crucial element of the respect that Greer insists be paid to the women writers she is republishing.

Technological Innovation

Stump Cross Books, although an interesting political and cultural case study, ultimately failed to navigate the shifting technological landscape of the twenty-first century. Alongside the drafts, research notes, correspondence and business records relating to the published Stump Cross volumes, the series also contains several full drafts and research notes for an unrealised collection of the poetry of Anne Finch, Countess of Winchilsea. The Finch volume was prepared in the late 1990s, with publication originally slated for around 2000, and was subsequently delayed multiple times. Correspondence held with the draft and research materials documents the difficulties of copyediting and typesetting the volume in an increasingly unfamiliar industry. Greer's comments in letters and printed emails reveal how these difficulties were compounded by the creep of technological change into the publishing process, expressing frustration with editorial quality, printing and binding in particular. Recognising these difficulties as indicators of a transforming industry, Greer considers turning to the production of an ebook volume:

Date: Thu, Aug 12, 2004, 10:40 am

Subject: e-book

Dear Ian,

I've been lying awake at night thinking about our e-book, and I've come to two rather depressing conclusions. One is that we had better start again. The other is that we need to raise some funding to develop the cyber-book format.

...

If you click on the question mark button you get a version with highlights on Anne Finch, G. Greer, H. Smith, and Stump Cross and an instruction to click on the highlighted terms for more information. Clicking on any of them will bring up a box with the relevant information. The Anne Finch box would contain a brief biography and a bracket (MORE). Click on 'more' and you get a more detailed biography. The Anne Finch box also has an ikon indicating that an image is available and such ikons appear in other boxes at all levels.

...

Set out like this it is obvious to me that there is a huge amount of work to do, and billions of key-strokes to make, in altering the vast mass of information in the book to fit into these compartments. You haven't time to do it and neither have I. We'd need funding to employ people to transform my hard copy into a cyber-book. I have no idea where to go to for it beyond asking Mr Gates himself.

Tell me what you think.

Germaine.[40]

---

40 Transcript, condensed, of email from Germaine Greer's Women and Literature series, University of Melbourne Archives, 2014.0047.00563.

Beyond painting a vivid picture of Greer "lying awake at night" stressing, Greer's email about the Anne Wharton "cyber-book", and the design challenges that this project threw up, reminds us that 2004 was before the widespread uptake of Kindle. It predates publishers' agreements on clear standards for ebook projects, let alone for digital scholarly editions. Although the Text Encoding Initiative, an international standard that set out best practice for the digital encoding of humanities texts, was established in 1987,[41] a "lack of investment" coupled with "resistance from the editorial community... prevent[ed] the agreement necessary to enable the development of effective tools".[42] Along with the description of a possible cyber-book, Greer's hyperbolic comments about "billions of key-strokes" and exaggerated joke about approaching Bill Gates for funding further reveal how daunted she is by this technological challenge.

Creating a hypertext ebook volume like Greer describes is typical of the one-to-many, document-based communication that characterises the pre-social media era of 'Web 1.0'.[43] Spinifex Press, like Stump Cross Books, shows persistent attachment to modes of innovation from the early 2000s. In their words:

Spinifex has always been at the forefront of technological change—publishing books about new technologies—we were the first Australian publisher to offer a web-based catalogue and the third to have our full catalogue available for purchase from our website. In 2006, Spinifex was the first small press in Australia to release eBooks through an eBookstore attached

---

41 TEI Consortium, "TEI: History," *TEI* <*Text Encoding Initiative*>, 2014, http://www.tei-c.org/About/history.xml.

42 Elena Pierazzo, "Digital Documentary Editions and the Others," *Scholarly Editing: The Annual of the Association for Documentary Editing*, 35 (2014): 12, http://scholarlyediting.org/2014/essays/essay.pierazzo.html; cf. also Tara Andrews, "The Third Way: Philology and Critical Edition in the Digital Age," *Variants* 10: 61–76. 2013.

43 Ulrike Gretzel, "Web 2.0 and 3.0," in *Communication and Technology*, ed. Lorenzo Cantoni and James A. Danowski (Berlin and Boston: Walter de Gruyter, 2015), 182.

to our website. We were the first publisher (1996) to set up an interactive site based on a book.[44]

A more successful adopter of technology than Stump Cross Books, Spinifex's key interventions in digital media, like those of Stump Cross, predate the move of other, bigger publishing players into this digital landscape. But unlike Stump Cross, Spinifex continues to intervene with their publications in the contemporary feminist landscape, and they are also active users of social media, particularly Twitter, a platform they joined in 2009 and on which they have 2,286 followers.[45] Although Greer does have a Twitter account, it was only used for about a week in early 2012. Greer, or one of her assistants, sent a total of fourteen tweets in this time, and despite this the account has 11,400 followers, testament to Greer's continuing and platform-independent high public profile.[46] Spinifex's Twitter functions in broadcast mode, primarily consisting of tweets and retweets sharing political news articles, and the promotion of new publications and book events. The Twitter accounts of Persephone (7,082 followers) and Virago (46,900 followers) are by contrast both highly visual, making consistent use of the attractive aesthetics of their high quality—or, indeed, highly Instagrammable—publications.[47] Both publishers' accounts regularly publish original, heavily posed photographs of their publications and share similar photographs from their readers. The Persephone account, in particular, joins in reader conversations. This social media use, interactive and heavy in original content, conforms with best-practice advice for publishers on social media,[48] but is also reflective of the

---

44 Spinifex Press, "About Us."

45 As at June 1, 2018; see https://twitter.com/spinifexpress.

46 As at June 1, 2018; see https://twitter.com/thefemalegreer.

47 As at June 1, 2018; see https://twitter.com/PersephoneBooks and https://twitter.com/ViragoBooks/.

48 Cf. Beth Driscoll, "Twitter, Literary Prizes, and the Ciriculation of Capital," in *By the Book? Contemporary Publishing in Australia*, ed. Emmett Stinson (Melbourne: Monash University Publishing, 2013), 104.

print-based ideals of aesthetics and community that these publishers espouse, as discussed above.

Conclusion

The logics of the twenty-first century—political, social, and technological—transformed the publishing industry and defeated Greer's efforts as an independent publisher, at least in terms of audience and commercial viability. While Greer's public profile as a media commentator survives, these same logics increasingly show her irrelevance to contemporary public debate. This irrelevance, with potential connections to technological and political advances, is an incremental development that could productively be traced and evaluated by future scholars examining the detailed archival records of Greer's engagements with other publishers and print media.

However problematic or ineffectual Greer's recent media forays, the undeniable aim of Stump Cross Books was, first and foremost, to create stable, critically thoughtful editions of the works of pioneer women poets, a scholarly intervention that would facilitate the sound critical appraisal of their works and lives. *Behn* is held in at least 140 libraries, scholarly and public, worldwide; *Wharton* in at least forty-seven; and the different volumes of *Philips* in at least 162.[49] The first volume of *Philips* is highly cited, with ninety citations aggregated by Google Scholar at the time of writing. Although a detailed examination of the reception of these volumes is beyond the scope of this chapter, these quantifications show that, despite the short-lived and commercially unviable nature of Stump Cross Books, it nevertheless has a considerable intellectual legacy. If the goal of feminist publishing is to "intervene in the processes of literary production to ensure that women's voices are made audible",

---

49 See entries for each book in WorldCat, an international network of library catalogues: http://www.worldcat.org/oclc/37970668; http://www.worldcat.org/oclc/884499856; http://www.worldcat.org/oclc/803494255; http://www.worldcat.org/oclc/612123900; http://www.worldcat.org/oclc/886005382.

Stump Cross Books and the other publishers examined in this chapter demonstrate the diverse ways in which this audibility is being sought and achieved, across the literary field—from the commercial to the scholarly; the avant-garde to the middlebrow.[50]

Works cited

Andrews, Tara. "The Third Way: Philology and Critical Edition in the Digital Age." *Variants* 10 (2013): 61–76.

Behn, Aphra. *The Uncollected Verse of Aphra Behn*, edited by Germaine Greer. Stump Cross, Essex: Stump Cross Books, 1989.

Bindel, Julie. *The Pimping of Prostitution: Abolishing the Sex Work Myth*. Melbourne: Spinifex Press, 2017.

Books+Publishing. "Over Half of Book-Industry Survey Respondents Report Sexual Harassment." *Books+Publishing*, December 12, 2017. https://www.booksandpublishing.com.au/articles/2017/12/12/99463/over-half-of-book-industry-survey-respondents-report-sexual-harassment/.

Bray, Abigail, and Melinda Tankard Reist, eds. *Big Porn Inc: Exposing the Harms of the Global Pornography Industry*. Melbourne: Spinifex Press, 2011.

Carmody, Broede. "Germaine Greer Announces New Book in Wake of #MeToo Backlash." *The Sydney Morning Herald*, March 28, 2018. https://www.smh.com.au/entertainment/books/germaine-greer-announces-new-book-in-wake-of-metoo-backlash-20180328-p4z6mk.html.

Clarke, Norma. "Review: Slip-Shod Musing. Germaine Greer. Slip-Shod Sybils: Recognition, Rejection and the Woman Poet." *History Workshop Journal* 41, no. 1 (March 1996): 263–66.

Cooke, Rachel. "Taking Women off the Shelf." *The Guardian*, April 6, 2008. https://www.theguardian.com/books/2008/apr/06/fiction.features1.

———. "One Shade of Grey: How Nicola Beauman Made an Unlikely Success of Persephone Books." *The Guardian*, November 25, 2012. https://www.theguardian.com/books/2012/nov/25/nicola-beauman-persephone-books-founder-interview.

Couper, Sarah. "Bookish Girls: Gender and Leadership in Australian Trade Publishing." In *The Return of Print? Contemporary Australian Publishing*, edited by Aaron Mannion and Emmett Stinson, 27–45. Melbourne: Monash University Publishing, 2016.

---

50 Simone Murray, *Mixed Media: Feminist Presses and Publishing Politics* (London: Pluto Press, 2004), 2.

Doody, Margaret Anne. "Poxy Doxies." *London Review of Books*, December 14, 1995. https://www.lrb.co.uk/v17/n24/margaret-anne-doody/poxy-doxies.

Driscoll, Beth. *The New Literary Middlebrow: Tastemakers and Reading in the Twenty-First Century*. Basingstoke: Palgrave Macmillan, 2014.

———. "Twitter, Literary Prizes, and the Circulation of Capital." *In By the Book? Contemporary Publishing in Australia*, edited by Emmett Stinson, 103–19. Melbourne: Monash University Publishing, 2013.

Dworkin, Andrea. *Woman Hating*. New York: Dutton, 1974.

———. *Pornography: Men Possessing Women*. New York: Perigee Books, 1981.

Erickson, Amanda. "Feminist Germaine Greer Says Most Rape Is Just 'Bad' Sex.'" *Washington Post*, May 31, 2018. https://www.washingtonpost.com/news/worldviews/wp/2018/05/31/feminist-germaine-greer-says-most-rape-is-just-bad-sex/.

Flood, Alison. "Germaine Greer Criticises 'Whingeing' #MeToo Movement." *The Guardian*, January 23, 2018. http://www.theguardian.com/books/2018/jan/23/germaine-greer-criticises-whingeing-metoo-movement.

Garner, Clare. "Fellows Divided over Don Who Breached Last Bastion." *The Independent*, June 25, 1997. http://www.independent.co.uk/news/fellows-divided-over-don-who-breached-last-bastion-1257781.html.

Gleeson, Kate. "From Suck Magazine to Corporate Paedophilia. Feminism and Pornography — Remembering the Australian Way." *Women's Studies International Forum* 38 (2013): 83–96.

Greer, Germaine. *The Female Eunuch*. London: MacGibbon & Kee, 1970.

———. *Slip-Shod Sibyls: Recognition, Rejection and the Woman Poet*. New York: Viking, 1995.

———. *The Whole Woman*. New York: Doubleday, 1999.

———. "Trans women 'not women'." Interview by Kirsty Wark, BBC Newsnight, October 24, 2015. http://www.bbc.com/news/av/uk-34625512/germaine-greer-transgender-women-are-not-women.

Gretzel, Ulrike. "Web 2.0 and 3.0." In *Communication and Technology*, edited by Lorenzo Cantoni and James A. Danowski, 181–90. Berlin and Boston: Walter de Gruyter, 2015.

Murray, Simone. *Mixed Media: Feminist Presses and Publishing Politics*. London: Pluto Press, 2004.

Norma, Caroline, and Melinda Tankard Reist, eds. *Prostitution Narratives: Stories of Survival in the Sex Trade*. Melbourne: Spinifex Press, 2016.

Persephone Books. "Home." Persephone Books. Accessed April 2018, http://www.persephonebooks.co.uk/.

———. "Frequently Asked Questions." Persephone Books. Accessed April 2018, http://www.persephonebooks.co.uk/faq/.

Philips, Katherine. *The Collected Works of Katherine Philips, the Matchless Orinda: Volume 1—The Poems,* edited by Patrick Thomas. Stump Cross, Essex: Stump Cross Books, 1990.

———. *The Collected Works of Katherine Philips, the Matchless Orinda: Volume 2— The Letters,* edited by Patrick Thomas. Stump Cross, Essex: Stump Cross Books, 1992.

———. *The Collected Works of Katherine Philips, the Matchless Orinda: Volume 3— The Translations,* edited by Germaine Greer and Ruth Little. Stump Cross, Essex: Stump Cross Books, 1993.

Pierazzo, Elena. "Digital Documentary Editions and the Others." *Scholarly Editing: The Annual of the Association for Documentary Editing,* 35 (2014): 1–20. http://scholarlyediting.org/2014/essays/essay.pierazzo.html

Roberts, Michele. "Books: Why Did Sappho Leap?" *The Independent,* September 16, 1995. http://www.independent.co.uk/arts-entertainment/books-why-did-sappho-leap-1601572.html.

Savonick, Danica, and Cathy N. Davidson. "Gender Bias in Academe: An Annotated Bibliography of Important Recent Studies." *LSE Impact Blog,* 2017. http://blogs.lse.ac.uk/impactofsocialsciences/2016/03/08/gender-bias-in-academe-an-annotated-bibliography/.

Schede, Alex, and Anna Theris. "Controversy in the Classroom." *Farrago,* May 26, 2014. https://umsu.unimelb.edu.au/farrago/controversy-in-the-classroom/.

Spinifex Press. "About Us." Spinifex Press. Accessed April 2018, http://www.spinifexpress.com.au/About_Us/.

Squires, Claire, and Beth Driscoll. "The Sleaze-O-Meter: Sexual Harassment in the Publishing Industry." *Interscript* (2018). https://www.interscriptjournal.com/online-magazine/sleaze-o-meter.

Stump Cross Books. "Welcome to Stump Cross Books." Accessed December 1, 2018, http://www.sxbxsx.com/

TEI Consortium. "TEI: History." *TEI <Text Encoding Initiative>,* 2014. http://www.tei-c.org/About/history.xml.

The Bookseller. "Sexual Harassment Reported by over Half in Trade Survey." *The Bookseller,* November 10, 2017. https://www.thebookseller.com/news/sexual-harassment-reported-over-half-trade-survey-671276.

The Stella Prize. "2016 Stella Count." The Stella Prize, 2016. http://thestellaprize.com.au/the-count/2016-stella-count/.

University of Melbourne Archives. "About the Collection." University of Melbourne Archives, 2018. https://archives.unimelb.edu.au/explore/collections/germainegreer/about-the-collection.

VIDA. "About the VIDA Count." VIDA: Women in Literary Arts. Accessed
April 2018, https://www.vidaweb.org/the-count/.

Virago. "About Virago." Virago. Accessed April 2018, https://www.virago.co.uk/
about/.

———. "Authors." Virago. Accessed April 2018, https://www.virago.co.uk/
authors/.

———. "Virago Modern Classics." Virago. Accessed April 2018, https://www.
virago.co.uk/books/virago-modern-classics/.

Wallace, Christine. *Germaine Greer: Untamed Shrew.* Sydney: Pan Macmillan
Australia, 2013.

Weber, Millicent. "At the Intersection of Writers Festivals and Literary
Communities." *Overland Literary Journal,* 2017. https://overland.
org.au/2017/09/at-the-intersection-of-writers-festival-and-literary-
communities/.

———. *Literary Festivals and Contemporary Book Culture.* London: Palgrave
Macmillan, 2018.

Wharton, Anne. *The Surviving Works of Anne Wharton*, edited by Germaine
Greer and Susan Hastings. Stump Cross, Essex: Stump Cross Books. 1997.

CHAPTER 7

Speculating on Gender

Investigating the Effects of Author and Reader Gender in the Speculative Fiction Field

MICHELLE GOLDSMITH

"How do you choose the books you read?" Outside of the world of publishing and publishing studies, when I ask this question the most common answer is some variation of, "I choose books I think I'll enjoy." To many of those who give it, this answer seems simple, even obvious. However, for those of us engaged in the study of books and reading, this statement engenders near-countless follow-up questions. Among the first might be, "How do you judge which books you're likely to enjoy before having read them?" Understandably, as readers of fiction, we may like to view our choice of books—whether for enjoyment, to discuss or to recommend to others—as largely based on, or at least closely related to, the actual content of the texts. While most of us acknowledge that our personal preferences and notions of value and quality are subjective, matters become more contentious when it comes to discussing to what degree these preferences may be shaped by outside influences, and how our choices may be affected by various implicit assumptions and biases we've unconsciously internalised.

In reality, we do not generally encounter and interact with books in a vacuum. As a result, the wider context in which we encounter a book, our own personal experiences and the ideas we bring with us to a text significantly affect our experience. So too does the book's paratext.

Gérard Genette defines "paratext" as the "accompanying productions" that "surround" and "extend" a text "to ensure the text's presence in the world, its 'reception' and consumption in the form (nowadays, at least) of a book".[1] A wealth of previous academic study has explored the ways in which paratextual factors and context contribute to shaping reader expectations, and how this in turn can have implications for the way readers engage with and interpret a book, and their perceptions of its value.[2] In the contemporary Anglophone publishing industry, books are often published with paratexts signalling aspects of author persona to the reader, including author gender. Author gender indicators may be peritextual (for example, the author's name or pseudonym, their biography or photo) or epitextual (for instance, interviews with the author, public appearances at literary events, or various other forms of publicity). While peritext can be controlled to obscure author gender or other aspects of personal identity if desired, doing so is more difficult for epitext, especially if the author is to take an active role in the promotion and marketing of the book, as is increasingly required of many contemporary authors. Ways in which technology-driven changes in the book industry have resulted in changes to the role of the author in book promotion and interaction with readers (e.g. the ubiquity of the "author platform") have been examined in previous scholarship, including, among others, Kim Wilkins's "Writing Resilience in the Digital Age"[3] and Simone Murray's "Charting the Digital Literary

---

1   Gérard Genette, *Paratexts: Thresholds of Interpretation*, (Cambridge: Cambridge University Press, 1997), 1.

2   Roger Chartier, "Texts, Printing, Reading," in *The New Cultural History*, ed. Lynn Hunt (Berkeley: University of California Press, 1989), 167; Barbara Herrnstein Smith, "Value/Evaluation" in *Critical Terms for Literary Study*, ed. Frank Lentricchia and Thomas McLaughlin (Chicago: University of Chicago Press, 1995), 185.

3   Kim Wilkins, "Writing Resilience in the Digital Age," *New Writing: The International Journal for the Practice & Theory of Creative Writing*, 11 (2014): 67–76.

Sphere",[4] and in the 2015 Macquarie University study *The Australian Book Industry: Authors, Publishers and Readers in a Time of Change.*[5] The Macquarie study further suggests that these changes, including those increasing author visibility to readers, are particularly relevant to authors of genre fiction.[6] The larger category of genre fiction includes books in the genres and subgenres encompassed by the umbrella term "speculative fiction"—Science Fiction, Fantasy and Horror, as well as their variations and combinations. This means authors of speculative fiction (and therefore aspects of their identity, such as gender) are increasingly visible to readers.

The gender of the author—or, more precisely, a reader's perception of the gender of an author—can come laden with assumptions that may spill over onto the text itself and play a role in shaping reader expectations and interactions with the book.[7] On the other hand, the gender of a potential reader could also have affected some of their prior experiences with texts and authors, altering the personal "context" they bring with them to their reader-book interactions.

While the "interactions" I mention may involve reading the book, they are not limited to such encounters—they can also occur before, after, or in the absence of actually reading a text. One such interaction that's especially important to authors, publishers and other parties involved in the production and distribution of books, and is the primary focus of this chapter, is a potential reader's decision whether or not to

---

4   Simone Murray, "Charting the Digital Literary Sphere," *Contemporary Literature* 56, no. 2 (2015): 311–339.

5   David Throsby, Jan Zwar and Thomas Longden. "Australian Authors," in *The Australian Book Industry: Authors, Publishers and Readers in a Time of Change* (Sydney: Macquarie University, Department of Economics, 2015), http://www. businessandeconomics.mq.edu.au/our_departments/Economics/econ_research/ reach_network/book_project/authors/1_Key_Findings.pdf.

6   Throsby, Zwar and Longden, "Australian Authors."

7   As I witnessed during my years as a bookseller, it is not unknown for readers to be wrong in their assumptions about an author's gender, especially when a gender-neutral pseudonym is employed.

purchase a particular book. So, how might readers' perceptions of the author's gender affect their likelihood of purchasing and/or reading a particular book? And how might the gender of the reader relate to their choice of books to read? Shortly, I'll explore some of these questions, and possible answers, using the field of speculative fiction as an arena.

Gender Bias in Literary Fields—A Conversation Spanning Decades

Gender bias within literary fields, explicit or implicit, has persisted as a topic of discussion to the present day, despite the steps taken by various parties to raise awareness and address issues of representation. Various disadvantages experienced disproportionately by female authors have been subject to previous scholarly and industry research. For instance, the annual VIDA Counts have highlighted discrepancies between the numbers of books written by women that receive reviews in major US and UK publications compared to books written by men, [8] while the Stella Counts have done similar, specifically for major venues in Australia.[9] Particular to Science Fiction and Fantasy, for a number of years online journal *Strange Horizons* undertook its own investigations into the gender and race balance of books reviewed in major speculative fiction review publications, as well as that of the individuals doing the reviewing. These counts also found that books by women were under-represented.[10] Other perspectives on the topic of potential gender bias within the speculative genres include those offered by Susan E. Connolly, who investigated the numbers of

---

8   VIDA, "The 2016 VIDA Count," 2017, http://www.vidaweb.org/the-2016-vida-count. Additionally, VIDA have now expanded their count to include non-binary writers and other identity categories such as age, education, race, disability and sexuality.

9   The Stella Prize, "2016 Stella Count," 2017, http://thestellaprize.com.au/the-count/2016-stella-count/.

10 Niall Harrison, "The 2014 SF Count," *Strange Horizons* (2015), http://www.strangehorizons.com/2015/20150330/sfcount-a.shtml.

authors of different genders published in some of the most prominent speculative fiction journals.[11]

Although, in light of previous research, it is difficult to convincingly argue against the existence of some degree of gender bias within literary fields, the question of where this bias originates and how it is maintained is more controversial. Many of the previous attempts to investigate, raise awareness of and address gender bias have focused on the books selected to be published, reviewed or to win awards. Or they have investigated gender-based differences in paratextual factors that the author or publisher has control over (for instance, the cover, the blurb and other elements of a book's marketing and promotion package). While these undoubtedly play an important role in the operation of gender bias within the field and deserve the attention they have received, other sources and operations of bias must be considered to comprehensively explore issues of gender disparity and representation, and to understand how these problems might be solved.

Furthermore, a distinction must be made between the subset of readers of any given genre who are heavily involved in and aware of the genre community and issues of discussion within it, and the entirety of the genre's pool of readers, who may engage or not engage with its community to various levels. This is important when considering indicators like gender balance in award short lists as a measure of the progress made addressing gender bias within a literary field. Due to processes of self-selection, the individuals who either volunteer as judges for a judged award (such as Australia's Aurealis), or nominate or vote for books in a fan-voted award (such as the Hugo) are generally from the "highly involved" pool of readers. Such readers are more likely to be aware of the topic of gender bias within the field, enabling them to try to limit any effect it could have on their decisions, assuming they wish to do so. And they are also more likely to encounter books that

---

11   Susan E. Connolly, "The Issue of Gender in Genre Fiction: A Detailed Analysis," *Clarkesworld* 93 (2014), http://clarkesworldmagazine.com/connolly_06_14/.

have not achieved the same level of visibility as others (especially in the case of awards with panels of judges who read every submitted work).

Viewed in isolation, an award short list featuring a high proportion of female authors, such as the 2017 Aurealis Award short list, may suggest an absence of bias against books authored by women in the field. However, the significance of literary awards to book sales numbers is questionable for all but a few of the largest awards, and sales figures suggest that the books that are short-listed for or win speculative fiction awards are not necessarily representative of the most visible, widely read or highest-selling books in the field. As a result, progress with regards to the number of female authors on awards lists or other such counts is not necessarily a precise indication of proportionate reductions in gender bias within the wider book-buying public—nor does it account for more subtle manifestations of implicit bias that may still affect many readers' book-buying choices, or even which books they are aware of in the first place. Addressing all the implicit ways bias may operate in such a heterogeneous group as "readers" with the aim to "level the playing field" is likely to be difficult and complicated. But an enhanced understanding of how such bias works—and how gender intersects with readers' purchasing choices more generally—is an important step to doing so.

In 2015, I undertook a study to gain insight into the author–reader relationship within the contemporary speculative fiction field. This included considering possible relationships between gender (of both authors and readers) and readers' expectations. To this end, I conducted a survey of 396 self-identified readers of speculative fiction, exploring topics that included gendered perceptions of different genres and subgenres, the effects of possible explicit or implicit bias in regard to author gender on readers' book choices, and the professed importance readers of different genders gave to an author's public persona and views on certain social and political issues when considering whether to purchase their books.

Surveying the Speculative Fiction Scene

The data was collected via an anonymous online survey consisting of 45 questions in total, investigating readership and authorship within the contemporary speculative fiction field, and author–reader interactions within this field. The survey included both multiple-choice questions and questions with open-ended long-answer boxes. The multiple-choice questions enabled the collection of quantitative data from which to identify trends, while the qualitative data from the long-answer questions facilitated a deeper understanding of individual participants' experiences and the rationale underlying their answers.[12] The first part of the survey was aimed at readers of any type of speculative fiction, while the optional second part of the survey included a number of questions for speculative fiction authors. The survey was designed on the assumption that speculative fiction authors were also readers of speculative fiction, and this assumption was supported by the fact that no author respondents failed to fill out answers to the questions for readers.

The survey began with a number of basic questions to provide a general overview of respondent demographics, after which it was broken into sections covering subjects such as reader genre and subgenre preferences, the influence of author identity on readers' book choices, the effects of author politics on reader book preference, author–reader interactions online and in person, the impact of author gender on reader expectations, and the role of the author in book promotion.

Survey respondents were initially recruited through my personal network of contacts in the speculative fiction community via Facebook

---

12 The results of the other sections of the survey, which explore the role of the author and author–reader interactions within the speculative fiction field without pertaining particularly to gender, can be found in Michelle Goldsmith, "Exploring the Author–Reader Relationship in Contemporary Speculative Fiction: The Influence of Author Persona on Readers in the Era of the Online 'Author Platform'" published in *LOGOS* 27, no. 1 (2016).

and Twitter, and from author community mailing lists on which I was active. Many of my primary contacts shared the survey with their own networks, broadening its reach. I also posted survey details and links on various active forums for discussing works in the speculative fiction genres, such as the "r/fantasy" and "r/science fiction" subreddits. Over the period that the survey was open, a total of 396 speculative fiction readers and/or authors responded. Nevertheless, when examining the data collected in this survey, some thought should be given to the probability that my sample of 396 survey participants is probably weighted more heavily towards politically progressive segments of speculative fiction readership. This is due to the identities of my personal contacts, as well as the likelihood of suspicion by more right-leaning potential participants towards research investigating any kind of implicit bias, which may have discouraged some from responding. Likewise, respondents to the survey are also more likely to come from an active and dedicated subset of speculative fiction fandom, meaning readers who interact with authors and are aware of various issues and ongoing conversations within the speculative fiction community may be over-represented in responses when compared to the totality of speculative fiction readership. Furthermore, due to the methods employed to distribute the survey, results are almost certainly weighted towards readers and authors who are at least reasonably active within online genre communities.

Who Reads Speculative Fiction?

Trends across answers to the survey's demographic questions provided a range of insights into online speculative fiction author and reader communities, some of which may help us understand the study's gender-related findings. Key findings in regard to demographics included that respondents to the survey were generally older than might be expected for a survey distributed primarily via social media, contained a relatively high proportion of established authors, and came from a wider range of countries outside of Australia than anticipated, while still including a large Australian contingent. A breakdown of respondent age is depicted in Figure 1.

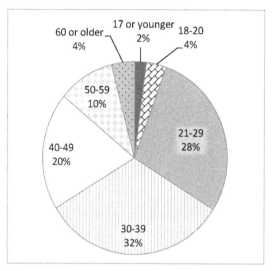

Figure 1. Respondent Ages.

The age breakdown of respondents may relate to another key demographic result—the high proportion of respondents who were authors of speculative fiction. Just over a quarter of respondents (26 percent) identified themselves as authors of one or more published works of speculative fiction. Although not specific to speculative fiction, half of the respondents to the Macquarie University study of Australian authors were aged 40–59 years, and nearly 40 percent were older.[13] After all, the older an individual, the more years they have had in which to potentially write books. As previously discussed, authors within the contemporary genre publishing industry are strongly

---

13 Throsby, Zwar and Longden, "Australian Authors."

encouraged to have an active online presence, regardless of age and, in some cases, of inclination. This, as well as the identities of my primary contacts to whom I distributed the survey, are likely among the factors that made the survey distribution method particularly effective at reaching and recruiting authors. The high percentage of author respondents may also reflect the relative importance of the survey's subject matter to authors. Authors are highly "interested" parties in regard to the research topic, as they have much to gain by successfully managing relationships with their existing readers and interactions with potential readers. Despite this, it must be understood that all respondents to the survey, whether or not they had ever authored a work of speculative fiction, should be considered "interested parties" to some extent. Readers are also agents and position-takers in the field with their own particular preferences and opinions on the topics explored by the survey. This was confirmed throughout their responses. Respondents frequently outlined their positions in the field and, in many cases, expressed strong personal investment in the production of their favoured books and in the careers of particular authors.

The range of different countries that survey respondents lived in (Figure 2) demonstrated both the transnational nature of the online speculative fiction community and the way Web 2.0 technologies have changed the ways online literary communities can interact, removing some of the barriers to communication between readers and authors in different geographic locations.

While I'm personally active mainly within the Australian speculative fiction community and initially distributed the survey primarily through my personal online networks, the highly interconnected nature of the Anglophone online speculative fiction community allowed it to reach readers and authors in a variety of different countries. Still, it is important to consider the possibility of national differences in speculative fiction communities and their implications for issues relating to gender.

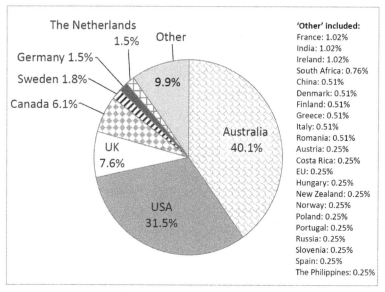

Figure 2. Country of Residence of Respondents.

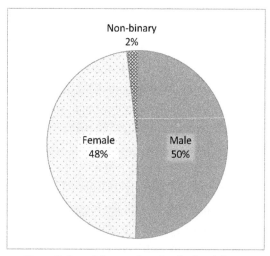

Figure 3. Overall Respondent Gender Breakdown.

For instance, the Australian speculative fiction community in particular has a strong tradition of successful female authors, especially within the Fantasy genre. Some have suggested this is linked to HarperCollins Australia launching its speculative fiction imprint Voyager with Sara Douglass's *Battleaxe* in 1995, and that her subsequent success paved the way for other female authors. When charting the history of the Australian fantasy fiction field, the vast majority of highly successful examples mentioned by Kim Wilkins are female.[14]

Overall, the numbers of male- and female-identifying respondents to the survey were close to even, while a smaller number identified as non-binary, as depicted in Figure 3.

Looking specifically at author respondents, approximately 56 percent were female, 42 percent male and 2 percent non-binary.[15] For reasons previously discussed, a majority of female speculative fiction authors was unsurprising due to the large proportion of Australian respondents. However, the percentage of women was still lower than the Macquarie study's gender breakdown for Australian genre fiction overall, which was 76.2 percent female and 23.8 percent male.[16]

Although the demographic results of this survey may not provide a completely comprehensive overview of contemporary speculative fiction readership, they offer a glimpse into a dedicated subset of the genre community and provide useful context for the other findings. For instance, respondent gender appeared to correlate with particular trends in answers relating to reading preferences and the influence of author persona. Additionally, confirmation of the presence of a substantial number of female speculative fiction authors problematises the ideas some reader respondents expressed regarding speculative fiction authorship,

---

14 Kim Wilkins, "Popular Genres and the Australian Literary Community: The Case of Fantasy Fiction," *Journal of Australian Studies,* 32, no. 2 (2008): 265–278.

15 The small sample size of non-binary respondents made it implausible to extrapolate any quantitative trends from their responses. Therefore, I excluded their responses from any purely quantitative analysis, drawing on them primarily for qualitative data.

16 Throsby, Zwar and Longden, "Australian Authors."

which I will discuss in more depth shortly. Questions investigating forms of diversity related to respondent identity categories other than basic gender identity (for example, race, sexuality or disability) were not included in the scope of the study due to project constraints and ethical considerations. Despite this, some of the information volunteered or hinted at by participants suggests that rich insights could be gained by future research into this area.

Gendered Genres

During the survey, respondents were asked to select both the speculative genres and subgenres they particularly enjoyed, as well as those that they actively disliked or avoided. Evident throughout the results was a correlation between a reader's gender and some of their most and least preferred speculative genres or subgenres. The differences between male and female readers' preferences were generally more pronounced when respondents were asked which genres or subgenres they particularly disliked than when they were asked about their preferred subgenres. This reflected a more general trend evident throughout responses to all sections of the survey, where respondents consistently reported stronger responses to negative stimuli (whether it was subgenres, books, genre tropes or authors they disliked) than to equivalent positive stimuli. Qualitative data collected by other survey questions indicated that in many cases general perceptions of a subgenre's amenability to readers of a given gender, or gendered concepts of genre hierarchy, were among the factors underlying readers' distaste for particular speculative subgenres.

The five subgenres with the greatest divergence between the numbers of male and female respondents who actively preferred them are depicted in Figure 4. Figure 5 displays results for the subgenres with the largest differences between the percentages of male and female readers who viewed them negatively or avoided books displaying the paratextual markers of that genre.

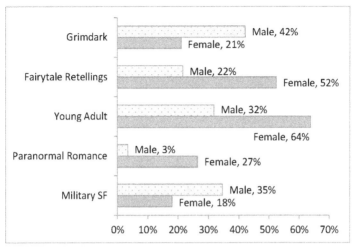

Figure 4. Percentages of male and female respondents
who enjoyed particular subgenres.

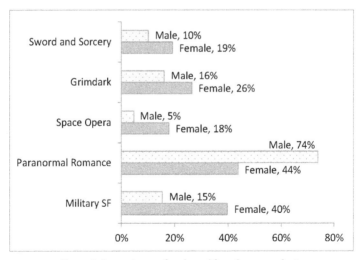

Figure 5. Percentages of male and female respondents
who disliked/avoided particular subgenres.

One such contentious subgenre was Grimdark. "Grimdark" is a loosely defined speculative fiction subgenre characterised by particularly grim, nihilistic, amoral or violent content, setting, tone or themes.[17] While 42 percent of male respondents enjoyed Grimdark fiction, only half that number of women listed it as one of their preferred subgenres. Likewise, female readers were significantly more likely to actively dislike the subgenre. On the other hand, Fairytale Retellings were popular with over half of the female respondents, while less than a quarter of men reported particularly enjoying them. At 64 percent, women were also twice as likely to enjoy Young Adult speculative fiction than men. Significantly fewer men than women professed a preference for Paranormal Romance, and almost three quarters of male respondents actively avoided it. On the other hand, almost twice as many men than women enjoyed Military Science Fiction, and women were more than twice as likely to avoid or dislike this subgenre. Female respondents were also much more likely to dislike Sword and Sorcery and Space Opera subgenres than male respondents. Although I did not explicitly ask respondents to explain why they particularly liked or disliked the subgenres they selected, the answers they provided for some of the other qualitative survey questions suggest that subgenre preferences were often related to perceptions regarding the "masculinity" or "femininity" of a subgenre, the dominance of authors of a particular gender within it, and its place in the genre hierarchy.

Gendered effects of genre hierarchisation—where books categorised by readers as belonging to particular subgenres are afforded greater or lesser value than others—were suggested by the particularly negative responses of many readers to the Paranormal Romance subgenre. A comparatively large percentage of readers, regardless of gender, listed Paranormal Romance as a genre they actively avoided. However, the percentage of women who listed it as one of their preferred genres

---

17 Teresa Frohock, "Is it Grimdark, or is it Horror?" *Tor.com* (2015), https://www.tor.com/2015/11/02/is-it-grimdark-or-is-it-horror/

was significantly higher than the percentage of men. The low status assigned to romance fiction in general and the relationship this has to gendered hierarchies of literary value has been subject to a wealth of previous scholarship, including Janice Radway's *Reading the Romance*[18] and contemporary investigations by academics including Beth Driscoll.[19] Further, examining the lists of major publishers suggests that Paranormal Romance novels frequently feature female protagonists, as do Fairytale Retellings. The subgenre is also generally perceived as dominated by female authors, as evident in qualitative survey responses.

> Subgenres are often very much dominated by one gender or the other... paranormal romance by females, epic fantasy by males etc... [Male respondent, age 30–39, USA]

The comparatively high number of male respondents who said they disliked speculative subgenres generally perceived as "feminine" could also tie in with suggestions by various feminist scholars and cultural critics that a lower cultural value is often allotted to stories written by and about women. The existence of such a bias in perceptions of cultural value appears to be supported by the results of data projects such as the aforementioned VIDA, Stella and *Strange Horizons* counts, as well as that overseen by author Nicola Griffith, which examined the percentage of prize-winning books featuring male or female protagonists and written by male or female authors. Griffith's data demonstrated an inverse relationship between the symbolic capital of a literary prize, its "prestige", and the likelihood of it being awarded to a book featuring a female protagonist or authored by a woman.[20]

---

18   Janice A. Radway, *Reading the Romance: Women, Patriarchy, and Popular Literature* (Chapel Hill: University of North Carolina Press, 1991).

19   Beth Driscoll, "Genre, Author, Text, Reader: Teaching Nora Roberts's Spellbound," *Journal of Popular Romance Studies* 4, no. 2 (2014): 1–16.

20   Nicola Griffith, "Books About Women Don't Win Big Awards: Some Data," 2015, http://nicolagriffith.com/2015/05/26/books-about-women-tend-not-to-win-awards/.

To date, one of the few studies attempting to gather systematic data on the actual prevalence of male and female authors in different book genres and subgenres is that undertaken by Mike Thelwall.[21] This study investigated a sample of data collected from the website Goodreads. Among other things, it found that many genres did display significant discrepancies between numbers of male and female authors. While Thelwall's study did not analyse all the speculative fiction subgenres included in my survey, some potentially relevant findings included that overall: a slightly higher number of Fantasy books were written by women than men; significantly more Young Adult books were authored by women; many more books by men than by women were categorised as Science Fiction; and that female authors dominated in the Paranormal Romance genre, as well as Paranormal Fantasy more generally.[22]

Because the data collected by my survey was self-reported, it is worth considering the possibility that different respondents had differing ideas about exactly what made any one book belong to a particular subgenre, and that their subgenre selections may have been influenced by factors related to their own self-image, and so to some extent may reflect the genres they thought they should like or dislike rather than providing a completely accurate breakdown of their reading habits. Genre preference itself represents a type of what Pierre Bourdieu calls, "position-taking" within the speculative fiction field.[23] As such, it is associated with symbolic capital and plays a role in defining an agent's (in this case a reader's) position within the field in relation to others. The importance of genre preferences—and, in many cases, the disavowal of genres perceived to be "frivolous", "unimportant" and highly

---

21   Mike Thewall, "Book Genre and Author Gender: Romance>Paranormal-Romance to Autobiography>Memoir," *Journal of the Association for Information Science and Technology,* 68, no. 5 (2016):1212–1223.

22   Thewall, 'Book Genre and Author Gender."

23   Pierre Bourdieu, *The Field of Cultural Production: Essays on Art and Literature,* ed. Randal Johnson (New York: Columbia University Press, 1993).

feminised, of which Paranormal Romance is a prime example—to the self-image of readers is explored in *Accounting for Tastes*.[24] Despite the consistently high sales of romance novels, both the male and female readers interviewed either expressed active distaste for them or, if they did admit to reading them, were almost unanimously apologetic for doing so.[25] Similar sentiments were expressed in a significant number of qualitative answers to my survey.

> The covers of books by female writers very often look like (paranormal) romance novels, and the blurbs tend to emphasise these aspects as well (regardless of how important they are to the main plot). That's pretty much guaranteed to turn me off a book instantly. [Male respondent, age 21–29, Germany]

> I hate romance fiction. This is not to say that there aren't any good women authors, it is just that, generally, a much higher proportion of authors I like are male. [Male respondent, age 18–20, Australia]

A direct conflation of female authors and "romance" was evident in a number of qualitative responses. In most cases, these responses were to questions that made no reference to subgenre at all and were about author gender in general, meaning the respondents were not prompted to make a connection between gender and subgenre.[26] On the other hand, the high percentage of female readers who disliked Grimdark fiction appeared to relate to their ideas about the way books in the subgenre treated female characters and suggestions that the subgenre as a whole (and sometimes its community) could be hostile to female authors and readers. A number of respondents who listed Grimdark as

---

24 Tony Bennett, Michael Emmison and John Frow. *Accounting for Tastes: Australian Everyday Cultures* (Cambridge, UK: Cambridge University Press, 1999).

25 Bennett et al., *Accounting for Tastes*, 145–147.

26 The exact wording of the question for the given example was, "Do you generally prefer authors of a particular gender?"

a subgenre they actively avoided mentioned having issues with sexism and the use of rape as a plot device in examples of Grimdark fiction they had read in the past.

The treatment of female characters within Grimdark fiction has been a topic of discussion within the speculative fiction community before, as has the use of sexual violence in Fantasy fiction more generally.[27] Some notable examples of this discourse include author Sophia McDougall's article about "rape as window dressing" and differences between acts of violence against male and female characters in genre fiction, and Jim C. Hines's frequently reprinted series of articles, "Writing About Rape".[28] Respondents also often expressed the belief that most authors writing in the Grimdark subgenre were male.

> Male writers often sacrifice character development to plot, and confuse trauma with character. See the entire grimdark genre for examples. [Female respondent, age 50–59, USA]

Overall, a significant number of the opinions that respondents expressed about different subgenres could be interpreted to suggest that some readers had specific preferences when it came to the gender of the authors of the books they read, a topic explicitly explored in another section of the survey.

The Effects of Author Gender on Reader Preferences and Expectations

The question of whether the gender of an author influences the reading or purchasing choices of some speculative fiction readers, directly or

---

27 Debra Ferreday, "Game of Thrones, Rape Culture and Feminist Fandom.," *Australian Feminist Studies* 30, no. 83 (2015): 21–36; Lenise Prater, "Monstrous Fantasies: Reinforcing Rape Culture in Fiona McIntosh's Fantasy Novels," *Hecate* 39, no. 1/2 (2014): 148–167.

28 Jim Hines, "Writing about Rape," *Apex Magazine* (2012), http://www.apex-magazine.com/writing-about-rape/; Sophia McDougall, "The Rape of James Bond," 2013, http://sophiamcdougall.com/2013/03/13/the-rape-of-james-bond/.

indirectly, and to what degree, have been debated for many years.[29] Likewise, differences in the reception of books by male and female authors are still frequently related anecdotally within writing communities, including speculative fiction communities. Personally, more than a few female authors have expressed to me the opinion that the issues explored by Science Fiction author Joanna Russ in her book, *How to Suppress Women's Writing*, are as relevant today as when she wrote about them over three decades ago.[30] While much of this discussion has related to implicit forms of bias, the possibility that some readers have explicit preferences in regards to author gender has been also raised. The data gathered throughout my survey suggests the existence of both explicit and implicit gender bias in the field, despite the fact that the majority of readers believed they were impartial in this regard.[31]

All in all, when a respondent professed to prefer books written by authors of a particular gender, they were significantly more likely to favour books by authors of their own gender. The proffered reasons for this were largely based on differing expectations of male, female and non-binary authors, and ideas about common differences in their writing. By the numbers, women were generally more willing to express an explicit preference for author gender than men, citing issues with female representation and the male gaze in male-authored speculative fiction as their rationale. The preferences of male and female respondents regarding author gender are represented in Figure 6 and Figure 7.

---

29 Cheryl Morgan, "Checking the Gender Balance.," *SFWA* (2011), http://www.sfwa. org/2011/06/guest-post-checking-the-gender-balance/; Tansy Raynar Roberts, "Tansy Rayner Roberts on Fantasy, Female Writers & The Politics of Influence," *SF Signal* (2015), http://www.sfsignal.com/archives/2015/06/guest-post-tansy-rayner-roberts-fantasy-female-writers-politics-influence/.

30 Joanna Russ, *How to Suppress Women's Writing*, (Austin, Texas: University of Texas Press, 1983).

31 It's also been suggested that these basic principles could be applied to books by authors belonging to other identity groups that are traditionally underrepresented in mainstream publishing. For example, Indigenous authors, transgender authors, disabled authors and many others.

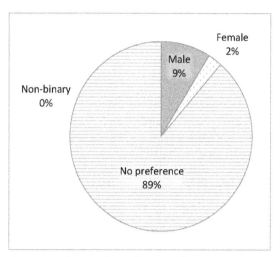

Figure 6. Author gender preferences of male respondents.

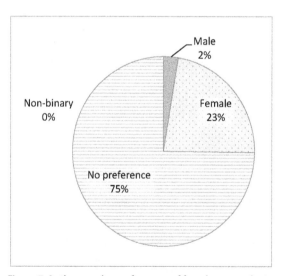

Figure 7. Author gender preferences of female respondents.

Of the readers who admitted to author gender influencing their reading choices, female readers usually preferred books written by women, while male readers more frequently preferred books written by men. Meanwhile, non-binary respondents all said that they preferred books by non-binary authors or had no preference. In many cases, respondent preferences appeared to be related to a belief that speculative fiction authors of different genders often wrote differently, in different genres, and about different things. The overall percentage of readers who believed there were general gender-based differences in authors' writing is shown in Figure 8.

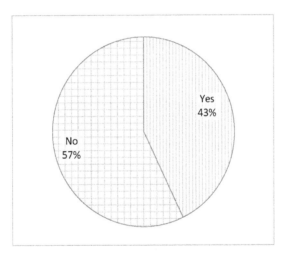

Figure 8. Overall answer percentages for the question "Have you noticed any general differences between the writing of speculative fiction authors of different genders?".

At 57 percent, the majority of readers did not believe that authors of different genders wrote differently. Some reported that they were frequently incorrect when they tried to guess the gender of a book's author when a gender-neutral pseudonym or initials were used. Regardless, a significant number of respondents still thought there were general differences between the writing of men and women, despite most saying that they had no preference between them. Many responses suggested that writers were more likely to write books featuring protagonists of their own gender, especially if they were men. Ideas that female authors were more likely to include significant female characters, non-binary characters were more frequently included by non-binary authors, and that authors tended to be better at writing characters of their own gender were also mentioned. There were also suggestions by some respondents that prose style or quality often differed between genders, as did the common themes and focuses of books. Traits frequently attributed to women's writing included "lyricism", "romance", "subtlety", "character development", "subverting tropes" and "feminism". On the other hand, traits commonly associated with men's writing included "grittiness", "action", "world-building", "plot", "sparse writing", "following tropes", "ideas", "violence" and "male gaze". Some responses also mentioned differences in the focus authors appeared to put on different aspects of a book, including female authors more frequently focusing on character and male authors focusing on action and plot development. Reponses also suggested that women were more likely to include romance and emotional nuance in their fiction, while men were more likely to include graphic gore and violence. Some readers also suggested that books written by women contained more minute details, such as descriptions of clothing, than those by men. Others expressed the opinion that women and non-binary authors were more likely to tackle social justice or feminist themes—however, opinion was divided as to whether this was a good or bad thing. A deeper understanding of the rationale underlying readers' preferences for author gender can be gained by examining some of the qualitative responses. For instance, the responses below are fairly typical examples by readers who preferred fiction written by men:

> I prefer classic plain text, with less elaboration and allusion.
> [Male respondent, age 60+, Australia]

I tend to enjoy world-building and magic system development, which I tend to find more from male authors. [Male respondent, age 30–39, USA]

Bit more of a bite—grittier. [Male respondent, age 50–59, Australia]

The distaste expressed by some respondents for the description and allusion they associated with women's writing often coexisted with a proclivity for other types of elaboration, such as world-building and magic system development, which these readers considered more worthwhile and as "belonging" within the speculative genres. Throughout responses, an association was often made between "gritty" and "plot-driven" content and male authorship, reflecting both the perceived male dominance of "gritty" subgenres like Grimdark and, potentially, more general perceptions of masculinity and femininity, with males associated with greater agency, action and violence, and females perceived as more passive, emotional and reactive.

The fact that female respondents were more likely to express an explicit preference relating to author gender than male respondents and, when they did, were much more likely to favour female authors over male authors, also appeared to be associated with perceived differences in writing and theme. Some female readers expressed frustration with the prevalence of the male gaze and absence of female characters in examples of speculative fiction written by men. Respondents also frequently attributed a greater tendency to include more diverse perspectives to female authors. Survey responses suggested that in many cases, a preference for female authors was a direct result of being disillusioned with the work of many male authors. This was not limited to female respondents; similar ideas were expressed in responses by some of the male and non-binary readers who believed there were often differences between the writing of speculative fiction authors of different genders. This is demonstrated in these responses from readers who preferred books by female authors:

> Male authors who write women (at all, let alone convincingly) are rare. I get sick of excusing golden age sci-fi for failing 50% of the population with "Oh, it was the time they were written in." Heinlein (nipples that go "sprung") is a classic example. [Female respondent, age 30–39, Australia]

> Male writers tend to reflect their gender privilege in terms of male gazey descriptions and "fridged" women. Women, I think, take far less of human interaction for granted and are more thoughtful about motivations. [Male respondent, age 30–39, India]

A number of respondents further clarified in their qualitative answers that they actually preferred books by women and non-binary authors equally, indicating that their preference was for books not written by men, rather than specifically written by women. Unfortunately, due to the format of the relevant survey question not enabling participants to select multiple responses, it was not possible to quantify to what exact extent this applied across all respondents.

Frequent use of terms such as "tired" and "sick of" throughout the responses illustrated the fatigue many readers expressed regarding the male gaze (as originally described by Laura Mulvey in relation to cinematic arts) in male-authored works.[32] Impassioned statements such as "failing 50% of the population" demonstrate the importance of seeing women represented within fiction to many female readers. Similarly, non-binary respondents who preferred books by non-binary authors cited representation as a key factor in their decision.

---

32 Laura Mulvey, "Visual Pleasure and Narrative Cinema," *Screen* 16, no. 3 (1975): 6–18, http://theslideprojector.com/pdffiles/art6/visualpleasureandnarrativecinema.pdf.

The characters are often more relatable to me, and the authors are far less likely to include transphobic or queerphobic content. [Non-binary respondent, age 30–39, New Zealand]

When outlining what they wanted in fiction that they believed they were not getting from books written by men, respondents expressed a desire for more diverse perspectives and characters of different genders, races and sexual orientations in speculative fiction books. Some male respondents stated that they were actively trying to read more books by women in an attempt to counter implicit bias. They said that they had chosen to do this as a result of having had their attention brought to issues of disparity in their personal reading habits and within the market in general by various campaigns, blog posts or informal discussions within speculative fiction, or larger literary, communities.

Readers with "No Preference" Read Mostly Men

Although the results of directly asking respondents about gender bias suggested that most did not factor author gender into their reading choices, and those that did more often favoured female authors than male authors, examining the books respondents listed as having recently read told a different story. Readers who reported that they had "no preference" with regard to author gender mentioned significantly more male authors than female authors.[33]

---

33 I chose to use authors rather than titles mentioned in order to reduce the impact of readers who were consecutively reading titles in a series on the results. Additionally, I sought to prevent results from being distorted by the large number of readers who were reading books by George RR Martin. However, most of the series being read consecutively and the books being read by more than ten different readers were authored by men. As a result of these attempts to avoid any inflation of the figures that may have caused excessive doubt to be cast on the results, it is possible that the figures presented actually underestimate actual author gender-based disparity. I also removed anthologies, journals, books with more than two authors, and the few books about which not enough information was given to identify the exact title.

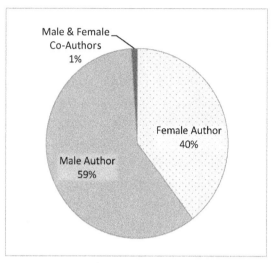

Figure 9. Gender breakdown of authors mentioned by respondents with "no preference".

Overall, 323 different readers professing to have "no preference" for author gender listed books by 536 different authors as included in the last five speculative fiction books they had read, with male authors outnumbering female authors and teams of male and female authors co-writing.

This result supported anecdotal suggestions in both the speculative fiction and larger literary community that readers who do not actively factor author gender into their book purchasing decisions often end up reading significantly more books by men than women. The reasons underlying this trend require further exploration, although some commentators have related them to subconscious bias against female authors based on (the previously examined) perceived gender-based differences in writing, differences in the paratext of books by authors of different genders, and a greater number of books by male authors achieving visibility to readers as a result of factors including receiving more reviews in major venues, being marketed differently, and being perceived as more "important" and imbued with a greater cultural value. The invisibility of all but the most well-known and bestselling female speculative fiction authors to some respondents was evident within a large number of qualitative responses by readers who said that author gender did not affect their reading choices.

> The overwhelming majority of authors that I read are male, I read really few female authors not by choice but because there is few ones [*sic*]. [Male respondent, age 21–29, France]

> I have not read much speculative fiction from female writers, though I am an aspiring female speculative fiction writer myself. [Female respondent, age 21–29, USA]

> Haven't read enough books by female authors to form an opinion. [Male respondent, age 21–29, Germany]

Such statements from speculative fiction readers are problematised by the number of female authors who answered the survey, the variety of female-authored titles listed by readers who favoured women authors, and previous research on the prevalence of female authors within speculative fiction genres. The fact that some readers did not believe that many female authors wrote within the speculative genres illustrates that at some point in the book publication or promotional process many books by women became "invisible" to these readers. This is despite the large number of Australian readers who completed the survey and the history of women authors dominating the most popular speculative genres in Australia.

Also worth noting is that the non-binary authors whose books were listed in the survey results were almost exclusively mentioned by non-binary respondents who reported actively seeking books by non-binary authors due to better (or any) representation of characters with a non-binary gender identity, and no books by non-binary authors were listed by respondents who chose "no preference".

When Authors' Opinions Get Personal

The survey asked readers a range of questions exploring how factors external to the text itself, such as their opinion of the author as a person, affected their decisions to read (or, more precisely, to pay for) books.[34] One key finding of this section of the survey was that, for the majority of readers, a negative opinion of an author appeared to have a stronger effect than a positive one. Although many of the trends identified in the data did not appear to vary by respondent gender, there were some notable exceptions. For instance, more women than men said that an author's social and political opinions could explicitly influence their book purchasing choices, as depicted in Figure 10.

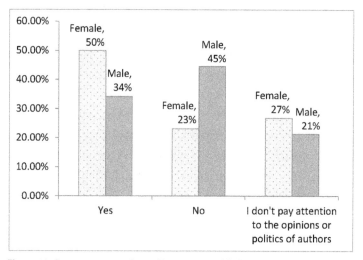

Figure 10. Answers to question—"Are you more likely to buy an author's book if you share a similar opinion on particular social or political issues?".

---

34 Throughout this section of the survey, respondents demonstrated high levels of awareness of the role of their book purchases in financially supporting authors in the creation of more books. Some readers also admitted to seeking alternative means, legal or otherwise, to access books written by authors they disliked in cases where they still wanted to read them, with the primary purpose being to avoid the author receiving money from the interaction.

Qualitative responses indicated that one possible factor underlying this discrepancy was that certain types of bigotry an author might publicly express, such as misogyny, felt more personal to female readers than to male readers and were therefore more difficult for them to overlook.

> I am unlikely to pick up anything from [Author name] as he has made it clear that I am one of the kinds of people that he particularly hates, and I understand from trusted sources that his work is openly discriminatory. [Female respondent, age 30–39, Australia]

> Authors who behave rudely to fans, or who express racist or sexist views aren't worth my reading time. Social media has weeded out a lot of authors for me. [Female respondent, age 30–39, USA]

> I'm less likely to buy someone's books if they're an asshole, particularly if they're an asshole in that they're racist, sexist, homophobic, and so on (chance of buying their stuff pretty much drops to zero). Occasionally if someone is known as being an asshole, but not in a way that triggers my social justice warrior tendencies (e.g. they say assholish things, but aren't actually a bigot) I might read their stuff out of morbid curiosity. [Female respondent, age 30–39, Australia]

> I will not buy books by authors who are overtly racist, sexist or homophobic. Not only am I unlikely to enjoy their characters (noting it's not necessarily impossible), I just don't want to support them at all. There are so many wonderful books in the world, it's not like I won't find anything else to read. [Female respondent, age 40–49, Australia]

Responses by non-binary readers generally reflected similar sentiments about purchasing books by authors who expressed opinions they considered bigoted, and a slight positive preference for authors who supported causes that respondents cared about.

> Finding out that the author is open-minded and for social justice tends to make me more likely to read their novels. [Non-binary respondent, age 30–39, Canada]

> [Author name]'s repeated racism and cissexism... have caused me to stop reading his books as they come out. I used to be a devoted reader. [Non-binary respondent, age 20–29, USA]

Likewise, responses from the male readers who suggested within other parts of the survey that they belonged to a minority identity, for instance in regards to race or sexuality, also generally supported the idea that readers who identified as belonging to a particular group or identity that an author disparaged were likely to decide not to purchase that author's work.

Importantly, the differences between the number of male and female respondents who reported that an author's social or political views influenced whether they chose to purchase a book must also be viewed with consideration given to the fact that responses to the relevant survey questions did not account for any implicit influence. Likewise, the data doesn't account for readers who may be reluctant to admit that factors external to a book's content influence their reception of it, due to reasons related to their self-image. For instance, it is possible that some male readers didn't respond in the affirmative to this question partially as a result of societal pressure on men to appear not to let their emotional reactions to various stimuli affect their decisions. As a result, it is possible that readers' opinions of an author affecting their book purchasing choices is even more common than the data implies.

A Reflection of Wider Issues

Viewed in their entirety, the findings of this study in relation to gender support suggestions that a degree of implicit gender bias still operates within the speculative fiction field and may influence the book purchasing choices of readers. However, in some cases, this implicit bias is being explicitly challenged by readers in light of greater awareness of gender disparity within literary fields. While efforts to address disadvantages disproportionately experienced by female authors appear to have made progress in a number of areas, such as recent award short lists, and to have made some readers aware enough of representational issues to go out of their way to counteract them, there is still scope for improvement. While addressing complicated manifestations of gender bias across the entirety of the potential audience for books is likely to be much more complicated than concentrating efforts on encouraging distinct entities (such as prize judges, review venues and publishers) to "lift their game", doing so is likely necessary to ever achieve true parity.

Another way gender and book choice intersect relates to how the prospective reader's gender may affect their reception of books displaying paratext associated with different speculative subgenres and, more broadly, their ideas about the attributes of these subgenres. Additionally, a reader's gender and their related lived experiences may also mediate the magnitude of their response to certain opinions about political or social issues an author might express. These factors can also influence how likely a particular reader is to buy any given book. Going back to the question raised at the start of this chapter, the gender of a reader and/or author can have significant effects on whether the reader perceives any given book as the "type of book" they "think they'll enjoy".

In examining the results of this research project, it is important to note that there is no indication that issues related to gender are restricted to the speculative genres. Instead, indications suggest bias exists to varying extents throughout the larger literary field. Therefore, the results of this research may be relevant to a broader audience throughout literary and publishing communities. Qualitative responses collected by my survey also support the idea, expressed before by other commentators, that disparity related to identity categories other than gender is prevalent within literary fields and warrants further investigation. If we are to truly attempt to 'level the playing field' and address these issues to better support and amplify the voices of authors from identity groups traditionally underrepresented in the Anglophone literary field, it is vital that we understand the full extent of any bias in the field, the intricacies of its operations and the rationale underlying it. Identifying and confronting the fundamental causes of bias and disparity, in addition to their symptoms and manifestations, provides us with the opportunity to create lasting change to the benefit of authors, readers, and all of us within wider literary communities.

Works cited

Bennett, Tony, Michael Emmison and John Frow. *Accounting for Tastes: Australian Everyday Cultures.* Cambridge, UK: Cambridge University Press, 1999.

Bourdieu, Pierre. *The Field of Cultural Production: Essays on Art and Literature*, edited by Randal Johnson. New York: Columbia University Press, 1993.

Chartier, Roger. "Texts, Printing, Reading." In *The New Cultural History*, edited by Lynn Hunt, 154–175. Berkeley: University of California Press, 1989.

Connolly, Susan E. "The Issue of Gender in Genre Fiction: A Detailed Analysis." *Clarkesworld* 93 (2014). http://clarkesworldmagazine.com/connolly_06_14/.

Driscoll, Beth. "Genre, Author, Text, Reader: Teaching Nora Roberts's Spellbound." *Journal of Popular Romance Studies* 4, no. 2 (2014): 1–16. http://jprstudies.org/2014/10/genre-author-text-reader-teaching-nora-robertss-spellboundby-beth-driscoll/.

Ferreday, Debra. "Game of Thrones, Rape Culture and Feminist Fandom." *Australian Feminist Studies* 30, no. 83 (2015): 21–36. https://doi.org/10.1080/08164649.2014.998453.

Frohock, Teresa. "Is It Grimdark, or Is It Horror?" *Tor.com* (2015). https://www.tor.com/2015/11/02/is-it-grimdark-or-is-it-horror/.

Genette, Gérard. *Paratexts: Thresholds of Interpretation*. Cambridge: Cambridge University Press, 1997.

Goldsmith, Michelle. "Exploring the Author-Reader Relationship in Contemporary Speculative Fiction." *LOGOS: The Journal of the World Book Community* 27, no. 11 (2016): 31–44.

Griffith, Nicola. "Books About Women Don't Win Big Awards: Some Data." 2015. http://nicolagriffith.com/2015/05/26/books-about-women-tend-not-to-win-awards/.

Harrison, Niall. "The 2014 SF Count." *Strange Horizons* (2015). http://www.strangehorizons.com/2015/20150330/sfcount-a.shtml.

Herrnstein Smith, Barbara. "Value/Evaluation." In *Critical Terms for Literary Study*, edited by Frank Lentricchia and Thomas McLaughlin, 177–185. Chicago: University of Chicago Press, 1995.

Hines, Jim. "Writing About Rape." *Apex Magazine (*2012). http://www.apex-magazine.com/writing-about-rape/.

Lamond, Julieanne. "Stella vs Miles: Women Writers and Literary Value in Australia." *Meanjin* 70, no. 3 (2011). https://meanjin.com.au/essays/stella-vs-miles-women-writers-and-literary-value-in-australia/.

McDougall, Sophia. "The Rape of James Bond." (2013). http://sophiamcdougall.com/2013/03/13/the-rape-of-james-bond/.

Morgan, Cheryl. "Checking the Gender Balance." *SFWA* (2011). http://www.sfwa.org/2011/06/guest-post-checking-the-gender-balance/.

Mulvey, Laura. "Visual Pleasure and Narrative Cinema." *Screen* 16, no. 3 (1975): 6–18. http://theslideprojector.com/pdffiles/art6/visualpleasureandnarrativecinema.pdf.

Murray, Simone. "Charting the Digital Literary Sphere." *Contemporary Literature* 56, no. 2 (2015): 311–339.

Prater, Lenise. "Monstrous Fantasies: Reinforcing Rape Culture in Fiona McIntosh's Fantasy Novels." *Hecate* 39, no. 1/2 (2014): 148–167.

Radway, Janice A. *Reading the Romance: Women, Patriarchy, and Popular Literature*. Chapel Hill: University of North Carolina Press, 1991.

Raynar Roberts, Tansy. "Tansy Rayner Roberts on Fantasy, Female Writers & The Politics of Influence." *SF Signal* (2015). http://www.sfsignal.com/archives/2015/06/guest-post-tansy-rayner-roberts-fantasy-female-writers-politics-influence/.

Russ, Joanna. *How to Suppress Women's Writing*. Austin, Texas: University of Texas Press, 1983.

The Stella Prize. "2016 Stella Count." 2017. http://thestellaprize.com.au/the-count/2016-stella-count/.

Thewall, Mike. "Book Genre and Author Gender: Romance>Paranormal-Romance to Autobiography>Memoir." *Journal of the Association for Information Science and Technology* 68, no. 5 (2016): 1212–1223.

Throsby, David, Jan Zwar, and Thomas Longden. "Australian Authors." In *The Australian Book Industry: Authors, Publishers and Readers in a Time of Change* (Sydney: Macquarie University, Department of Economics, 2015). http://www.businessandeconomics.mq.edu.au/our_departments/Economics/econ_research/reach_network/book_project/authors/1_Key_Findings.pdf.

VIDA. "The 2016 VIDA Count." Accessed June 2017. http://www.vidaweb.org/the-2016-vida-count/.

Wilkins, Kim. "Popular Genres and the Australian Literary Community: The Case of Fantasy Fiction." *Journal of Australian Studies* 32, no. 2 (2008): 265–278.

———. "Writing Resilience in the Digital Age." *New Writing: The International Journal for the Practice & Theory of Creative Writing* 11 (2014): 67–76.

CHAPTER 8

Shared Reading in the Victorian Mallee

BRIGID MAGNER AND EMILY POTTER

This chapter emerges from our literary history project *Reading/Writing the Mallee*, which utilises shared reading methodology as a way of generating new knowledge about the Victorian Mallee region. We discuss a series of four events we have recently coordinated—in the rural cities of Mildura and Swan Hill and the smaller towns of Quambatook and Hopetoun—which have produced evidence of rich localised reading practices.

The Mallee region may be defined biogeographically as any semi-arid area of mainland Australia that has Mallee scrub as its principal natural vegetation; this includes parts of South Australia, New South Wales and southern Western Australia. Our focus in this chapter is the informally defined Mallee region of north-western Victoria. Kerang and the Loddon River are the usually accepted eastern boundary of the Mallee. The southern boundary is often depicted as a line extending through Lake Hindmarsh to the South Australian border.[1]

Colonisation of the Mallee region began in 1846, and spread rapidly from 1950, violently dispossessing Indigenous groups including the Latji Latji, Paakantji (Barkindji), Ngiyampaa, Mutthi Mutthi, Wemba Wemba, Tati Tati and Barapa Barapa peoples. Due to the widespread clearing of the Mallee vegetation, settlers endured a series of disasters, namely plagues (rabbits, mice, grasshoppers), drought

---

1 "Mallee," Victorian Places, accessed March 20, 2018, http://www.victorianplaces.com.au/mallee.

and dust storms.[2] The dust "monsters" of the 1930s were attributed to rapid expansion of land cultivation, overstocking with sheep and cattle, "bad seasons", and government advice to "grow more and more wheat".[3] Deb Anderson argues that, for those who stayed, "that history of survival, of endurance, has prevailed as cultural capital for generations to come".[4]

The Victorian Mallee has tended to be associated in the Australian imagination with wheat production—and the tribulations of farmers and their families—rather than its literary production. Literary entries on the Mallee tend to be dominated by references to its desolation and barrenness instead of its potential as a site of literary creativity. Entries in standard literary histories of Australia tend to focus on three figures: Rolf Boldrewood, John Shaw Neilson and Nancy Cato. In *Australian Readers Remember: An Oral History of Reading 1890–1930*, Martyn Lyons and Lucy Taksa note that conventional literary histories have concentrated on writers and placed primary value on the creativity of authors.

Only rarely do publishers, booksellers and the mass of readers themselves figure in the history of Australian literature. We need to question this obsession with the author, and to widen our vision of literary culture. We need a reader's version of literary history or, more accurately, a history of the Australian reader.[5]

Following Lyons and Taksa's call for a reader's version of literary history, we seek to explore readers' perceptions of local literature through reading groups located in different rural cities and towns around the Mallee. In these encounters, we have tried to find out

---

2   Paul Dee, "The Mallee," *State Library of Victoria*, May 11, 2016, https://blogs.slv. vic.gov.au/such-was-life/the-mallee/.

3   Deb Anderson, *Endurance: Australian Stories of Drought* (Melbourne: CSIRO Publishing, 2014), 191.

4   Ibid.

5   Martyn Lyons and Lucy Taksa, *Australian Readers Remember: An Oral History of Reading 1890–1930* (Melbourne: Oxford University Press, 1992), 2.

how contemporary Mallee books might be received by readers who are residents of this region and what patterns of sociability they might give rise to.

Textual Communities

"Textual communities"—or groups of readers in close communication with each other through books—that date back to the twelfth century have been identified by scholars such as Brian Stock.[6] After the invention of printing, there were a myriad of "book based communities" according to Elizabeth Eisenstein and Adrian Johns.[7] Seventeenth-century salons were forums for discussions of literature, politics and culture.[8] These led onto nineteenth-century literary societies, which comprised mostly women (in the US context) and were responsible for founding up to 75 percent of public libraries in North America.[9] Contemporary book clubs resemble these associations in various ways; however, they are much less formal, with fewer rules and regulations.

Marilyn Poole notes that in Australia reading groups constitute one of the largest bodies of community participation in the arts.[10] In Australia, the most successful movement that auspices reading groups is the Council of Adult Education (CAE), which began in 1946. In

---

6   Brian Stock, *The Implications of Literacy*: Written language and Models of Interpretation in the Eleventh and Twelfth Centuries (Princeton: Princeton University Press, 1983).

7   Elizabeth Eisenstein, *The Printing Press as Agent of Change: Communications and Cultural Transformation in Early Modern Europe* (Cambridge and New York: Cambridge University Press, 1979).

8   Adrian Johns, *The Nature of the Book: Print and Knowledge in the Making* (Chicago: Chicago University Press, 1998).

9   Barbara Sicherman, "Sense and Sensibility: A Case Study of Women's Reading in Late-Victorian America," in *Reading in America*, ed. Cathy Davison (Baltimore: John Hopkins University Press, 1989), 209.

10 Marilyn Poole, "The Women's Chapter: Women's Reading Groups in Victoria," Feminist Media Studies 3, no. 3 (2003): 263–281.

2017, there were 534 CAE book groups, averaging 10–11 members each, with the majority located in Victoria.[11] Libraries around the country also administer reading groups and it's this network that we are utilising for our project.

Along with Danielle Fuller and DeNel Rehberg Sedo, we understand "shared reading" as both a social process and a social formation that involves intersubjectivity and even interdependence.[12] Joan Swann and Daniel Allington have shown that shared reading is a complex process in which much interpretative work is done "on the hoof", as members collaboratively co-construct textual interpretations within specific contexts of reading.[13] We are especially interested in local reading groups as sites of discussion, contestation and creativity in the context of the Mallee region.

Marguerite Nolan and Robert Clarke have utilised book group methodology to analyse discussions of reconciliation in relation to Kate Grenville's controversial book *The Secret River*.[14] Nolan's more recent collaboration with Janeese Henaway explores the workings of a Murri reading group in Townsville and the ways in which it enables cross-cultural empathy and subverts assumptions about book clubs as reading formations.[15] Both articles demonstrate the usefulness of book group methodology for understanding the dialogical nature of

---

11 Jessica Zibung, personal communication with author, 2017.

12 DeNel Rehberg Sedo, "An Introduction to Reading Communities: Processes and Formations," in *Reading Communities from Salons to Cyberspace*, ed. DeNel Rehberg Sedo (Basingstoke: Palgrave Macmillan, 2011), 2.

13 Joan Swann and Daniel Allington, "Reading Groups and the Language of Literary Texts: A Case Study in Social Reading," *Language and Literature* 18, no. 3 (2009): 253.

14 Robert Clarke and Marguerite Nolan, "Book Clubs and Reconciliation: A Pilot Study on Book Clubs Reading the 'Fictions of Reconciliation,'" *Australian Humanities Review* 56 (2014).

15 Maggie Nolan and Janeese Henaway, "Decolonizing Reading: The Murri Book Club," *Continuum* 31, no. 6 (2017).

reading and of the need to critically account for the politics and ethics of reading in process.[16]

Wendy Griswold's book *Regionalism and the Reading Class* discusses the importance of the "reading class" to regional communities in America, but many of her observations can also be usefully applied to the Victorian Mallee region.[17] She notes that every community has a "reading class" that gives rise to informal discussion groups such as book clubs, where "intense personal, intellectual, and occasionally even political bonds are forged".[18] Griswold contends that regular participants tend to become more involved in wider community affairs by converting a solitary intellectual activity into one which is social and civic.[19] The existence of a regional literature, Griswold argues, depends upon state and institutional support, the market, and a reading class that is interested in reading about place.[20]

The adjective regional can be attached to a particular work of literature or to an author who is strongly associated with a certain place. Unlike other well-known regional literatures, Mallee literature has not been defined and discussed in any comprehensive way. As mentioned earlier, the only authors who have been consistently connected with the region are Rolf Boldrewood, John Shaw Neilson and Nancy Cato—and of these, only Cato's work is known to the wider public, largely due to the television series based on her *All the Rivers Run* trilogy. We have sought to interact with members of the reading class in Mildura, Swan Hill, Quambatook and Hopetoun in order to gauge local perceptions of novels that could be classified as examples of an emergent Mallee literature.

---

16 Clarke and Nolan, "Book Clubs," 137.

17 Jenny Griswold, *Regionalism and the Reading Class* (Chicago: Chicago University Press, 2008).

18 Ibid., 161.

19 Ibid., 161.

20 Ibid., 70.

Methodology

Initially, we sought to access already existing reading groups by utilising the networks of the Mildura library, Swan Hill library, and the John Gorton library in Kerang. Librarians in Mildura, Swan Hill and Kerang, along with the coordinators of the Quambatook Resource Centre and the Hopetoun Neighbourhood House, assisted by recruiting participants and distributing the books on our behalf. Due to the small number of reading groups—and possibly the time involved with reading three Mallee novels in advance of a meeting—we were only able to engage with one already existing reading group, which was in Swan Hill. Therefore, we decided to artificially assemble groups for events in Mildura, Quambatook and Hopetoun, which meant that participants had not operated as reading groups previously. A more appropriate term would be "research reading groups", given they were thrown together for a one-off event, purely for the purposes of our project.

One-hour discussion sessions were filmed for transcription purposes. We used open-ended questions to start the conversation but we emphasised that the participants could take the discussion in any direction. Afterwards, we emailed a brief follow-up survey to collect demographic information and offer another opportunity for participants to comment on the books and the session itself.

All participants signed consent forms agreeing to the use of their transcribed talk in our published research. Individual group members are anonymised through the removal of identifying names and attributes. The actual locations—Mildura, Swan Hill, Quambatook and Hopetoun—have been retained as we wish to reflect the issues of place, which are central to our project, and to acknowledge the rich contributions of participants from these communities.

Most of the respondents were in the 61–70 age group, with around 20 percent of respondents in the 31–40 age group. Only 45 to 50 percent of participants had a university qualification, with some not having completed high school. The level of education varied between groups—for example, the Mildura group contained a number of librarians and the Quambatook group featured some retired schoolteachers, while in the Swan Hill and Hopetoun groups, few participants had completed high school. This contrasts with many other studies of book groups, in which the participants are usually university educated. In their British survey, Hartley and Turvey found that most book club members were "highly educated".[21]

The Swan Hill group had been running for three or four years, while the Mildura group was a composite made up of people from different groups and included librarians, meaning participants weren't all known to each other beforehand. The Quambatook and Hopetoun groups were also assembled for the occasion, as mentioned previously. The smallest group was in Hopetoun, with only three participants present on the day even though ten people had received and partially read the books. Some of the Quambatook participants had experience with book groups individually but they hadn't been in one together. To our knowledge, none of the Hopetoun readers had ever been involved with reading groups before.

Three groups of between nine to eleven people were made up almost entirely of women, with one man in each of the Mildura, Quambatook and Hopetoun groups. We were told that there had been a male farmer in the Swan Hill group but he had recently dropped out. The remaining members told us that it was a Monica McInerney book that had driven him to leave. This suggests that the prevalence of "female" book choices was alienating for the male participant.

In *The Reading Group Book*, Jenny Hartley suggests that 69 percent of members in her sample belonged to all-female groups.[22] Marilyn

---

21   Jenny Hartley, *The Reading Groups Book: With a Survey Conducted in Association with Sarah Turvey* (Oxford; New York: Oxford University Press, 2001).
22   Ibid.

Poole and Frances Devlin-Glass have also observed that reading group membership in Australia is made up mostly of women.[23] Janice Radway and Elizabeth Long have both focused attention on the "ways of talking" used by female participants in book group formations.[24] Radway and Long inaugurated the tradition of observational research on reading groups that is drawn upon by our own research in the Victorian Mallee.

Along with other researchers who use book groups as their methodology, we recognise that it is problematic in some ways—and not fully representative—especially since we tend to attract people of a similar demographic—females, usually older than fifty, and almost always of Anglo-Celtic background. We also recognise that our own participation in the discussion, including our posing of questions, has an effect on what is said and how it is said, in the context of a research reading group rather than a normal reading group situation.

As Bethan Benwell notes, this issue of mediation by the research process is one that has troubled many researchers undertaking ethnographically oriented research in the social sciences, and is a particularly vexed issue in audience and reception studies, where the views of participants are often found to be difficult to access in any kind of authentic way. Like Benwell, we are alert to the fact that our presence and the questions we pose to the readers almost certainly alter our participants' behaviour and partially shape their responses.[25] We

---

23 Poole, "The Women's Chapter." Frances Devlin-Glass, "More Than a Reader and Less Than a Critic: Literary Authority and Women's Book Discussion Groups." *Women's Studies International Forum* 24, no. 5 (2001): 571–85.

24 Janice Radway, *A Feeling for Books: The Book-of-the-Month-Club, Literary Taste and Middle Class Desire* (Chapel Hill: University of North Carolina Press, 1997); Elizabeth Long, "Women, Reading, and Cultural Authority: Some Implications of the Audience Perspective in Cultural Studies," *American Quarterly* 38, No. 4 (Autumn, 1986).

25 Bethan Benwell, "'A Pathetic and Racist and Awful Character': Ethnomethodological Approaches to the Reception of Diasporic Fiction," *Language and Literature* 18, no. 3 (2009): 301.

found that the participants could initially be reluctant to say anything critical, through politeness or hesitation, about the books we have chosen until we let them know of our interest in all responses both positive and negative.

There may have been some trepidation involved with the process for some participants, particularly those who had not been within school or university contexts for some time. The Swan Hill group met at the library a week prior to our official reading event because they were worried that they would not have anything "intelligent" to say. One of the Hopetoun participants told us that they had discussed *The Salt of Broken Tears* during their crochet group earlier in the month: "I just thought it was me until I sat here at crochet and there was four of us that sat here and had the same. I was disappointed that I couldn't read that one."

During the research process, we have encountered problems of translation, indicating a distance between our own experience and that of the local readers. As Melbourne-based academics, albeit fairly regular visitors to the Mallee, we could not always follow all the geographical specificities in the discussions—we recognise that most participants, except for those who have recently come to the area, tend to share a complex mental geography that we do not. At times we would ask them to explain what they meant if it was vital for understanding their point, sometimes interrupting the flow of discussion.

To begin the discussion, we asked about their book group and how it might contribute to their lives. A younger Mildura reader, who works from home, described the benefits succinctly:

> I love being able to discuss books face to face. It gives me a chance to meet with like-minded people. I talk a lot to people online—BookTube, Twitter, Goodreads etc—but it is nice to chat in a social setting as we often go off on tangents as well. With the added bonus of getting me out of the house.

A Swan Hill member also used the term "like-minded" in her response, describing "conversations with like-minded people where you can disagree without fear of prejudice". For this reader, the "like-mindedness" may centre around an interest in books rather than expecting other members to share the same opinions. As with other reading groups documented by scholars, reading group members generally value disagreements because they make discussions more lively. Marguerite Nolan and Robert Clarke have noted the capacity for the book group to foster conversations that allow for "dissensus".[26] This was borne out by comments made at our events, with a Mildura participant saying that her regular book group helped her to understand "the differences in opinions and emotions and their relevance to the book".

The Texts

The texts under discussion were Michael Meehan's *The Salt of Broken Tears* (1999), Carrie Tiffany's *Everyman's Rules for Scientific Living* (2005) and Kerry McGinnis's *Mallee Sky* (2013). The Meehan and Tiffany titles can be classified as literary fiction, while *Mallee Sky* is genre fiction—a hybrid crime-romance novel. *The Salt of Broken Tears* is now out of print, while the other two books are classified as midlist titles.

The Salt of Broken Tears features a ten-year-old boy travelling around the Mallee in the 1920s with a horse and dog in search of a missing girl, and a hawker who may know something about her disappearance. Set in the 1930s, *Everyman's Rules for Scientific Living* centres around two characters, Jean and Robert, on the Better Farming Train, which travelled through Victoria in the 1920s and 30s. When the pair marry, they take up land (albeit unsuccessfully) in Wycheproof. *Mallee Sky* is set sixty years later, in an invented place called Laradale. The plot

---

26 Clarke and Nolan, "Book Clubs."

features a woman named Kate returning to her home town after a failed marriage, following her involvement with an old murder mystery and her entanglement in a new romance.

These three texts offer differing degrees of accessibility, raising questions about the styles the novels are written in and how this might affect their reception by Mallee readers who have varying levels of education, cultural capital and generic preferences. We distributed the novels at the same time, without instructing readers what order to read them in.

We were interested in the relationship between the three chosen texts and the participants' previous experiences, if any, of Mallee literature. Most participants had not read any Mallee literature. Names that were mentioned included Rosalie Ham's *The Dressmaker* (2000), Danny O'Neill's *Ancestral Streams: Notes from the Murray Valley* (2005), *Old Riverboats of the Murray* (1985), Max Jones's *A Man Called Possum* (1984), Nancy Cato's *All the Rivers Run* (1958) and Carrie Tiffany's *The Mateship of Birds* (2012). Of these titles, only the Tiffany and Ham novels were not orientated around the Murray river. One of the by-products of our study is the recognition that the participants might have an enhanced awareness of the existence of Mallee literature, a category which is rarely discussed.

Through our conversations with readers, we found that the "easiest" book to read—*Mallee Sky*—produced the least commentary. And the "toughest" text—*The Salt of Broken Tears* (hereafter known as *Salt*)—generated the most discussion. *Salt* was repeatedly described as "too difficult" or "hard going". One Swan Hill reader submitted a hand-written note when returning the books that read:

> I can't really get into this book. It chops and changes too much. So much I cannot follow the story. It will not hold my interest. I kept on reading but after half way through I gave up still none the wiser. My apology to the author of Salt of Broken Tears.

This note reveals the reader's struggle to fulfil her obligations as a member of the book group and to make sense of a book that she saw as incapable of holding her interest. Another Swan Hill participant had written summaries of the books, which she handed to us and quoted from in her survey response:

> This was an extremely difficult book to read. The times must have been so hard to live through… This book depicts the Mallee as a totally barren land, but it's during the years between the wars when depression hit the land and there were many drought years as well as the mouse plague.

A number of readers identified this godforsaken, desolate quality of the landscape in *Salt* but did not comment on its depiction of the Mallee as a space for dreaming, as proposed by a character called the 'Bag Sewer' based on the poet John Shaw Neilson. The negative attributes of the Mallee tended to prompt more responses than the creative potential of the region obliquely suggested by the author.

Seeking Connection

In relation to mass reading events, Fuller and Sedo have argued that the "fantasy of connection between people who are at once private and public persons, can, however fleetingly, become realized as a book becomes subject to a rereading or point of departure for the sharing of emotional knowledge."[27] During our Swan Hill reading event, two women told very personal stories about their failed marriages in response to the experience of women in *Mallee Sky* and *Everyman's Rules*. The stories of female protagonists who had survived bad marriages prompted their own painful accounts of emotional abuse and

---

27 Danielle Fuller and DeNel Rehberg Sedo, *Reading Beyond the Book: The Social Practices of Contemporary Literary Culture* (New York and London: Routledge, 2013), 211.

estrangement. Although we were not actively trying to elicit such personal revelations, we noted the power of these narratives—when discussed in a sympathetic group situation—to create a sense of intimacy, albeit evanescent. It should be noted that this degree of sharing was perhaps partly enabled by the fact that it was an all-female group that had already established rapport during previous book group sessions.

We also noted that these books provided an opportunity to share knowledge of place. In all three discussions, we observed a degree of dissensus about some topics, including respective degrees of affection for the Mallee itself, with some participants declaring ambivalent or even hostile feelings towards it. Through discussion, participants expressed affective attachment to or a sense of estrangement from the Mallee in various ways. Although not all participants grew up in the Mallee, with some describing themselves as newcomers, most expressed some degree of connection with it, due to their current location there and/ or their familial and experiential backgrounds. Sometimes this was expressed as an ambivalent connection, with at least two implying that they were essentially trapped there through circumstances largely beyond their control.

We were most interested to know how the representations of the Mallee in the three books might coincide with their own lived experience, or that of their families and friends, if at all. As mentioned earlier, the Mallee region has shifting definitions, depending on whether it is mapped according to government boundaries or in terms of its bioregionality. When asked if they recognised the Mallee in the novels, Quambatook participants made very clear distinctions between the Victorian and South Australian Mallee regions, while acknowledging that Quambatook is located in the "southern Mallee". For these readers, the Mallee does not extend across state boundaries.

A: Kerry McGinnis's book didn't feel like the Mallee to me.

B: I think it's an appalling book.

C: I agree.

A: Being based in South Australia as well—that doesn't feel like the Mallee to me.

D: But we're only on the fringe of the Mallee in Quamby.

B: How she described the landscape—a lot of it is around harvest time and they just go and have morning tea—where are they working? There's no real understanding of Mallee life in it—it's just a Mills & Boon in the Australian bush.

D: She talks about the forest where they live and to me— and to me the word forest is wrong.

B: I call the Mallee the area where there's a short scrubby vegetation.

D: Not the lushness that the word forest suggests.

Here participants are criticising the choice of the word forest as it simply does not fit into their understanding of their place. One participant observes that when you're working during harvest in the Mallee, you cannot easily stop for morning tea, therefore this part of the narrative does not ring true for her. The description of the book as "appalling" is perhaps shaped by the participant's personal regime of value, which serves to denigrate romance as a genre. This participant's designation of *Mallee Sky* as "appalling" meant that others felt embarrassed to say that they liked it, though it was fairly well regarded by at least three participants who found it easy to read.

The person who disliked *Mallee Sky* was keen to signal to us that she was an educated member of the reading class and largely out of place in the Mallee despite her long-term residence there. In response to her avowed dislike of the Mallee, we observed gentle teasing by one or two participants who playfully suggested they should warn her husband about her imminent departure. Joan Swann has noted that teasing in a reading group context can serve to "take the edge off" any threat that might be posed by a particular topic.[28]

It was in the discussions of *Mallee Sky* that we were most aware of the tendency to disparage romance fiction as trashy entertainment. In *Accounting for Tastes: Australian Everyday Cultures*, Tony Bennett, Michael Emmison and John Frow found that only one woman in their interview sample displayed an unambiguous preference for romance fiction, outlining her reasons in ways that were not apologetic, explaining her reading habits without feeling any need to explain them away.[29] They found that other women readers, if often ambivalently, tended to disavow an interest in romance fiction.[30] There was only one vocal fan of genre fiction in the Mildura group, who unapologetically explained why she liked it. Being a member of a younger demographic—in the 31–40 age range—she did not feel the need to disparage her own reading tastes.

Male Responses

As discussed previously, there was a marked gender imbalance in the groups we surveyed. During discussions, and through the process of transcription, we noticed that the male participants usually talked about local history rather than engaging directly with the texts. The male participant in Quambatook, an ex-schoolteacher, had only been able to absorb *Everyman's Rules* as an audio book due to eye problems. However, he was full of praise for the novel's evocation of the Mallee:

> I listened to it and I thought the writer had a real insight into the Mallee. I was lucky enough... I came here in 1962... they

---

28 Joan Swann, "How Reading Groups Talk About Books," *The Readers Voice Online*, accessed February 10, 2018. https://sites.google.com/site/thereadersvoiceonline/home/how-reading-groups-talk-about-books.

29 Tony Bennett, Michael Emmison and John Frow, *Accounting for Tastes: Australian Everyday Cultures* (Melbourne: Cambridge University Press, 1999), 145.

30 Ibid., 146.

were still bagging wheat... when they tried to set up between Wyche and Towaninie... I could relate to the hardships that he went through and she went through.

He went on to point out the existence of ghost towns in the area where nothing remains but trees:

To me just listening to it... if you go out the Charlton road, if you cut back toward Wyche... there are peppercorn trees, sugar gum trees, every half mile and nothing, no-one there, not any evidence of the town, yet these were the people who were hit by smut, rust... the years they were trying to make a living.

Here he pays homage to the backbreaking work of the pioneers and the disasters that befell them. Being a son of a family who stayed in the Mallee and survived, arguably this participant carries his hard-won knowledge as a kind of cultural capital.[31]

The male participant in the Mildura group, a retired scientist and amateur historian, may not have read any of the texts in depth, as he offered no reflections on their themes or plotlines. Instead, he sought to provide information about the Mallee environment as background to the books rather than engaging with characters like the other readers. The comment he wrote in the follow-up survey indicates that he understood that the authors of the novels used artistic licence to some degree and that he didn't expect the books to be exactly true to the "real world": "Perhaps there was an expectation, that the novels discussed, provide a technical description of the mallee, rather than telling a story that may have just been set in the mallee, in whole in in part."

In Hopetoun, the male participant arrived with a handful of self-published local histories, which he exhorted us to consider, indicating that they were "true Mallee", unlike the novels we had asked him to

---

31 Anderson, *Endurance*.

read. He had read *Mallee Sky* and recounted the plot with enthusiasm but described the other novels as "total crap". This opinion was re-iterated by his comments in the follow-up survey: "The book by Kerry McGinnis was great but the other two were total rubbish not even fiction." The claim that they were "not even fiction" was intriguing for us, indicating that he thought they could not even be classified as fiction. Rather than talking about the books in terms of his own taste, or in relation to their perceived inaccessibility, he chose to challenge their very status as fiction. This approach contrasted with all the other participants, who generally talked about their inability to "get into" a book—*Salt* in particular. He was the sole participant to discount these novels entirely, instead affirming local histories written by male contemporaries and antecedents.

Common Ground

Book groups can generate a feeling of community and give readers a chance to articulate a sense of belonging, however illusory.[32] Book groups offer the promise of finding common ground with other people, even if you have never encountered them before. In the places where we ran these research groups, the chance of not knowing others at all was slim, particularly in the town of Quambatook, with its tiny population. Nevertheless, the format of the events, with their special focus on reading and place, provided the possibility of interacting with other locals (previously known or unknown) in a new way.

During our reading group sessions, we discovered that some themes were especially galvanising for participants. There were a number of topics that arose in each of the discussions, including wheat varieties, dust storms, mouse plagues, farm inheritance—especially women's traditional inability to inherit—and the Afghan and Indian hawkers who used to travel the Mallee selling goods door to door.

---

32 Fuller and Sedo, *Reading Beyond the Book*, 211.

Many of the older participants could remember the Indian and Afghan hawkers who feature in all three books. This was a shared motif that we didn't register ourselves until a reader pointed it out. The Swan Hill readers took pains to emphasise the importance of these hawkers to extremely isolated Mallee communities in the "olden days":

> A: The hawkers were very popular and they were very religious.
>
> B: We had a Hal Singh when I was a kid. He came around with the horse and the buggy with all sorts of things, ribbons and lace. He used to come into our house, he even nursed my brother when he was a baby.
>
> A: I can remember an old gentleman telling me, when he was eight years old, witnessing an Indian funeral, on a pyre, at the Quambatook cemetery actually... and he went through the graphic details of watching it.
>
> C: There was one in Swan Hill too, when we were kids... an Indian pyre and half of Swan Hill went to it.

A member of the Quambatook reading group passed around obituaries for Afghan hawkers from the defunct *Quambatook Times*, which she had accessed via the National Library of Australia's Trove database. This prompted another member to take us to the cemetery after the reading event to see hawker Cabel Singh's headstone in person. Singh's gravesite is set apart from the others, due to his cultural and religious difference. His remains were actually cremated but the headstone was erected in his memory, given that he was a respected member of the community.

The Better Farming Train, which features in *Everyman's Rules*, was another major topic of discussion for both groups, possibly because it still resides in living memory. It was envisaged as an "agricultural college on wheels" to teach skills to farmers, and cooking and infant welfare to farmers' wives.[33] At all three book events, we observed participants articulating their own memories of the train or referencing the memories of it of people they knew. Two Swan Hill readers responded:

> I'm a carer and there's a couple of ladies I care for who still remember the train when it came through Manangatang. They were about five at the time and they recall that they got all dressed up and went into the town to see the train and treated it as an outing at the time. It was all buggies and horses in those days… This lady is 90 and she was about five she reckons when it came through Manangatang.
>
> We had those sorts of trains here when I was at school. It goes back a long way but it was also in my time—I know I'm getting close to 80. You know, it was in my time at school.

People in the Swan Hill group agreed that the scientific principles taught to farmers by the Better Farming Train in *Everyman's Rules* were alright in theory but did not allow for the variables of the Mallee climate.

> A: In all those experiments suggested by the train none of it related to rain and if it would rain.
>
> B: That's why I had no sympathy with Robert [the scientist character] because it was all high on science.
>
> C: It was all scientific not realistic.

Being long-term residents of the Mallee in most cases, they were sceptical of the schemes proposed by Robert, a scientist and avid soil-taster in *Everyman's Rules*.

Participants appeared to bond over aspects of everyday life in the Mallee, such as the prevalence of mice and dust. The Swan Hill readers surprised us with the graphic nature of their discussion about the

---

33   Editorial, "'Better Farming' Train," *The North Eastern Ensign* (Benalla, Victoria), August 14, 1925, https://trove.nla.gov.au/newspaper/article/70773761.

mouse plagues of the 1980s. The function of these stories, aside from elaborating on the texts, was to deepen connections between readers through recollection of shared experiences.

> A: The ground actually used to move with the mice… it was just horrible.
>
> B: I had one eating my hand when I was asleep. I woke up and moved and the mouse scuttled away.
>
> C: They had to put the legs of baby cots in tins of water.
>
> B: I did that with my kids in Sea Lake.
>
> A: My son was on Channel 10 with the most awful rash from the mice, from top to toe—he must've been allergic to it, from a flea or something.
>
> B: One of my sons had an air rifle and he put a hole in the flywire in the window and was shooting the mice as they ran up the birdcage.
>
> D: I'm thinking of all the games we used to play with the mice. We'd tie them by the tails to the tank stand just out of the cat's reach. We'd wait and see how long it would take them.
>
> E: They tied Tom Thumb crackers to mice tails then they'd explode.

Dust appears prominently in all three books and was a galvanising topic for readers because everybody could relate to this topic. The following exchange took place while discussing Michael Meehan's *Salt*:

> A: I'd like to count the number of times he used the word dust.
>
> B: But isn't that so much part of our life?
>
> C: Yes!
>
> A: You can't get away from it!

Mildura readers referred to the famous dust storms experienced by their parents in the 1920s, who had to "put on kerosene lamps and so on because it was just black". One person made the point that "you couldn't seal your house like you can now". Then another added: "But it still gets in."

Participants acknowledged that mistakes were made in the management of land in the Mallee, causing considerable environmental degradation. One reader referred to the dust storm featured in *Everyman's Rules*:

> I think they've re-planted some of those trees that they cut down which caused those dust storms cos that was a big problem. They got rid of all that vegetation.
>
> They talk about the one that reached Melbourne in that book.

In this way, discussion of the three novels serves to activate the readers' latent knowledge, garnered through familial and community networks.

Gaps and Silences

As mentioned earlier, participants were quick to point out the negative themes in the books like isolation and barrenness, but there was less identification of positive traits in the representation of the Mallee. When asked whether anything was missing from the texts, participants noted that the Murray River is hardly mentioned in the three texts, which they found surprising.

A Swan Hill book group member noted that "the river didn't come up much". We then asked whether the river was a big part of living there. To which she replied, "I think so… you just say you live on the Murray or you say you live in the Mallee and everybody knows where that is."

A Mildura participant also noted the absence of the river:

> I felt the presence of the Murray was missing from these three books—it was in this one [*Salt*] briefly but not strongly.

> To me the Murray is an integral part of the Mallee and it
> has transformed the Mallee… if you think about what the
> river did for Mildura, it was turned from a dustbowl to a
> magnificent agricultural basin. Mildura could never have been
> the success it was without the Murray—to me that's a really
> important part of the Mallee that's not represented in these.

Mildura readers also noted that the more positive aspects of life in the
Mallee tended to be lacking in the books under discussion.

> A: I could recognise the Mallee in it, certainly the salt
> pans like around Swan Hill but it was an alien landscape, very
> frightening, without the beauty.
>
> B: The sea of Mallee, that undulating sea that you see
> when you come up the Ouyen road—that wasn't quite
> described right, for me. No-one got that.

Another person agreed that it was a "very harsh version" that was
represented in *Salt*. A younger member of the Mildura group commented: "This reminded me of Mad Max in that everybody has
their own stories and they are all a bit weird and it's lost in space
and time."

A Mildura reader was disconcerted by the number of errors she
noticed in the books. In the survey this participant wrote: "There
were some typing errors in the pages and some fallacies which should
not have been there had the subject been studied or edited carefully."

A Hopetoun reader noted problems with the route the Better
Farming Train took in *Everyman's Rules:* "How they got there was a
little bit twisted. There's no train line between here and there. I know
that from the structure around here. But that's fine."

Readers from all the groups attempted to work out the boy's route
around the Mallee in *Salt* but felt frustrated by the inconsistent use
of place names. As one Mildura reader commented:

When you're reading about an area that you're familiar with, you feel a sense of ownership—you want it to be right. When I was reading this [Salt] I was desperately trying to work out where he was going. I knew the names of all the places but I couldn't quite get the route. I was actually going to get a map and track it. You sort of want it to be accurate. It's important isn't it?

A Hopetoun participant was annoyed because the boy's journey did not make sense to him given that he was travelling on horseback. This error seriously shook his faith in the book, leading him to question its overall value:

A: The kid walked with his horse to Underbool and the next chapter is at Hattah. Now how could a kid with a horse walk from Underbool to Hattah through the scrub? He never took anything with him.

B: And the timeframe was wrong.

A: Yeah, it was just far out… and yet it's won an award in New South Wales.

B: They were cheap that year, they gave them away.

A: I think some money might have changed hands there.

Readers sometimes became frustrated because they couldn't map their own mental geographies onto the fictional texts—because *Everyman's Rules* and *Salt* use real names, there was an expectation amongst readers that the fictional places would match existing places exactly, in every detail.

A Mildura reader noted that the sense of community in the Mallee did not feature enough except in *Everyman's Rules*, which is set partly in Wycheproof:

I think there is a strong sense of community in the Mallee isn't there—like the little towns… the Wycheproofs and the Sea Lakes… they seem to be very close-knit and supportive. They stick together and that probably comes from the hardship of the environment.

Another reader noted: "[T]hat community feel is still here."

A Hopetoun participant mentioned that newcomers have moved into the town, reducing the percentage of people that she is now related to. She recounted that she used to be able to call most people uncle, aunty, cousin, sister and so on due to the close interrelation of people in the town but noted, sadly, that this was not the case anymore.

However, overall, readers' comments suggest they acknowledge that the communities of the Mallee remain strong despite, or possibly because of, threats such as diminishing populations and the already apparent effects of climate change.

In all three sessions, we asked whether the readers had noticed any traces of pre-colonial settlement in the novels. Some Mildura readers noted that the bones found on a farm in *Mallee Sky* possibly related to the colonial violence perpetrated in that area. The Swan Hill readers began a discussion about which Indigenous groups "owned" the town before settlement. They referred to people they knew who had studied Indigenous history in the area but could not answer these questions from their own knowledge. Readers in the Quambatook group noted the references to genocide, as uncovered by a character in *Mallee Sky* who was writing a local history.

> A: Harry Quigley in *Mallee Sky* was interesting… a lot of knowledge there. He didn't care about ticking people off as long as it was true to what had happened. Even if they were pillars of community.
>
> B: Well they were pillars based on mud, weren't they? Not solid foundations.

Here they recognise that so-called "pillars of [the] community" in the novel—and possibly even their own ancestors—may be implicated in acts of violence against the first peoples of Australia.

We noticed that when the subject of colonial violence against Indigenous peoples is broached in these book group discussions, participants are hesitant to respond. With other topics such as dust or mouse plague, or hawkers, they enthusiastically joined in with anecdotes and stories; however, cross-cultural conflict prompted less response, possibly due to its divisive potential. As researchers, we are keen to follow this line of enquiry but we have found that participants seem less interested or more tentative.

Marguerite Nolan and Robert Clarke have noted that book clubs provide spaces for discussions of fictions of reconciliation such as Kate Grenville's *The Secret River* (2005). They argue that "such texts and spaces do facilitate the evolution of understandings of reconciliation between Indigenous and non-Indigenous Australians".[34] Their pilot study was designed specifically to approach issues to do with reconciliation while our book group research is not explicitly orientated toward this topic. Our participants signed up to talk about Mallee novels rather than frontier violence or institutionalised racism; nevertheless, these issues did emerge as marginal subjects, partly due to our line of questioning.

Relationships Between the Region and the Metropolis

During the Quambatook reading event, two participants asked us about our broader project and wondered aloud about why Mallee literature does not have a greater public profile. Another reader suggested that it might be because the writers didn't tend to get together into organisations as in other states or regions. She observed that none of the authors of the three novels under discussion actually still live in the Mallee:

---

34 Clarke and Nolan, "Book Clubs," 138.

A: It's because so many people who have written about the Mallee have run from it because they don't want that connection.

B: Run screaming you mean?

A: Almost exorcising the horror of the Mallee.

C: She's hit one too many kangaroos I think.

D: I can't imagine a Mallee writer wanting to go to Melbourne. Sorry—I'm the opposite to you. Melbourne would be the last place I would go to.

B: I loved Melbourne when I lived there.

D: I love the country.

B: Both places offer such diverse things.

D: It's not very far away.

Differing views of the Mallee are being expressed in this exchange, with one reluctant resident of thirty years wholeheartedly disliking it, even referring to the "horror of the Mallee", while another local cannot imagine ever wanting to live in Melbourne. A third person— who lived in Quambatook when young, moved away with her family and returned in middle age—can see the benefits of both country and city. This person sought to defuse a potentially volatile exchange by using humour, making a comment about hitting kangaroos. This intense conversation originally spiralled out from the discussion of Kerry McGinnis's rendering of the South Australian Mallee in *Mallee Sky*. As Bethan Benwell observes, the reading of texts in this group context is "very much a negotiated, often contested, collaborative process, which is informed by and responds to the conditions and context of its production".[35] The Quambatook participants knew each other well enough to be able to use humour to smooth over moments of disagreement or potential conflict. We noted that participants can feel reluctant to praise a book that has been criticised by others,

---

35   Benwell, "'A Pathetic and Racist and Awful Character,'" 308.

but equally they might be emboldened by others' negative responses, enabling them to say what they really think.

Place-Based Understandings

Though the effects of the gender imbalance in the reading groups cannot be thoroughly canvassed here, we did establish that female readers we encountered could sometimes be uncertain about the worth of their contributions. Martyn Lyons and Lucy Taksa identify a strong tendency for women readers to engage in "cultural self-devaluation".[36] The women readers in our reading group sessions would often display this tendency to downplay their own cultural competence, with the exception of ex-schoolteachers and librarians, who were generally more confident about their opinions. As Lyons and Taksa observe, the defensive attitudes of some participants could be the understandable reaction of people who had had only a "sketchy formal secondary education and were faced with academics with tape-recorders".[37] We acknowledge our role as organisers of these sessions and the effect that our questions might have had on the flow of discussion, as well as the power differential between us and our participants.

Bennett et al note that the role of education in organising reading practices is both clear and marked. Levels of education significantly affect the extent to which reading is a regular activity and what kinds of books people buy and collect, as well as their preferences between different genres.[38] We found that the Swan Hill readers were perhaps the least critical in terms of assessing the value of the books and this correlates with their lower levels of education compared with the Mildura and Quambatook groups, which contained higher proportions of people with tertiary education.

---

36 Lyons and Taksa, *Australian Readers Remember,* 160.

37 Ibid., 160.

38 Bennet et al., *Accounting for Tastes,* 158.

A nervousness about the import of their comments was exemplified by the Swan Hill readers' perceived need for a warm-up session a week earlier to work out whether they had anything "intelligent" to say to us as researchers. Yet the Swan Hill group members were more forthcoming with details of their personal biographies, including painful details of their mistreatment at the hands of men. These participants wrote considerably more on the follow-up survey, including raw anecdotes about life in the Mallee:

> I lived on a Mallee farm for many years and heard many
> ladies—their husbands had selected their land & cleared
> it—talk of their lives. Some of the talk: some sold butter.
> Left horse harnessed after driving children to school saved
> time for return trip to collect children. Milking cow just got
> one woman out of the house for a few minutes. Sometimes
> still hanging washing by the time children came home
> from primary school. When they killed a sheep one woman
> cooked joints of lamb in kerosene buckets and the fat
> which rose to the top protected meat from going bad in hot
> weather.

This collection of memories, which reads like oral history, is offered as a continuation of the discussion of women's experiences in the Mallee. Even though these reflections are not directly linked to the books under discussion, the participant wished to tell us more about how exhausting life was for women so that we might begin to understand it better, as outsiders to the community. This comment shows us the power of the book group to encourage subjective engagement with local history and to encourage personal storytelling.

Rather than interrogating the texts with the tools of the literary critic, these lay readers tend to use them as starting points for their own "interpretive acts of domestication" to help define their own claims and judgements.[39] For example, the hardships experienced by characters, especially in *Salt* and *Everyman's Rules*, which are set in the early twentieth century, elicited affective outpourings about the sufferings of people known to them.

There are many aspects of our pilot study that we are unable to discuss in depth here, including the book group participants' identification with particular characters and their varying responses to the literary styles of the texts themselves. For the purposes of this chapter, our focus has primarily been on place and the ways in which readers identify or recognise their region in these texts. We found that the three Mallee novels prompted participants to locate themselves geographically, which provided us with better understanding of their lived experience.

These four reading events have shown us definitively that the same books do not reliably produce similar responses. Readers who are "calling" the book, encounter it with such richly differentiated previous experiences that in turn influences the aspects of a book's "face" or presence they attend to.[40] We found that the same three books were revered, resisted, embraced, criticised and interrogated by the participants. A bunch of complex factors related to education, life experience and class help to shape their responses. Some readers only felt confident to critique the books at the level of the "real world"—in other words, they identified mistakes in geography or terminology (as in the discussion of the word "forest"), while others felt more able to discuss the books at the level of literary style (as in the discussion of the "expressionistic" style of *Salt*.

Through this preliminary research, it has become clear to us that book groups perform important "identity work". As Elizabeth Long

---

39   James Procter and Bethan Benwell, *Reading Across Worlds: Transnational Book Groups and the Reception of Difference* (London: Palgrave Macmillan, 2015), 75.

40   Elizabeth Long, *Book Clubs: Women and the Uses of Reading in Everyday Life* (Chicago: University of Chicago Press, 2003), 28.

has argued, the intersubjective aspect of book club reading can be "profoundly transformative" for participants.[41] Although we cannot know how transformative these four events might have been for individuals, without undertaking in-depth interviews, we have received some anecdotal feedback that suggests that the Quambatook group may reconvene in the future despite being artificially constructed by us. The Mildura group has continued in a slightly reconfigured form, attesting to the participants' engagement with the process.

The data these reading groups yield comprises opinion, interpretation, anecdote and accounts of personal life experience. Nevertheless, these responses offer a sense, however partial, of what it's like for locals to read Mallee books in the Mallee. The readerly comments generated by our shared reading events constitute an important resource, adding to our understanding about the relationship between reading and place. After coordinating and analysing four reading events, we are convinced that Mallee-based readers bring very different understandings and identifications to these texts, which would otherwise be unavailable to us as city-based researchers. We found evidence of the production of local readings of the three texts, however we have not yet tested this in a non-Mallee location. We found that local readers brought their own mental geographies to bear on the texts, reading them attentively for traces of the Mallee landscape and culture they recognise.

The narratives tended to elicit the readers' own stories of hardship, and those of their wider network, especially in relation to farming and domestic practices, leading to emotive discussions that brought the participants closer—albeit momentarily—and allowed us to apprehend the texture of everyday life in the Mallee.

---

41 Ibid., 144.

Works cited

Anderson, Deb. *Endurance: Australian Stories of Drought*. Melbourne: CSIRO Publishing, 2014

Bennett, Tony, Michael Emmison, and John Frow. *Accounting for Tastes: Australian Everyday Cultures*. Melbourne: Cambridge University Press, 1999.

Benwell, Bethan. "'A Pathetic and Racist and Awful Character': Ethnomethodological Approaches to the Reception of Diasporic Fiction." *Language and Literature* 18, no. 3 (2009): 300–315.

Clarke Robert and Marguerite Nolan. "Book Clubs and Reconciliation: A Pilot Study on Book Clubs Reading the 'Fictions of Reconciliation'." *Australian Humanities Review* 56 (2014): 121–140.

Dee, Paul. "The Mallee." *Such Was Life*. [Blog]. State Library of Victoria, May 11, 2016. https://blogs.slv.vic.gov.au/such-was-life/the-mallee/.

Devlin-Glass, Frances. "More Than a Reader and Less Than a Critic: Literary Authority and Women's Book Discussion Groups." *Women's Studies International Forum* 24, no. 5 (2001): 571–85.

Eisenstein, Elizabeth. *The Printing Press as Agent of Change: Communications and Cultural Transformation in Early Modern Europe*. Cambridge and New York: Cambridge University Press, 1979.

Fuller, Danielle and Sedo, DeNel Rehberg. *Reading Beyond the Book: The Social Practices of Contemporary Literary Culture*. New York and London: Routledge, 2013.

Griswold, Jenny. *Regionalism and the Reading Class*. Chicago: University of Chicago Press, 2008.

Hartley, Jenny. *The Reading Groups Book: With a Survey Conducted in Association with Sarah Turvey*. Oxford; New York: Oxford University Press, 2001.

Johns, Adrian. *The Nature of the Book: Print and Knowledge in the Making*. Chicago: Chicago University Press, 1998.

Long, Elizabeth. "Women, Reading, and Cultural Authority: Some Implications of the Audience Perspective in Cultural Studies." *American Quarterly* 38, no. 4 (Autumn, 1986): 591–612.

———. *Book Clubs: Women and the uses of reading in everyday life*, Chicago: University of Chicago Press, 2003.

Lyons, Martyn and Taksa, Lucy. *Australian Readers Remember: An Oral History of Reading 1890–1930* Melbourne: Oxford University Press, 1992.

Nolan, Maggie and Henaway, Janeese. "Decolonizing Reading: The Murri Book Club." *Continuum* 31, no. 6 (2017): 791–801.

North Eastern Ensign, The. "'Better Farming' Train." Editorial. August 14, 1925 (Benalla, Victoria). https://trove.nla.gov.au/newspaper/article/70773761.

Poole, Marilyn. "The Women's Chapter: Women's Reading Groups in Victoria." *Feminist Media Studies* 3, no. 3 (2003): 263–281.

Procter, James and Benwell, Bethan. *Reading Across Worlds: Transnational Book Groups and the Reception of Difference*. London: Palgrave Macmillan, 2015.

Radway, Janice. *A Feeling for Books: The Book-of-the Month-Club, Literary Taste and Middle Class Desire*. Chapel Hill: University of North Carolina Press, 1997.

Sedo, DeNel Rehberg. "An Introduction to Reading Communities: Processes and Formations." In *Reading Communities from Salons to Cyberspace*, edited by DeNel Rehberg Sedo, 1–24. Houndmills, Basingstoke, Hampshire: Palgrave Macmillan, 2011.

Sicherman, Barbara. "Sense and Sensibility: A Case Study of Women's Reading in Late-Victorian America." In *Reading in America*, edited by Cathy Davison, 201–225. Baltimore: Johns Hopkins University Press, 1989.

Stock, Brian. *The Implications of Literacy: Written language and Models of Interpretation in the Eleventh and Twelfth Centuries*. Princeton: Princeton University Press, 1983.

Swann, Joan and Allington, Daniel. "Reading Groups and the Language of Literary Texts: A Case Study in Social Reading." *Language and Literature* 18, no. 3 (2009): 247–264.

Swann, Joan. "How Reading Groups Talk About Books." *The Readers Voice Online*. Accessed February 10, 2018, https://sites.google.com/site/thereadersvoiceonline/home/how-reading-groups-talk-about-books.

Victorian Places. "Mallee." Accessed March 20, 2018, http://www.victorianplaces.com.au/mallee.

CHAPTER 9

Small Publishers, Symbolic Capital and Australian Literary Prizes

EMMETT STINSON

In 2016, I wrote an essay which examined the relationship between the Miles Franklin Award and small publishers.[1] This relationship matters because the mediation of literary works has changed in the twenty-first century, and small publishers[2] have now become the primary producers of Australian literary titles.[3] Through an analysis of data on what kinds of publishers had produced longlisted, shortlisted and winning titles, I argued that there was a disjuncture between small publishers' importance for literary publishing and the symbolic recognition of such publishers by the Miles Franklin Award, which

---

1   Emmett Stinson, "Small Publishers and the Miles Franklin," in *The Return of Print? Contemporary Australian Publishing* eds. Emmett Stinson and Aaron Mannion, (Melbourne: Monash University Publishing, 2016), 132–42.

2   The term "small publisher" is an inherently relative and slippery one, and multiple definitions have been offered even in the Australian context. For my purposes, I am following the membership guidelines created by the Small Press Network, which includes both small and independent publishers. In practice, this definition includes essentially all Australian publishers except for the large multinationals and Allen and Unwin. This means, by my accounting, that Text Publishing—which, in terms of size and turnover would be classed as a mid-sized independent—is treated as a small publisher. If anything, then, focusing only on the truly "small" publishers would make the results of this research even more bleak. For this reason, I have generally noted the number of times that Text, in particular, has been recognised for various awards. For more on the definition of a small publisher, see Nathan Hollier, "*Austral*ian Small and Independent Publishing: The Freeth Report," *Publishing Research Quarterly* 24, no. 3 (2008): 165–74.

3   Emmett Stinson, "Small Publishers and the Emerging Network of Australian Literary Prosumption," *Australian Humanities Review* 59 (April/May 2016): 23–43.

had disproportionately gone to titles from large and multinational houses.[4] I also found that Miles Franklin shortlistings were not evenly distributed among small publishers and tended to over-represent two highly regarded publishers: Giramondo and Text. As a result, the Miles Franklin seemed to be a prize that was disconnected from the material means by which Australian literature had been produced and brought to market over the previous decade.

In the intervening two years, however, there appears to have been a significant change in the way that the prize values small publishers: the last two works to win the prize—Alec Patrić's *Black Rock White City* (Transit Lounge) and Josephine Wilson's *Extinction* (UWA Publishing)—have both been produced by small publishers with no significant track record of Miles Franklin success. Given this unexpected development, I want to return to the question of small publishers and literary prizes to examine whether or not a legitimate shift appears to be occurring in the symbolic recognition of texts and their mediators. I will extrapolate on my previous analysis by incorporating data on the two other major prizes that are seen by publishers and booksellers to have a broad public impact that can translate into higher book sales: the Prime Minister's Literary Award for Fiction (PMLAF) and the Stella Prize. As I will argue, the shortlisting practices of these three prizes suggest there has been increasing recognition of small publishers in major Australian literary awards, but the degree and timing of this recognition still differs among them. I will further consider the causes of this shift and its effects—specifically the (potentially deleterious) consequences that broader recognition of small press titles might have on the status and value of literary prizes themselves. Finally, I will argue

---

4   This tendency appears to reflect international Anglophone trends; as Jody Mason has noted of the Giller Prize, Canada's most significant literary prize, "45 percent of Giller winners and 47 percent of the titles in the Finalist category between 1994 and 2015 are products of the big two transnational publishing companies, Penguin Random House and Harper Collins"; *see* Jody Mason, "'Capital Intraconversion' and Canadian Literary Prize Culture," *Book History* 20 (2017): 430.

that the increasing recognition of small publishers can also be viewed as an institutional reassertion of the value of explicitly literary writing at a moment when popular forms of writing seem, if not increasingly dominant, at least ascendant in Australian book cultures.

Literary prizes have a significant influence in Australian book culture, both as taste-making institutions, and in relation to the careers of authors and other agents in the literary field. It remains possible to have a long literary "career" as an Australian author without winning or being shortlisted for a major prize for an individual work (as is the case for Gerald Murnane, who had never been recognised by the Miles Franklin or the PMLAF before 2018, but has won major lifetime achievement awards, such as the Melbourne Prize for Literature and the Patrick White Award). But most contemporary Australian authors who have published multiple books have also had some success with literary prizes. Indeed, many authors even find their careers started by prizes, such as the Vogel or various state-based awards for unpublished manuscripts. Major literary prizes have become the key mediator of literary value for the broader book-reading public that does not attend literary events, or regularly read book reviews in newspapers or publications like *The Sydney Review of Books* and *Australian Book Review*.

Prizes are not only highly regarded by the book-reading public, but they are also extremely important within the book industry and the broader literary field. In examining prizes, I am relying on the sociological frameworks developed by Pierre Bourdieu, and more specifically, his notion of symbolic capital; as Bourdieu argues, symbolic capital is typically "unrecognized as capital and recognized" instead as a form of "authority" that is pervasive in "markets in which economic capital is not fully recognized", as is often the case in cultural markets.[5] Bourdieusian sociology has rightly been critiqued for what Simone

---

5   Pierre Bourdieu, "The Three Forms of Capital" *in Handbook of Theory of Research for the Sociology of Education*, ed. J. E. Richardson (Westport: Greenword Press, 1986), 49.

Murray has described as the "alleged universality of [its] structuralist-inflected 'rules' of cultural functioning" that nonetheless have a "French (and especially Parisian) specificity".[6] Nonetheless, I think that the Bourdieusian notion of symbolic capital remains particularly useful for indexing the relative prestige and influence of institutions like prizes, whose value cannot be captured in economic terms alone.

As John B. Thompson argues, prizes are so important because they add "symbolic value to every individual and organization associated with the book" while also potentially contributing to sales.[7] In the case of major prizes, such as the Man Booker, this sales bump is enormous: "Get on the Booker shortlist and you could sell another 25,000 copies... And if you won it you could sell possibly another 200,000 copies."[8] The importance of increased sales cannot be overstated, especially for literary works, which are typically not bestsellers unless they have been propelled to this status by an outside event, such as a prize or a film or television adaptation. Prizes are thus particularly valuable to authors, because they offer a source of direct revenue (from winnings), indirect revenue (from increased sales) and symbolic capital that helps to extend their influence within the literary field and make it more likely that publishers will publish and distribute their future works. Prizes are valuable to publishers for the same reasons, more or less: they increase sales and also reflect well on the publishing house as a prestigious destination for other authors in the future—and in this sense, prizes index symbolic capital.

However, not all prizes are equal. Not only do some prizes have more symbolic capital than others, but also some prizes have significantly more social capital (i.e. they have relationships with readers, the media, or booksellers and other agents in the field). As Beth

---

6   Simone Murray, "Charting the Digital Literary Sphere," *Contemporary Literature* 56, no. 2 (2015): 325.

7   John B. Thompson, *Merchants of Culture: The Publishing Business in the Twenty-First Century* (Cambridge: Polity Press, 2010), 277.

8   Ibid.

Driscoll has argued, however, "no single prize can be the ultimate consecrator".[9] In this sense, prizes do compete for the same cultural position and often have a complex set of interrelations, as in the case of the Stella Prize, whose name foregrounds its connection to the Miles Franklin Award. Only a select few of the many Australian literary prizes generate significant sales, because these prizes are effectively recognised markers of quality by the broader reading public. Indeed, James English has even argued that prizes are the "most effective institutional agents of *capital intraconversion*" in a Bourdieusian sense, which is to say that they are particularly good at exchanging symbolic capital into economical capital.[10]

Not all prizes convert capital at the same rate. As director of UWA Publishing Terri-Anne White noted in her decision no longer to submit UWA books for prizes (a decision that occurred prior to a UWA novel winning the 2017 Miles Franklin award), "The returns from our very substantial investment every year in shortlisted and winning entries and the minimal sales results from our winning entries tell us something about the way awards and prizes operate these days."[11] Her implication was that many prizes are essentially parasitic, using entry fees to subsidise their administrative costs while delivering little material benefit to winning authors and publishers. In particular, many publishers complain about the various state-based awards, which are great for winning writers, who take home a cash prize and increase their symbolic capital, but do little for book sales. This is also the case for a variety of other awards—such as the ALS Gold Medal for Fiction

---

9   Beth Driscoll, *The New Literary Middlebrow: Tastemakers and Reading in the Twenty-First Century* (London: Palgrave Macmillan, 2014), 124.

10   James F. English, *The Economy of Prestige: Prizes, Awards, and the Circulation of Cultural Value* (Cambridge, MA: Harvard University Press, 2005), 10.

11   Susan Wyndham, "The Hidden Costs that Threaten Australian Literary Awards," *Sydney Morning Herald*, December 3, 2018, https://www.smh.com.au/entertainment/books/the-hidden-costs-that-threaten-australian-literary-awards-20161202-gt32wc.html.

or the Kibble Literary Awards—which are very well-regarded awards within the literary field and the publishing industry, but do not have broader recognition among the general public or even the reading class. As a result, winning one of these prizes does not necessarily increase sales.

Small press works have been significantly recognised by many prizes of this kind, which are symbolically important but lack broader public recognition. Most poetry prizes, for example, would almost certainly be dominated by the small publishers, since none of the large or multinational publishers have significant investments in publishing new poetry. My contention, however, is that small presses—in general—have not been proportionally recognised by large, prestigious prizes with high public visibility—which are, of course, also the kind of prizes that increase sales. It is for this same reason that I have focused on prizes for fiction (although the Stella, as I will discuss, is a multi-genre award, it primarily recognises works of fiction); fiction prizes produce much higher sales than awards for other genres, and also appear to generate much greater public interest. This is generally true across the Anglophone world: the Man Booker Prize remains the most significant award in the UK, and news about the Pulitzer Prize for Fiction typically gets far more publicity than other winning genres do.

Only a handful of Australian prizes reliably boost sales. After Alec Patrić's *Black Rock White City* won the Miles Franklin Award in 2016, his publisher, Barry Scott, of the small press Transit Lounge, noted that while the book had "sold reasonably well... before the award" at "close to 3000 copies", the Miles Franklin Award means that Transit Lounge "printed another 20,000 and sold a lot of them. There has been interest from overseas and interest in Alec's next book. It's going to help our bottom line eventually."[12] The Miles Franklin remains one Australian literary prize that definitely has a saleable recognition among

---

12 Ibid.

the reading public. Although it has been running for only six years, the Stella Prize has already established a significant public profile and developed a reputation for influencing sales.[13] Sophie Cunningham, one of the prize's founders, notes that "Charlotte Wood's *The Natural Way of Things* tripled its sales after winning the Stella in 2016", and that other winning and shortlisted titles have seen sales bumps.[14] Among independent booksellers, in particular, the Stella is viewed as a prize whose effect on sales is nearly on par with the major award (the Miles Franklin) that it shadows. Although it is the richest award in Australia with a payout of $100,000, the PMLAF has a more ambiguous relationship to sales; Patrick Allington, for example, has argued that the award needs to improve "the quality and focus of [its] publicity and marketing".[15] But there is no question that it enjoys a very high profile and significant media coverage, as a result of the fact that it is associated with the Prime Minister and is thus always also a political event deemed inherently newsworthy. For this reason alone, the PMLAF has established itself as one of Australia's most significant prizes.

But while prizes are important as mediators of literary value, their practices are not always (or even necessarily) tied to the broader material practices of the literary field. Indeed, as Beth Driscoll notes, contemporary literary prizes typically reflect "elite literary values associated with the quality of a work's prose and themes".[16] The critique I previously

---

13 The Stella Prize was inspired, at least in part, by the historical gender imbalance in the awarding practices of the Miles Franklin, which has overwhelmingly gone to men. The Stella Prize is named after Miles Franklin's first name, as a reminder of her gender, but, in doing this, the Stella also inherently links itself to the Miles Franklin Award.

14 Sophie Cunningham, "Making Waves: Stella Turns Six," *Kill Your Darlings*, February 5, 2018, https://www.killyourdarlings.com.au/article/making-waves-six-years-of-the-stella-prize/.

15 Patrick Allington, "Why the Prime Minister's Literary Awards Need an Urgent Overhaul," *The Conversation,* June 22, 2016, https://theconversation.com/why-the-prime-ministers-literary-awards-need-an-urgent-overhaul-61300.

16 Driscoll, *The New Literary Middlebrow*, 120.

offered of the Miles Franklin ran along these lines, arguing that the prize's institutional values were out of step with contemporary literary production insofar as they did not recognise works by small publishers. Since 2000, only 21% of Miles Franklin shortlisted works have been produced by small presses, a figure that is disproportionately low given that small publishers now produce the majority of Australian literary titles. Indeed, from 2002–5, no small press titles were shortlisted. Only in three years (2006, 2016 and 2017) have small publishers' titles constituted 40% or more of the shortlist, and from 2007 to 2015, small presses' share of the shortlist varied between 20% and 33%. In 2017, however, small press titles suddenly comprised 80% of the shortlist—more than double the highest previous total. As Figure 1 shows, the last two years do suggest a strong upward trend for small publishers in relation to the Miles Franklin, but the question at this stage is whether this reflects a broader shift in the symbolic valuation of small publishers. As I will argue by looking at data from the Stella Prize and the PMLAF, there is good reason to suspect that this is part of a broader trend among literary prizes.

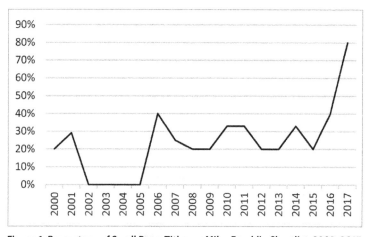

Figure 1. Percentage of Small Press Titles on Miles Franklin Shortlist, 2000–2017.

At the same time, it is unlikely that small press titles will continue to dominate the Miles Franklin shortlist to this degree. Indeed, looking at the data from the Miles Franklin longlists helps to reinforce both that there is a trend upward in small press representation and that the 2017 result is probably not sustainable. As I have previously noted, small press titles have typically been better represented on the longlist, and comprise around 26% of all longlisted titles since 2005 (the year in which the prize began publicly releasing its longlist data). Indeed, this data shows significant representation of small press titles in both 2011 (44%) and 2014 (45%), although these trends did not hold in the subsequent years. Nonetheless, the longlist displays a clear boost for small presses in 2016 and 2017; in both years, small press titles comprised 55% of longlisted titles. In other words, the 2017 shortlist went against the Miles Franklin's historical trend in that a higher proportion of small press titles made the shortlist than made the longlist. This, in and of itself, is significant insofar as it suggests an overturning of long-term biases against small publishers.

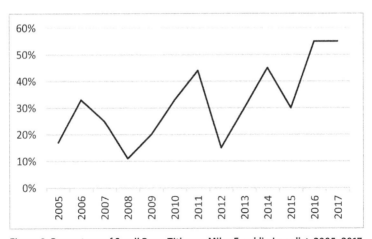

Figure 2. Percentage of Small Press Titles on Miles Franklin Longlist, 2005–2017.

Established in 2008, the PMLAF already has a better track record of recognising small publishers: four of the twelve (33%) winning titles (there have been dual winners in two years) have been produced by small publishers. These winning small press works are *Dog Boy* by Eva Hornung (Text) in 2010, *Traitor* by Stephen Daisley (Text) in 2011, *The Life of Houses* by Lisa Gorton (Giramondo) in 2016, and *Their Brilliant Careers* by Ryan O'Neill (Black Inc.) in 2017. Like the Miles Franklin, then, the PMLAF has mostly awarded prestigious small presses.

The PMLAF and the Miles Franklin have a similar track record with small publishers on their shortlists, however. Small presses account for just under 29% (16 out of 56 titles) of shortlisted works for the PMLAF. Again, however, Text and Giramondo dominate these shortlists: of the 16 shortlisted small press titles, seven have been produced by Text (44%), and three have been produced by Giramondo (19%). No other small publisher has been shortlisted more than once; the other small publishers to have been shortlisted are Australian Scholarly Publishing, Black Inc., Island Magazine, Sleepers Publishing, University of Queensland Press and UWA Publishing. This is significant because it suggests that the Miles Franklin's historical treatment of small publishers is not unusual among prestigious literary awards, and that there has been a tendency to privilege works from large publishing houses over those produced by small publishers.

At the same time, however, the shortlisting data from the PMLAF shows a nearly identical trajectory to the Miles Franklin data over the last two years, as Figure 3 illustrates. Like the Miles Franklin, the PMLAF also saw a jump in shortlisted small press titles in 2016 (40%) and 2017 (80%) in the exact same proportions. In 2017, in fact, both awards shortlisted the same four small press titles: Josephine Wilson's *Extinction* (UWA Publishing), Ryan O'Neill's *Their Brilliant Careers* (Black Inc.), Mark O'Flynn's *The Last Days of Ava Langdon* (University of Queensland Press), and Phillip Salom's *Waiting* (Puncher & Wattmann). The fifth shortlisted title—*The Easy Way Out* by Steven

Amsterdam (Hachette)—is also interesting insofar as its author published his previous two books with small publisher Sleepers Publishing (and won the now-defunct Age Book of the Year in 2009 for his debut, *Things We Didn't See Coming*). In this sense, he is also an author with a small-press pedigree. On the one hand, this suggests an enormous shift in the way that the PMLAFs value small publishers; on the other hand, the unusual—and even bizarre—correlation between the shortlists of the Miles Franklin and the PMLAFs suggest that this particular instance of small press dominance may be anomalous.

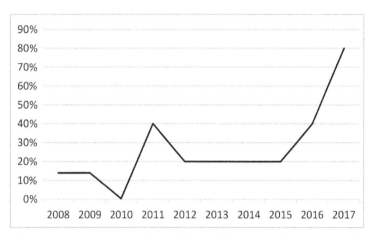

Figure 3. Percentage of Small Press Titles on Prime Minister's Literary Award for Fiction Shortlist, 2008–2017.

Analysis of the shortlisting practices of the Stella Prize also suggests that significant prizes have begun to recognise small press titles, but it presents a very interesting—and quite different—set of trends to the Miles Franklin and the PMLAF. It is first necessary to consider some of the key differences between the Stella and these other prizes. First of all, the Stella is the youngest of the three prizes, having been founded in 2013, and, as a result, there are only six years of data to analyse. Secondly, the Stella differs from the other two in that it only recognises female-identifying authors (a response to the disproportionate recognition of male authors by the Miles Franklin Award). Thirdly, the Stella is open to a wide array of literary forms, including "novels of all genres, collections of short stories by a single author, memoirs, biographies, histories, verse novels, and novellas of at least 20,000 words" as well as illustrated books and graphic novels, "provided they are accompanied by a substantial quantity of text".[17] Poetry collections and children's literature, however, are mostly ineligible. Given these differences, it might appear that the Stella is a prize that cannot be compared with the other two.

But the very name of the Stella Prize intentionally (and quite cleverly) positions itself in relation to the Miles Franklin. Moreover, despite its multi-generic brief, the Stella Prizes primarily recognises works of fiction, and, indeed, mostly works of fiction that could be classed as novels. Four of the six winners of the Stella Prize have been novels; of the two non-fiction works to have been awarded, one—Alexis Wright's *Tracker* (Giramondo, which won in 2018)—was written by an author who has written three novels, one of which (*Carpentaria* (2006)) won the Miles Franklin Award in 2007. Indeed, of the 36 works that have been shortlisted for the Stella, 27 (75%) have been works of fiction, and the vast majority of those have been novels. This is not to criticise the Stella Prize in any way, but simply to note that—based on its record so far—it can be described as *primarily* an award for literary fiction, and, in this sense, it is more similar to the Miles Franklin and PMLAF than it might initially appear.

Looking at the Stella Prize longlists and shortlists absolutely demonstrates that small publishers are being recognised by the prize; where the Stella differs, however, is the timing and trend of this recognition. Aside from one lower result in the Stella's inaugural year (33%), at least *half* of its shortlisted titles have been produced by small publishers in every other year, as Figure 4 demonstrates.

---

17 "Submission Guidelines," The Stella Prize, http://thestellaprize.com.au/prize/guidelines-submission/.

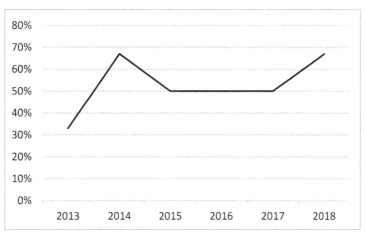

Figure 4. Percentage of Small Press Titles on Stella Prize Shortlist, 2013–2018.

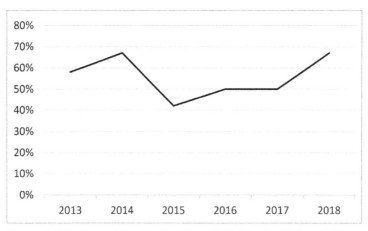

Figure 5. Percentage of Small Press Titles on Stella Prize Longlist, 2013–2018.

Small publishers comprise a small majority of Stella Prize shortlisted titles, with 19 of the 36 (53%) shortlisted works coming from the small press. Similarly, three of the six winning titles have been produced by small publishers (Text, Giramondo and Affirm Press). In other words, the Stella Prize has recognised small presses at effectively double the rate of both the Miles Franklin and the PMLAF. The dominance of small publishers in the Stella is also replicated in the longlists, with 40 of 72 titles (55%) being produced by small publishers. It's also worth noting that the shortlists are not as dominated by Text and Giramondo as the other prizes: four of the 19 small press shortlisted titles are from Text (21%), and three are from Giramondo (16%). Three other small publishers (Black Inc, Scribe and University of Queensland Press) have been shortlisted twice while five other publishers (Affirm Press, Five Islands, Seizure, Transit Lounge and Wild Dingo Press) have been shortlisted once.

There are material reasons why the Stella Prize has probably been more open to small publishers than the other two awards. For one, the Stella Prize was created in Melbourne—traditionally viewed as the home of much of Australia's small-publishing activity—and those involved with the prize have either worked for or published with small publishers. For example, co-founder and former executive director, Aviva Tuffield, is a highly regarded editor, who has worked at small publishers such as Scribe, Affirm and Black Inc. The original prize manager, Megan Quinlan, previously worked at Text publishing and *The Monthly* (which has the same ownership as Black Inc.). Many of the Stella Prize judges past and present, such as Tony Birch and Julie Koh, have published their fiction solely through small publishers. In other words, the Stella Prize has been largely staffed by people who know small presses, are familiar with the value of what they produce, and are therefore unlikely to have biases (unconscious or conscious) toward works produced by large publishers.

I suspect it is also not coincidental that a prize that champions women's writing and gender equity would also tend to recognise small publishers. Indeed, small publishers, as Sarah Couper has demonstrated, have a significantly better track record in terms of gender equity, and have a significantly higher proportion of female executives than large publishers do.[18] Moreover, I suspect that small publishers are probably more diverse and inclusive on the whole, both in terms of the authors they publish and the kinds of views and perspectives that they present. This is so because small publishers, as Aaron Mannion and Amy Espeseth have argued, frequently seek to support social causes rather than simply pursuing returns for shareholders, as most large, publicly held companies are legally and ethically obliged to do.[19] In this sense, the dominance of small publishers' titles in the Stella is unsurprising given that it is an award that seeks to champion diversity as well as literary quality.

The last component I want to consider is the *timing* of the Stella Prize's recognition of small publishers. As Figure 4 and Figure 5 demonstrate, the Stella has recognised small press works more or less since its inception, and therefore anticipates the current upward trends in the Miles Franklin's and the PMLAF's recognition of small publishers by four years. I do not think this is merely a case of the Stella anticipating a future trend; rather, I would suggest that the Stella's willingness to consider such works is *a major cause* of the Miles Franklin and PMLAF taking small press books more seriously. The routine appearance of such works on the Stella lists has normalised the recognition of small press books by a prestigious prize and thus made it more acceptable for other such prizes to do the same.

I suspect the Stella has been able to do this (perhaps unintentionally) because it has been so effective at intervening in public debates and engaging with the literary field and publishing industry. The Stella's yearly Stella Count—which tracks the gender ratios of both book reviewers and reviewed authors—is always a significant news

---

18 Sarah Couper, "Bookish Girls," in *The Return of Print? Contemporary Australian Publishing*, *ed*s. Emmett Stinson and Aaron Mannion (Melbourne: Monash University Publishing, 2016), 24–42.

19 Aaron Mannion and Amy Espeseth, "Small Press Social Entrepreneurship: The Values of Definition" in *By the Book? Contemporary Publishing in Australia, ed.* Emmett Stinson (Melbourne: Monash University Publishing, 2013), 74–88.

item, and its founders and board have regularly produced articles that intervene in various debates. The Stella has also received significant buy-in from booksellers, particular independent booksellers, who have become even more essential for the literary market with the collapse of Borders and REDgroup Retail in 2011; for example, Chris Gordon, Events Manager at Readings Books, Melbourne's most significant independent book chain, was among the founders of the prize. For this reason, the Stella's interventions have been particularly significant and have arguably permeated the literary field more than any other prize in recent years. Aviva Tuffield has made precisely this argument, claiming that the Stella has increased the Miles Franklin's recognition of women writers and has helped encourage local VCE lists to achieve gender parity.[20] In this sense, the Stella's listing of small press books has almost certainly influenced the Australian literary field.

The second likely cause of the current trend toward acknowledging small press works can be attributed to the judges of these prizes. Both the PMLAF and the Miles Franklin have changed some or all of the judges on their panels, and these changes are probably at least partially responsible for the increasing recognition of small press works. As Beth Driscoll has noted, judges play a significant role in the awarding of prizes. Awards, as she argues, are dependent on the prestige of the judges, but her historical analysis of the Man Booker prize also demonstrates that its various judges "have been unable to present a coherent idea of literary value through consistent decisions that build a recognisable canon of winners."[21] In other words, judges' decisions are not based on the application of a rule (and this is not surprising since, from a Kantian perspective, aesthetic judgements are *never* based on a rule), but rather are highly idiosyncratic, and

---

20 Aviva Tuffield, "Bold Interventions Can Change the Game for Women, Just Look at the Stella Prize," *Women's Agenda*, https://womensagenda.com.au/latest/soapbox/six-years-of-stella-the-importance-of-symbolic-acts/.

21 Driscoll, *The New Literary Middlebrow*, 128.

necessarily based on personal taste.[22] Moreover, judges' decisions are necessarily contingent insofar as they arise out of the dynamics of the judging committee; oftentimes, a winning work is not every judge's favourite title, but rather a compromise. As Driscoll argues, judges' decisions do not therefore define literary value, but rather "unsettle literary value".[23] Rather than producing coherent arguments about literary worth or adhering to clear and explicit criteria, literary prizes instead simply produce judgements, which, even after the fact, cannot be schematised. For this reason, changes to judging panels can have a major effect on the kind of works selected.

The final likely cause, as I have argued in the past, is that larger publishers have increasingly scaled back their literary publishing programs in favour of more profitable forms of popular fiction. In this sense, there is less competition within elite literary space and small presses are increasingly—if belatedly—coming to fill this gap. In this sense, small publishers' higher success rate is due to the fact that the kinds of values their works project are more in line with the expectations of literary "elites" (a term, it must be emphasised, that does not necessarily reflect the economic status of such judges, who may in no way be economically "elite") that typically comprise judging panels.

Having considered the likely causes of this trend toward recognition of small presses, I now want to turn to the possible effects of this shift. Before doing so, I want to emphasise again that I suspect the dominance of small press titles in 2017 is unlikely to be a sustainable phenomenon, but I do think that a general increase in the proportion of small press titles is likely, probably in-line with the Stella Prize, which has drawn half of its winners and slightly more than half of its shortlistees from small presses. In the short term, the valuation of small presses is a good thing, because it increases the diversity

---

22 Immanuel Kant, *Critique of Judgment*, trans. James Creed Meredith, ed. Nicolas Walker (Oxford: Oxford University Press, 2007), 138–9.

23 Driscoll, *The New Literary Middlebrow*, 124.

of the titles brought to the attention of the reading public, and decreases the unfair advantage historically held by larger publishers, who have decreased their investments in literary publishing. But in the longer term, the recognition of small press titles—especially if those titles are regularly selected as winners and fail to appeal to a broader reading market—could have potentially negative effects on prizes themselves.

This is so because, as Driscoll argues, "the authority of the literary prize is strikingly vulnerable"; even prominent awards, such as the Man Booker, cannot definitely claim to recognise the best book in a given year, since these judgements are intensely scrutinised and debated by commentators who "continually set the awards against one another".[24] The main way that prizes tend to guarantee their ongoing relevance and social prestige is through *scandal*; Driscoll again quotes an administrator of the Booker Prize noting as early as 1972 that: "It may be argued too that no prize was ever really successful unless surrounded by a fearful hullaballoo of controversy!"[25] While more niche or intellectual titles can be useful as *occasional winners* that generate their own kind of controversy or scandal, repeatedly awarding such works will not generate this discussion. Moreover, the goal of such prizes, which Driscoll terms the middlebrow dream, is "to secure both cultural legitimacy and commercial success".[26] Small press works, which are often (though not always!) more niche or explicitly literary, might not appeal to the broader reading class and therefore may have difficulty attaining this status.

In this sense, literary prizes are put in a complex situation by the changes to the mediation practices of Australian publishers. Literary prizes are reliant on notions of literary prestige. Large publishers' decreasing investments in literature have meant that prizes appear

---

24 Ibid., 124.
25 Ibid., 140.
26 Ibid., 141.

now to be looking more carefully at small-press works, which often appeal to the forms of literary prestige that prizes have traditionally championed. Indeed, it could be argued that the last winners of the Miles Franklin Award (Josephine Wilson's *Extinction*) and the PMLAF (Ryan O'Neill's *Their Brilliant Careers*) are books that may have been selected for the fact that they so clearly and explicitly signal their literary investments. Wilson's *Extinction,* for example, openly connects itself to the work of Austrian writer Thomas Bernhard, both in almost exactly appropriating the title of his final novel, *Extinctions* (1986), and in making its protagonist a concrete manufacturer, a further reference to Bernhard's *Concrete* (1982). Ryan O'Neill's *Their Brilliant Careers* is not only explicitly literary in its allusion to Miles Franklin's most famous novel, but also presents a rhetorically complex and highly ironic re-imagining of Australian literary history. In creating a series of false biographies of Australian writers (a technique not dissimilar to that applied in Roberto Bolano's *Nazi Literature in the Americas* (1996)), O'Neill also repeatedly shadows *real* Australian literary history in a way that gives it continuing force and relevance. In other words, both of these books are unashamedly literary in their subject matter, but also argue (implicitly) for the continuing value and relevance of literary history and literary values. To be clear, I do not mean this as a critique of these novels, both of which are excellent and deserving winners. Rather, I am focusing on the mediation practices of judging to argue that the selection of these specific texts at this specific time can be understood as a meaningful intervention in broader Australian literary discourse.

In this sense, I think the 2017 Miles Franklin and PMLAF could be read as a defense or reassertion of the literary at a moment when popular or commercial fiction seems increasingly influential in Australian book culture. Recently, for example, David Carter has noted that genre fiction (in terms of titles and sales) is growing faster than literary fiction, and argued for replacing the term "Australian literature" with the term "Australian writing", which, as he claims, better describes "a dispersed, disaggregated field, mobilised in diverse ways in diverse institutions".[27] While this argument is clear and well-supported by evidence, it is also representative of a broader de-centring of capital-L literature in favour of a diversity of writing practices. Often, though not always, these scholarly de-centrings are an implicit valorisation of popular fiction over literary values that are seen as elitist and exclusionary. Mark Davis presented a view that resonates with Carter's in a 2017 speech at the Independent Publishing Conference, in which he provocatively depicted the Australian literary field by showing a photograph of the apocalyptic wasteland from *Mad Max*. His point, like Carter's, was that the institutions surrounding the literary field have changed to such a degree that it may no longer even constitute a field, as such. Whether or not one accepts these arguments in their strongest forms, it nonetheless seems reasonable to assert that both reading culture and institutions are changing in ways that threaten literary writing's traditional hegemony over "elite" writing culture. In this context, the choice of two, highly literary texts for major prizes in the same year, both of which are produced by smaller publishers, hardly seems unrelated.

This brings up a final point, which is that the increasing recognition of small publishers is based on tenuous and contingent circumstances. If 2017 was a banner year for small presses at the literary awards, it also seems that this surge has been motivated by a set of preferences and values that have been traditionally associated with what is, for better or worse, called "elite" literary culture. Similarly, the increase of these titles also derives from large publishers vacating the cultural space of the literary for increasingly commercial reasons. But there is absolutely nothing stable about this state of affairs. If

---

27 David Carter, "The Literary Field and Contemporary Trade-Book Publishing in Australia: Literary and Genre Fiction," *Media International Australia* 158, no. 1 (2016): 56.

large publishers did increase their literary publishing programs even modestly, for example, it is conceivable that small publishers' share of prize recognition could decrease. On the other hand, it is also conceivable that activist judges or future prizes may seek to foreground popular fiction in a fashion similar to the Stella's elevation of small publishers. Indeed, the Miles Franklin has (rarely) gone to works of popular fiction in the past, such as when the prize was awarded to Peter Temple's *Truth* in 2010. Such competition from works of popular fiction would similarly undermine the gains that small publishers have made—although it would also open elite literary institutions to a much broader range of writers and writing practices.

Works cited

Allington, Patrick. "Why the Prime Minister's Literary Awards Need an Urgent Overhaul." *The Conversation*, June 22, 2016. https://theconversation.com/why-the-prime-ministers-literary-awards-need-an-urgent-overhaul-61300.

Bourdieu, Pierre. "The Three Forms of Capital." In *Handbook of Theory of Research for the Sociology of Education*, edited by J. E. Richardson. Westport: Greenword Press, 1986.

Carter, David. "The Literary Field and Contemporary Trade-Book Publishing in Australia: Literary and Genre Fiction." *Media International Australia* 158, no. 1 (2016): 48–57.

Couper, Susan. "Bookish Girls." In *The Return of Print? Contemporary Australian Publishing*, edited by Emmett Stinson and Aaron Mannion, 24–42. Melbourne: Monash University Publishing, 2016.

Cunningham, S. "Making Waves: Stella Turns Six." *Kill Your Darlings*, February 5, 2018. https://www.killyourdarlings.com.au/article/making-waves-six-years-of-the-stella-prize/.

Driscoll, Beth. *The New Literary Middlebrow: Tastemakers and Reading in the Twenty-First Century*. London: Palgrave Macmillan, 2014.

English, James. *The Economy of Prestige: Prizes, Awards, and the Circulation of Cultural Value*. Cambridge, MA: Harvard University Press, 2005.

Hollier, Nathan. "Australian Small and Independent Publishing: The Freeth Report," *Publishing Research Quarterly* 24, no. 3 (2008): 165–74.

Kant, Immanuel. *Critique of Judgment*. Translated by James Creed Meredith, edited by Nicolas Walker. Oxford: Oxford University Press, 2007.

Mannion, Aaron, and Amy Espeseth. "Small Press Social Entrepreneurship: The Values of Definition." In *By the Book? Contemporary Publishing in Australia* edited by Emmett Stinson. Melbourne: Monash University Publishing, 2013: 74–88.

Mason, Jody. "'Capital Intraconversion' and Canadian Literary Prize Culture," *Book History* 20 (2017): 424–46.

Murray, Simone. "Charting the Digital Literary Sphere." *Contemporary Literature* 56, no. 2 (2015): 311–39.

Stinson, Emmett. "Small Publishers and the Emerging Network of Australian Literary Prosumption." *Australia Humanities Review* 59 (April/May 2016): 23–43.

———. "Small Publishers and the Miles Franklin." In *The Return of Print? Contemporary Australian Publishing,* edited by Emmett Stinson and Aaron Mannion. Melbourne: Monash University Publishing, 2016. 132–42.

The Stella Prize. "Submission Guidelines." Retrieved April 15, 2018, http:// thestellaprize.com.au/prize/guidelines-submission/.

Thompson, John B. *Merchants of Culture: The Publishing Business in the Twenty-First Century.* Cambridge: Polity Press, 2010.

Tuffield, Aviva. "Bold Interventions Can Change the Game for Women, Just Look at the Stella Prize." *Women's Agenda* April 13, 2018. https:// womensagenda.com.au/latest/soapbox/six-years-of-stella-the-importance-of-symbolic-acts/.

Wyndham, Susan. "The Hidden Costs That Threaten Australian Literary Awards." *Sydney Morning Herald*, December 3, 2016. https://www.smh. com.au/entertainment/books/the-hidden-costs-that-threaten-australian-literary-awards-20161202-gt32wc.html.

Chapter 10

Literary Prizes and Book Reviews in Australia since 2014

Melinda Harvey and Julieanne Lamond

This essay seeks to characterise the relationship between two key institutions in the contemporary Australian literary field: book reviews and literary prizes. We find that the relationship between literary prizes and book reviews is one of interdependence and amplification. By "interdependence", we mean that there is significant movement of agents between the two sectors as well as a mutual influence of the sectors upon each other. By "amplification", we refer to the fact that attention in one sector often leads to heightened attention in the other. Reviews value many of the same works as prizes—especially in the case of works of fiction—and their value assessments are magnified when those works go on to win prizes. Prizes also implicitly and explicitly evidence responses to reviews. Furthermore, success in prizes usually leads to better review coverage for the author's subsequent publications.

Our study reveals certain crucial differences between literary prizes and book reviews, especially when genre and publisher are scrutinised. Reviews value a greater range of works, and are thus vitally important for the many species of books that tend to be excluded from, or do not go on to win, prizes. The review mediates books' encounters with judges and readers, whereas the purpose of prizes is explicitly to rank certain works at the top of a hierarchy of value—although we do notice the contemporary phenomenon of prizes giving more and more attention to their shortlists via events, bookshop collateral and social media. While prizes might seem to be doing some of the work of reviews in terms of consecrating and promoting books in the Australian literary field, they cannot replace them: without reviews, many excellent works would not receive the opportunity to be appraised in the public eye.

These findings draw on data collected in collaboration with the Stella Count for the years 2013–17 as well as newly compiled data on twenty-two prize categories of Australia's most important literary awards since 2014: the Miles Franklin Literary Award, the Stella Prize, all six prizes that constitute the Prime Minister's Literary Awards,[1] nine of the thirteen prize categories that constitute the New South Wales Premier's Literary Awards,[2] and five of the eight prize categories that constitute the Victorian Premier's Literary Awards.[3] This constitutes 108 instances of prize-giving, ninety winning books and ninety-four judges. For each prize, we have recorded the following information: prize year, book title, book author, author gender, book genre, book publisher, and prize judges.[4] We acknowledge that this data is more indicative than exhaustive. Our decision to focus on these four prizes—of the more than fifty awarded in Australia—is based upon our assessment of them as the most lucrative, highest profile national or state-based prizes in the country. The review data we have collected with the Stella Count casts a much wider net but

---

1   The PM's Literary Awards, since 2012, consists of six separate prizes: for fiction, nonfiction, young adult fiction, children's literature, poetry and Australian history.

2   For this study, we count the Christina Stead Prize for Fiction, Douglas Stewart Prize for Nonfiction, Kenneth Slessor Prize for Poetry, Ethel Turner Prize for Young People's Fiction, Patricia Wrightson Prize for Children's Literature, UTS Glenda Adams Award for New Writing and annual overall prize called the Book of the Year. We also count the NSW Multicultural and Indigenous Writers' Awards since their inauguration in 2016. The remaining prize categories are for playwriting, screenwriting and translators (two prizes), which we do not count.

3   We count the prizes for fiction, nonfiction, poetry, writing for young adults and the annual overall award called the Victorian Prize for Literature. We do not count the prize for drama, People's Choice Award or Unpublished Manuscript Award.

4   Our judges data is complete for the Prime Minister's Literary Awards, Stella Prize and the Victorian Premier's Literary Award but is exclusive of the NSW Premier's Literary Award. It is also inclusive of 2013 judges data for these three prizes.

is also not all-encompassing. It includes 17,786 instances of books reviewed over five years in twelve different publications: *The Australian*, *Australian Book Review*, *Australian Financial Review*, *The Age/Sydney Morning Herald*, *The Courier Mail*, *The Advertiser*, *The West Australian*, *The Mercury*, *Sydney Review of Books*, *The Monthly*, *The Saturday Paper* and *Books+Publishing*.[5] However, we recognise that our reviewing data does not wholly capture genres such as poetry and specific subgenres of fiction such as children's and young adult literature, which have their own reviewing networks that are internet-based and operate outside of the conventions of the largely print-based periodicals in our data.

Background to this Study

In our 2016 essay, published in *Australian Humanities Review*, we noted that the size of the field of Australian book reviews was shrinking: the total number of reviews published in Australia declined by 457 between 2015 and 2017. We also noticed the scrutiny of Australian books diminishing in the outlets where you would expect it to be a priority. Take, for example, *Australian Book Review*: in 1985, it devoted 97% of its total number of reviews to books by Australian authors; in 2013, that number dropped to 69% and since then it has dropped to 65% in 2015 and 63% in 2017. This is despite the fact that *Australian Book Review*'s total number of reviews has remained steady since 2013, hovering around the 300 mark.[6] There have been concerns expressed about the declining attention paid to Australian books in review pages over the past decade. This period has seen the increased, then total, syndication of reviews across *The Age* and the *Sydney Morning Herald*, and the departures of the literary editors at the *Canberra Times* (in 2012) and *The Sydney Morning Herald* (in 2017). This is part of the

---

5   *The Age* and *Sydney Morning Herald* were counted separately in 2013.
6   *Australian Book Review*'s annual numbers of reviews for the period are: 284 (2013), 327 (2014), 310 (2015), 346 (2016) and 319 (2017).

sector-wide restructuring that is taking place in the news media in the face of dramatic digital disruption and declines in the sale of print newspapers.[7]

Meanwhile, prizes multiply. The Stella Prize—a response to the "sausage fest" shortlists of the 2009 and 2011 Miles Franklin Literary Awards—was inaugurated in 2012. Numerous publishing houses and literary magazines have now entered the field, offering prizes of their own where once there might have been a slush pile: there is, for example, the Scribe Nonfiction Prize for Young Writers, *Seizure*'s Viva La Novella Prize and *Griffith Review*'s Novella Project (all since 2012), Hachette's Richell Prize (since 2014), UWA Publishing's Dorothy Hewett Award (since 2015), *Kill Your Darlings*' Unpublished Manuscript Award, and the Penguin Random House Australia Literary Prize (both since 2017). This is not even to mention the multitude of prizes for shorter works run by magazines, literary organisations, universities, festivals and libraries, and the prizes run by bookshops (such as the Readings Prize). This prize frenzy is not just happening in Australia: James English argues in *The Economy of Prestige* that prizes have enjoyed "feverish proliferation in recent decades"[8] and are "expanding in number and in economic value much faster than the cultural economy in general".[9] It was not, then, surprising to find that Beth Driscoll's contribution to the 2017 *Oxford Research Encyclopedia of Literature* names "Australia's calendar of literary prizes" as one of six "networks" that "are key to Australia's literary culture". The literary prize, Driscoll writes, "supports writers, builds canons, and maintains the visibility of literary culture". A starting point for this chapter was this: should the shrinking and diminishing of book reviews and the

---

7   Sybil Nolan and Matthew Ricketson, "Parallel Fates: Structural Challenges in News-paper Publishing and their Consequences for the Book Industry," in *Sydney Review of Books* (February 22, 2013), https://sydneyreviewofbooks.com/parallel-fates-2/.

8   James English, *The Economy of Prestige: Prizes, Awards and the Circulation of Cultural Value* (Cambridge, MA: Harvard University Press, 2005), 2.

9   Ibid., 10.

growing numbers of prizes be interpreted as evidence of book reviewing's increasing insignificance to Australian literary culture? While they have been given much less scholarly attention than prizes on the whole, reviews are often described in much the same terms as prizes: they "build careers and reputations" and are vital to authors' public profile and sales figures,[10] and they pave the way for the book's acceptance by the academy.[11] However, none of the six networks judged "key to Australia's literary culture" by Driscoll overtly includes book reviews or even newspapers—for which the majority of book reviews are still produced in Australia. We argue, on the contrary, that book reviews are a key institution in contemporary Australian literary culture because they are, more often than not, the primary evaluative and promotional mechanism through which books travel on their way to longevity and canonicity—or, in less fortunate cases, obscurity. As we shall show, prizes bear the imprimatur of book reviews in their adjudications, both by virtue of decisions made and stated reasons for them. As Robert J. Meyer-Lee argues, "individual ascriptions of literary value are always performed in some relation to... other agents' ascriptions of literary value".[12] Our study understands reviewers and judges as agents in the networks of literary value that sustain Australian literature as a field.

Prize Winners in Book Reviews

We began our study by asking this question of our data: are Australian book reviews paying attention to Australian prize winners? What we found is that there is a significant, but not complete, overlap between

---

10 Gail Pool, *Faint Praise: The Plight of Book Reviewing in Australia (Columbia: University of Missouri Press, 2007)*, 9; Nolan and Ricketson, "Parallel Fates."

11 C. J. Van Rees, "How a Literary Work Becomes a Masterpiece: On the Threefold Selection Practised by Literary Criticism," *Poetics* 12 (1983): 403.

12 Robert J. Meyer-Lee, "Toward a Theory and Practice of Literary Valuing," *New Literary History* 46, no. 2 (2015): 341.

the books that have won prizes and the books that were reviewed in Australia over this period. Our data shows that 92% of books that have won prizes since 2014 received at least one book review. In the vast majority of cases (86%), books that won prizes had already been reviewed. Only two out of ninety books—both nonfiction—received their only reviews after they won prizes, which we discuss in further detail below. For works of fiction—the genre that most "depends on the oxygen of reviews pages"[13]—reviews precede prizes in every single instance in our data. These figures prove that—notwithstanding the emergence of the pre-publication prize in Australia—reviews are the earliest consecrating mechanism a new book encounters. Indeed, the fact that reviews have this kind of stranglehold on initial reception might explain the eagerness of publishers to set up pre-publication prizes. Unpublished manuscript awards disrupt the temporal order of the consecratory chain for the most vulnerable titles—new books—such that they seek to undermine book reviewing's priority in the chain without inhibiting a book's chances of being noticed through externally administered prizes later on. Several novels in our period won such awards, went on to be very well reviewed, and then won prizes: this was the case for Josephine Wilson's *Extinctions*, Emily Bitto's *The Strays* and Melanie Cheng's *Australia Day*. The pre-publication prize is something to continue to watch closely.

In *Merchants of Culture*, John B. Thompson argues that prizes are particularly important for regulating the reception of "literary fiction and serious nonfiction".[14] Fiction is the genre in which, by and large, reviews and prizes tend to value the same books, which we discuss in further detail below. Nonfiction, however, is a slightly different case. While nonfiction is very well represented in Australian reviews pages (especially in *The Australian*, *Australian Book Review* and *The Age*), this

---

13 Nolan and Ricketson, "Parallel Fates."

14 John B. Thompson, *Merchants of Culture: The Publishing Business in the Twenty-First Century* (Cambridge: Polity Press, 2010) 277.

coverage is spread across more titles. As Figure 1 shows, works of prizewinning fiction receive significantly more reviews than individual works of other genres. Fifteen prizewinning works of fiction received six or more reviews each in our period of study, while only six works of nonfiction, one work of poetry and no children's/young adult fiction did so. A book is also more likely to be reviewed more than once if it is a work of fiction: in 2014–16, 20% of fiction titles received more than one review compared to 15% for nonfiction. In other words, the reviewing of fiction is concentrated: fewer books are reviewed, but they receive more attention. For many prizewinning works of fiction, receipt of a prize amplifies its presence in the public eye, which already has been initiated, even fortified, by repeated reviews. For other works, a literary prize might be the primary consecrating factor in play.

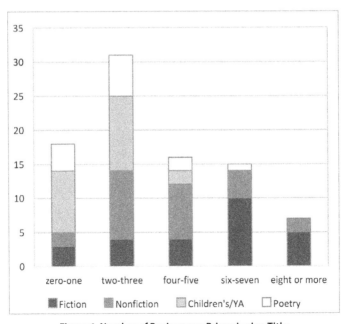

Figure 1. Number of Reviews per Prizewinning Title.

Reviewing clearly plays an important early role in the assessment of works of fiction. There are, however, other kinds of books that do not receive as much attention in the reviews pages. Forty percent of prizewinning books in our data—that is, thirty-seven books—received two or fewer reviews. Of these, nineteen (51%) were works of children's/young adult fiction, eight (22%) works of poetry, six (16%) nonfiction, and two each (5%) of fiction and drama. Of the ninety prizewinning books across this period, seven received no reviews at all. These books included two works of poetry, one of nonfiction, one of drama and three of children's/young adult fiction. Genre would appear to be a crucial point of difference that undergirds the ways in which prizes and reviews value books.

Children's and young adult fiction, poetry and nonfiction are the genres in which the values of prizes and reviews would seem to diverge from one another. Children's and young adult fiction, for example, is well represented in the field of prizes and poorly represented in book reviews. Australian book reviews across this period covered fiction (47%), nonfiction (37%), children's and young adult fiction (12%) and poetry (4%). This coverage varies significantly between publications. Children's and young adult fiction is much more strongly represented in the reviews pages of state-based newspapers than national ones. For example, in 2017 the highest proportion of reviews constituted by children's/young adult fiction is 22% in *The West Australian*, followed by 12% in *The Advertiser* and 10% in *The Courier Mail*. Poetry, however, is poorly represented in the state-based papers and well represented in review-specific and national publications. In 2017, poetry reviews constituted 22% of all reviews at *Sydney Review of Books*, 8% at *Australian Book Review* and 7% at *The Australian*. The works of poetry that received the most reviews were by well-established poets: Jill Jones (three reviews), Jennifer Maiden (four), David Malouf (four), Maxine Beneba Clarke (three), and Sarah Holland-Batt, for *The Hazards* (three). Holland-Batt is an interesting case as she appears in our data as an author, reviewer and judge. De Nooy notes in relation to judging panels that "members of the literary field will transfer the prestige of a position to its holder and the authority of the expert to the position held".[15] English, likewise, writes of "the social and symbolic rewards that accrue to judges" and that "the stature of judges guarantees the stature of the prize".[16] Holland-Batt is a good example of how prestige—which is also, of course, generated by the quality of the work itself—flows both ways and is amplified between book reviews and prizes.

In the realm of nonfiction, some works receive repeat reviews. These are, by and large, works of life writing—specifically, memoir or biography: for example, Maxine Beneba Clarke's *The Hate Race* (nine reviews), Helen Trinca's *Madeleine* (six), and Sarah Krasnostein's *The Trauma Cleaner* (six). It would seem that the typical chronology of the review then the prize can also, in the case of some nonfiction, be reversed. There are two works in our data that only received a review after they had won a literary prize: Geoffrey Blainey's *The Story of Australia's People* and Bruce Pascoe's *Dark Emu, Black Seeds: Agriculture or Accident?* Blainey's history received no reviews until after the Prime Minister's Literary Award announcement on early November 2016. This precipitated a flurry of three reviews across the following two months. *Dark Emu, Black Seeds* was only reviewed in our surveyed publications in 2017 after winning Book of the Year in the 2016 NSW Premier's Awards. *The Australian* covered Pascoe's book in a long composite review in July 2017, describing it as "his recent award-winning book". *Dark Emu, Black Seeds* was published by small press Magabala Books, which only received a total of eight reviews in 2016. This might be the case of a small publisher without the publicity resources to leverage space in the reviews pages. It is certainly a case in which the literary

---

15   Wouter De Nooy, "Gentlemen of the Jury... The Features of Experts Awarding Literary Prizes," *Poetics* 17 (1988): 532.

16   English, *The Economy of Prestige* 121–123.

prize does the purported work of the review—that is, brings the book to public attention—and then the review belatedly follows. In the case of nonfiction, poetry and children's and young adult literature, it would seem that prizes are valuing different books from reviews by noticing books that went relatively undiscussed in the field of book reviewing. We could even speculate that, despite the fact that fiction prizes attract more press, prizes are more important for poetry, children's and young adult fiction, and nonfiction books because books in these genres rarely get the notice that repeat reviewing generates.

We were keen to know which reviewing outlets covered more of the same books that were rewarded by prize committees. Of the publications included in our data, *The Australian* is noticing the highest proportion of books that later go on to win prizes, reviewing between 57% and 72% of prizewinning books over this period, followed by *The Age*, which reviews between 52% and 72%. It is not surprising that these two publications review the most prize winners as, across the period, they publish more reviews than any other publication. *The Age* remains the major publisher of book reviews in Australia, publishing some 3060 (17% of the total) reviews between 2014 and 2017. The next most significant publication in the field is *The Australian*, which published 2401 reviews (13% of the total) across this period. The other important player in the field is *Australian Book Review*, which publishes 7% of all reviews in our data and covered between 38% and 52% of our prize winners. Despite a recent reduction in the number of book reviews it publishes, *The Advertiser* publishes more book reviews than any other state-specific publication, publishing 13% of total reviews in our survey, and between 24% and 50% of the prizewinning books in our survey.

When scale is taken into account, however, it appears to be the smaller book reviewing outlets that notice more of the books that go on to win prizes. Considered as a percentage of the total number of books reviewed by individual outlet, prizewinning works constituted

6.2% of all books reviewed in *The Monthly* over this period, and 5.1% of books at *Sydney Review of Books* (see Table 1). This may be because the larger review outlets are conceiving of the purpose and audience of their book pages differently. For example, *Sydney Review of Books* publishes the longest reviews in the field and offers peer review to its contributors. This suggests an editorial imperative that leans towards books that are expected to have longer afterlives beyond prizes in the arenas of academic research and teaching. Newspapers include book reviews as part of a much broader ambit to inform and entertain readers. For example, a specific nonfiction book might allow for the review to double as a feature article on a specific topic. Our data suggests that some review publications are more like prizes in their orientation towards prestige than others.

Table 1. Prize Winners Reviewed per Publication.

Publisher of Review	Total Prize Winners Reviewed	Total Reviews	Prize Winners as % of Total Reviews
The Monthly	9	145	6.2
Sydney Review of Books	13	257	5.1
The Saturday Paper	16	432	3.7
Australian Book Review	44	1312	3.4
The Courier Mail	21	723	2.9
The Australian	59	2401	2.5
The Advertiser	33	1389	2.4
The Age	52	3060	1.7
The Mercury	9	673	1.3
Australian Financial Review	2	188	1.1
The West Australian	3	681	0.4

Fiction Prize Winners in Book Reviews

As we noted earlier in this chapter, review coverage of fiction prize winners is generally more comprehensive than that of the other genres. We now drill down into these numbers to discover which particular works of prizewinning fiction were given more notice in book reviews than others (see Table 2).

Table 2 shows that prizewinning works of fiction in this period were very widely reviewed in Australian publications. To provide some context: in 2017, only 3% of all titles reviewed in Australia received more than five reviews. The majority (69%) of prizewinning works of fiction fall within this very privileged category. This suggests that, in most cases, the book review and the literary prize are working in concert with one another. We should note, however, that there are many works that receive this same number of reviews but were not awarded prizes.

We might have expected the books that win prizes to also sit at the top of the list of most reviewed titles, but this is not quite the case (see Table 3). Table 3 is a reminder that, if prizes are primarily a consecrating mechanism, then reviews are more than this. They are evaluative but also have a journalistic function, providing an opportunity for more general discussion of a writer in the context of their works and career, and the literary world more generally. Reviews mediate, rather than simply bestow, value—they can, of course, be negative. Reviews, like prizes, are also promotional mechanisms; reviews pages necessarily promote, and value, a much wider range of works.

There are also certain kinds of fiction that are not well recognised in Australia's most prestigious national and state-based prizes. This includes works that might fall into the "genre" rather than "literary" category, however porous we might think these categories.

Table 2. Fiction Prize Winners by Number of Reviews, 2014–17.

Year	Prize Winner	No. of Reviews
2014	Richard Flanagan, *The Narrow Road to the Deep North*	11
2015	Joan London, *The Golden Age*	10
2014	Steven Carroll, *A World of Other People*	8
2015	Charlotte Wood, *The Natural Way of Things*	8
2017	Kim Scott, *Taboo*	8
2014	Fiona McFarlane, *The Night Guest*	7
2015	Emily Bitto, *The Strays*	7
2015	Mark Henshaw, *The Snow Kimono*	7
2015	Rohan Wilson, *To Name Those Lost*	7
2014	Alex Miller, *Coal Creek*	7
2017	Georgia Blain, *Between a Wolf and a Dog*	7
2016	Lisa Gorton, *The Life of Houses*	7
2015	Luke Carman, *An Elegant Young Man*	7
2014	Evie Wyld, *All the Birds, Singing*	6
2016	A. S. Patrić, *Black Rock White City*	6
2016	Mireille Juchau, *The World Without Us*	6
2016	Sonja Dechian, *An Astronaut's Life*	6
2017	Melanie Cheng, *Australia Day*	6
2014	Michelle de Kretser, *Questions of Travel*	6
2017	Ryan O'Neill, *Their Brilliant Careers*	5
2017	Heather Rose, *The Museum of Modern Love*	5
2017	Bram Presser, *The Book of Dirt*	5
2016	Josephine Wilson, *Extinctions*	4
2015	Sofie Laguna, *The Eye of the Sheep*	3
2016	Merlinda Bobis, *Locust Girl: A Lovesong*	3
2017	Michelle Cahill, *Letter to Pessoa*	3
2016	Ellen van Neervan, *Heat and Light*	3

Table 3. Most Reviewed Australian Fiction Titles, 2014–17, with Prizewinning Books in Our Data Indicated with an Asterisk.[17]

Title	No of Reviews
Amanda Lohrey, *A Short History of Richard Kline*	10
Steve Toltz, *Quicksand*	10
Sofie Laguna, *The Choke*	10
Hannah Kent, *The Good People*	10
Susan Johnson, *The Landing*	10
Gregory Day, *Archipelago of Souls*	9
A.S. Patrić, *Atlantic Black*	9
James Bradley, *Clade*	9
Joan London, *The Golden Age**	9
Malcolm Knox, *The Wonder Lover*	9
Gail Jones, *A Guide to Berlin*	8
Ceridwen Dovey, *Only the Animals*	8
Kim Scott, *Taboo**	8
Robyn Cadwallader, *The Anchoress*	8
Janette Turner Hospital, *The Claimant*	8
Eva Hornung, *The Last Garden*	8
Dominic Smith, *The Last Painting of Sara de Vos*	8
Charlotte Wood, *The Natural Way of Things**	8
Alex Miller, *The Passage of Love*	8
Sam Carmody, *The Windy Season*	8
Debra Adelaide, *The Women's Pages*	8
Robert Drewe, *Whipbird*	8

17 Some of the book titles in Table 2 do not appear in Table 3, despite being well reviewed. This is because they were reviewed in 2013, and we cannot include 2013 data in Table 3 because it does not distinguish between Australian and other titles.

Many of the works that received repeat reviews in our data are firmly works of literary fiction that simply did not win prizes. In some cases, this is due to the sometimes idiosyncratic conditions imposed by funding bodies and individuals on prizes. Most famous in this respect, of course, is the Miles Franklin Literary Award's stipulation that winning works must "present Australian life in any of its phases", which has controversially excluded some works of Australian fiction.[18] These conditions can be more implicit, as in the case of the Prime Minister's Literary Awards, which "celebrate outstanding literary talent in Australia and the valuable contribution Australian writing makes to the nation's cultural and intellectual life".[19] Writers whose work is less clearly engaging with Australian cultural imperatives might find themselves, if not ineligible, then less likely to succeed.

Prize Winners, Book Reviews and Publishers

Books do not find their way into reviews pages and prize lists on their own. Publishers play a role in determining how books enter, and are received, in the public arena. We now ask: how have books published by large multinationals and Australia's own array of large and small independent publishers fared in Australian prizes and book reviews?

Allen & Unwin and Text Publishing were the publishers of the most prizewinning books in our sample across 2014–17, winning twelve prizes each of the total of ninety awarded, followed by Penguin Random House with eight, Giramondo at six, UQP at five and Macmillan, NewSouth, Scholastic and HarperCollins with four each. Of the ninety prizewinning books in our survey, we find that the 'Big Five'—that is,

---

18 Patrick Allington, "'What Is Australia Anyway?' The Glorious Limitations of the Miles Franklin Literary Award," *Australian Book Review* (June 2011): 24.

19 "About Awards," Department of Communications and the Arts, Australian Government, https://www.arts.gov.au/pm-literary-awards/about-awards.

Penguin Random House, Hachette, Simon & Schuster, Macmillan and HarperCollins—published only nineteen (or 21%) of them. The annual share of prize winners published by the Big Five has varied from between 28% in 2014 and 5% in 2016. Small publishers have won 64% of the prizes in our survey.

These findings would appear to temper Emmett Stinson's claim in his 2016 essay "Small Publishers and the Miles Franklin Award" that "there is a disjuncture between the way that Australian literary works are produced and brought to market and the way that this same culture is received, shaped and symbolically recognised".[20] Stinson argues that small presses are responsible for publishing the bulk of literary fiction in Australia but that they "do not generally receive adequate recognition in national literary prizes".[21] However, our data shows that if one looks beyond fiction and the Miles Franklin, one sees that small presses have been well represented in literary prizes. And it is worth noting here that the last two Miles Franklin awards have gone to books by small presses: Transit Lounge for A. S. Patrić's *Black Rock White City* and UWA Publishing for Wilson's *Extinctions*.

When it comes to the wider consecratory field, our statistics show that books published by small presses are also being reviewed strongly. Across the period 2014–16, the Big Five publishers accounted for only 24%–34% of all books reviewed in our surveyed publications. As you can see from Figure 2 over page, the conglomerate Penguin Random

---

20 Emmett Stinson, "Small Publishers and the Miles Franklin Award," in *The Return of Print? Contemporary Australian Publishing*, eds. Aaron Mannion and Emmett Stinson (Melbourne: Monash University Publishing, 2016), 139.

21 We note that since we presented a version of this paper at the SPN Conference in November 2017, Stinson has publicly modified his stance, stating that there has been "a particularly dramatic spike" for small press books on prize shortlists since 2016. See Stinson, "Friday Essay: the Remarkable, Prize-winning Rise of Our Small Publishers", *The Conversation*, 4 May 2018, https://theconversation.com/friday-essay-the-remarkable-prize-winning-rise-of-our-small-publishers-95645.

House unsurprisingly publishes most of the books reviewed (12%), followed by Allen & Unwin (10%). Text, however, is the third most reviewed publisher at 5.7% of all reviews, ahead of the other four of the Big Five: Macmillan (5.5%), HarperCollins (4.5%), Hachette (4.5%) and Simon & Schuster (1.4%).

Figures 2 and 3 together provide a snapshot of the ways in which publishers are represented across the fields of prizes and reviews from 2014 to 2016. Small presses are more strongly represented in the field of prizes than in reviews, but when the relative scale of the publishing houses featured in this chart is taken into account, Black Inc., UWA Publishing, UQP, Scribe, Transit Lounge, Affirm and Giramondo are all strongly represented in the reviews pages, too. These publishers' books all received more than seventy reviews across this three-year period. John B. Thompson notes, in the American context, that small publishers find it difficult to access space in the reviews pages for their books.[22] This does not seem to be so true in the Australian context.

Indeed, some small-to-medium presses are punching above their weight in the fields of both prizes and reviews in Australia. The most conspicuous example of this is Text Publishing. In a paper we presented at the Small Press Network conference in 2014, we first noticed what we coined "the Text Effect"—that is, the fact that Text publications were being represented in our reviews pages to an extent that belied the scale of its operations. The book review data we have since gathered from 2014 to 2016, in addition to our prize data, confirms that the Text Effect is real and not a blip, but also positions this publisher's figures in light of the overall success Australian small, medium and independent publishers are having in these spheres.

---

22 Thompson, *Merchants of Culture*, 162–163.

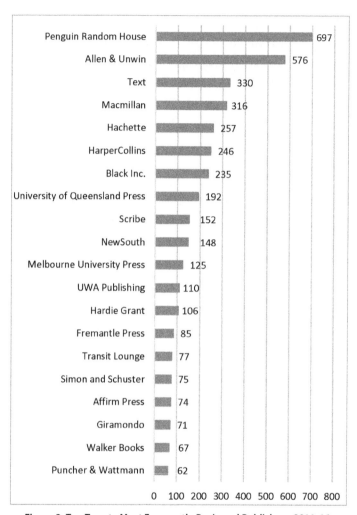

Figure 2. Top Twenty Most Frequently Reviewed Publishers, 2014–16.

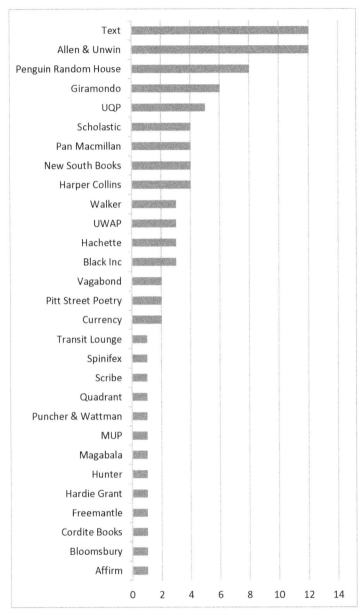

Figure 3. Prizes Won per Publisher, 2014–16.

Text's books have been enjoying an increasing prominence in the reviews pages across the publications we survey. Text was ranked sixth most reviewed publisher in 2014 and fourth in 2015. In 2016, it was the third most reviewed publisher behind Penguin Random House and Allen & Unwin. As far as prizes are concerned, we have already noted that Text, alongside Allen & Unwin, is the publishing house with the highest number of award-winning books in our survey. This is despite the fact that Text publishes, at a conservative estimate, 100 fewer titles each year than Allen & Unwin.[23] Text's books have won more awards than any other publisher in two of the four years of our survey: that is in 2016 (14% of the total number of prizewinning books) and 2017 (17%). Indeed, Text's proportion of the total number of prizes annually has only once fallen below 14% in the other years of our survey. That was in 2015, when Text books constituted only 5% of the total number of prize winners. We now refine "the Text Effect" to refer to this nexus of strong performance in prizes and representation in the book review pages—that is, in more than one of the sections of the Australian literary field that serve a consecratory function.

While Text is the most reviewed and awarded small-to-medium publisher in our survey, we would also like to draw attention to Giramondo. Giramondo is almost as well-represented in literary prizes as Text. In terms of prizes, Giramondo is ranked equal fourth most successful publisher in our survey. This is a remarkable achievement considering its small output. In the years 2014–17, Text has published an average of over nine times the number of books Giramondo has, though it

---

23 We calculate Text's annual publication rate at an average of 117 new books per year, based upon their bi-annual catalogues. See https://www.textpublishing. com.au/catalogue. Allen & Unwin claim on their "About Us" webpage that they publish "around 250 new titles each year", though the company's response to the Productivity Commission's draft report (dated April 2016) into Intellectual Property Arrangements states the figure for 2015 at 375. See, https://www. allenandunwin.com/about-allen-and-unwin and https://www.pc.gov.au/__data/ assets/pdf_file/0016/201247/subdr473-intellectual-property.pdf.

has won exactly double the number of prizes that Text has. For the 2014–17 period, Giramondo consistently won 10% of the total number of prizes, with a slump to only 3% in 2017. Giramondo was the 18th most reviewed publisher of Australian books from 2014–16. Its books received seventy-one reviews across these three years: this is significant attention in the reviews pages, considering its scale. We can conclude from this that reviews and prizes are both working well in the Australian field to promote—and consecrate—books published by small, medium and independent publishers in Australia, especially in relation to publishers of literary fiction.

Prizes, Book Reviews and Writers' Reputations

The data we have presented thus far indicates some strong overlap, and some specific domains of difference, between the books noticed by prizes and reviews. We would now like to trace the role of reviews and prizes in the reception of two books published in 2015: Charlotte Wood's *The Natural Way of Things* and A. S. Patrić's *Black Rock White City*. We will do this by comparing the reception of these novels with other books in our data, with the aim of bringing to light the nature of the temporal relationship between reviews and prizes. We also aim to establish the interdependence of these two consecratory mechanisms by demonstrating the ways in which their qualitative assessments of value mirror each other.

Wood's *The Natural Way of Things* was accorded value across the consecrating acts of book reviewing and prizes, which had an almost immediate flow-on effect in terms of university syllabuses. There are only two other books in our data that have received similar levels of attention across these three arenas in the literary field: Richard Flanagan's *The Narrow Road to the Deep North* and Kim Scott's *Taboo*.[24] Flanagan is,

---

24 Note that Scott's *Taboo* was only published in July 2017 so we are yet to know the full extent of its prize and syllabus reach.

by almost any criteria, a canonised contemporary Australian writer: he may have never won the Miles Franklin but he has received multiple awards, been the subject of some 128 works of criticism, had his works taught on some thirty-three university syllabuses and was the Boisbouvier founding Chair in Australian Literature at the University of Melbourne.[25] Of the authors in our data, Flanagan comes a close second to Kim Scott, whose works have received multiple prizes, including the Miles Franklin Award (twice), attracted 122 works of criticism and been taught on 109 courses.[26]

Wood was an established author when she published *The Natural Way of Things*: she had released four previous novels, won the Dobbie Literary Award and been shortlisted for the Miles Franklin and the Christina Stead Prize for Fiction; she was also Chair of Arts Practice, Literature at the Australia Council for the Arts during the period of our study. Her work pre-*The Natural Way of Things* was widely reviewed and discussed in the press[27] but rarely taught (three courses) or given scholarly attention (three journal articles).[28] It was over the period of our data that her work began to attract significantly more attention. We speculate that our prize and review data circumstantiates the process of Wood's transformation from an established to a canonical Australian writer.

The Natural Way of Things was published by Allen & Unwin on 1 October 2015. It received advance reviews that year in *Books+Publishing* (July) and *The Australian* (September). In the month of its publication, it was reviewed in *Sydney Review of Books*, *The Saturday Paper*, *The Advertiser* and *The Age*. *Australian Book Review* published its review in November, and *The Monthly* in December. Within the first three

---

25 "Richard Flanagan," Austlit, Richard Flanagan, http://www.austlit.edu.au/austlit/page/A10641.

26 "Kim Scott," Austlit, http://www.austlit.edu.au/austlit/page/A13678.

27 There are 67 works about Charlotte Wood's writing listed in Austlit prior to the publication of *The Natural Way of Things*.

28 "Charlotte Wood," Austlit, http://www.austlit.edu.au/austlit/page/A36080.

months of its publication, it had received reviews in eight of the twelve publications surveyed in the Stella Count. This is, in part, an effect of a new book by an established author, as well as a strong promotional campaign, complete with book trailer that included blurbs by established authors Joan London, Christos Tsiolkas and Malcolm Knox, and drew comparisons to Margaret Atwood's *The Handmaid's Tale* and William Golding's *The Lord of the Flies*.[29] This was also a novel that arrived at, and participated in, a particular cultural moment of unprecedented (at least since the 1980s) public interest in and discussion of sexual harassment and violence, especially domestic violence: for example, 2015 was the year in which Rosie Batty was named Australian of the Year.

Reviews of *The Natural Way of Things* emphasised its timeliness, associating it with contemporary discussions around gender, misogyny and violence. Reviewers report that the novel "lays bare the rape culture and slut-shaming associated with contemporary misogyny and the tyranny of corporate control over consumers and workers",[30] and is a "searing exploration of the most frightening elements of contemporary gender relations".[31] The reviews are also very strongly positive and evaluative. Stephen Romei describes it in *The Australian* as "one hell of a novel by one of our most original and provocative writers".[32] Rosemary Sorensen, writing in *Sydney Review of Books*, asserts it as "masterful" and "a virtuoso performance".[33] Kerryn Goldsworthy, in *The Age*, writes that it is "a profoundly

29 Online promotional material, Allen & Unwin, 2015, https://www.allenandunwin. com/browse/books/fiction/literary-fiction/The-Natural-Way-of-Things-Charlotte-Wood-9781760111236.

30 Portia Lindsay, "Fiction Reviews," *Books+Publishing* 95, no. 1 (2015): 21.

31 Portia Lindsay, "Horrors of Misogyny in Charlotte Wood's *The Natural Way of Things*," *The Australian*, September 26, 2015.

32 Stephen Romei, "Gripping from the Outset," *The Australian*, September 4, 2015.

33 Rosemary Sorenson, "Listen to the Sirens: *The Natural Way of Things* by Charlotte Wood," *Sydney Review of Books* (October 2, 2015), https://sydneyreviewofbooks. com/the-natural-way-of-things-charlotte-wood/.

literary novel".[34] It is tempting to speculate about the extent to which promotional material influences how reviewers describe a work: the references to Golding and Atwood are repeated in nearly all the reviews of Wood's novel. Nonetheless, it is clear that these reviews are assessing Wood's novel as having literary value, in part because of its critique of contemporary gender relations.

On March 10, 2016, some three months after the reviewing had died down, Wood's novel was announced as part of the shortlist for the 2016 Stella Prize: a prize established out of a specifically feminist imperative to promote and recognise Australian women's writing. Later that month, it won the Indie award for fiction, and in April won the Stella Prize. It was announced as the joint winner of the Prime Minister's Literary Award for fiction that November, and was shortlisted for the NSW and Victorian Premier's Literary Awards, the Voss Literary Prize, the IMPAC Dublin Literary Award, and the Australian Book Industry Award Book of the Year. Most of these shortlists, and all of these prizes, prompted further newspaper discussion of Wood's work.

From this, we can conclude that prizes were not the only, or even the primary, force at work in the consecration of *The Natural Way of Things*. This was a novel that articulated a form of feminism that was, two years later, to find a fuller public voice in the #metoo movement. It was also a novel whose literary qualities were recognised, described and promoted by reviewers prior to its entering the prize circuit, in ways that were informed and perhaps inflected by publishers' marketing efforts. Prizes, as Claire Squires notes, "demonstrate the fusion of cultural and economic capital, mediated by journalistic capital".[35] Reviews are a key way in which journalistic capital is brought to bear

---

34 Kerryn Goldsworthy, "Food for Thought as Women Prove the Great Survivors," *The Sydney Morning Herald*, October 10, 2015.

35 Claire Squires, "A Common Ground? Book Prize Culture in Europe," *Javnost—The Public* 11, no. 4 (2014): 41.

on the question of how a particular work is esteemed, alongside what we have noted elsewhere as the burgeoning of non-review coverage in the books pages.[36]

Wood's novel is also an example of the remarkable speed with which novels that have garnered significant public attention through reviews and prizes make it onto university syllabuses. *The Natural Way of Things* was taught on five courses across five different universities in 2016: one before the novel was shortlisted for the Stella Prize, and four after it had won.[37] Wood's novel is not alone in this: other novels that won prizes in this period entered university syllabuses very soon afterwards: Luke Carman's *An Elegant Young Man* was taught on three courses in 2015, the year after the author won the *Sydney Morning Herald* Best Young Novelist of the Year.[38] Likewise Evie Wyld's *All the Birds, Singing*, Fiona McFarlane's *The Night Guest* and Emily Bitto's *The Strays* were taught in university courses within a year of winning prizes.[39] These findings confirm that there is indeed a correlation between Australian literary prizes and educational reading lists, as noted by Sophie Allan and Beth Driscoll.[40] Our point is that these books were also widely reviewed—in ways that were explicitly evaluative—before they went on to win the prizes and make their way on to university courses, and that this part of the value chain should not be underestimated in the making of writers' reputations.

---

36 Melinda Harvey and Julieanne Lamond, "Taking the Measure of Gender Disparity in Australian Book Reviewing as a Field, 1985 and 2013," *Australian Humanities Review* 60 (2016), http://australianhumanitiesreview.org/2016/11/15/taking-the-measure-of-gender-disparity-in-australian-book-reviewing-as-a-field-1985-and-2013.

37 "Charlotte Wood," Austlit.

38 "Luke Carman," Austlit, http://www.austlit.edu.au/austlit/page/A118240.

39 See "Evie Wyld", Austlit, http://www.austlit.edu.au/austlit/page/A125611; "Fiona McFarlane", Austlit, http://www.austlit.edu.au/austlit/page/A69636; "Emily Bitto", Austlit, http://www.austlit.edu.au/austlit/page/A110320.

40 Sophie Allan and Beth Driscoll, "Making the list: The Value of Prizes for Women Writers in the Construction of Education Reading Lists," in *By the Book? Contemporary Publishing in Australia*, ed. Emmett Stinson (Melbourne: Monash University Publishing, 2013).

The role of reviews in this process is just as, if not more, important in the case of less established writers. A. S. Patrić's 2016 Miles Franklin win for his debut novel, *Black Rock White City*, published by Melbourne-based Transit Lounge, was claimed as a triumph for small presses.[41] At this stage in his career, Patrić had attracted some, but not many, of the measures of literary esteem that we have seen shoring up the reputations of Wood, Scott and Flanagan: he had published one novella and two collections of stories, all with small presses, and had won two short story prizes and been shortlisted for one. His work was not taught or written about in the academy.[42] Patrić, then, presents a good case study for how reviews and prizes treat a work that does not bring with it a major marketing campaign and previous acclaim.

Black Rock White City was published on April 1, 2015. It received six reviews, all within just over a month of its publication date, which is very good coverage for a less-established author—in 2015, only 2% of books reviewed received six or more reviews—and suggests that his previous collections had made some impact. However, the novel was not reviewed in the *Sydney Review of Books* or *Australian Book Review*: its reviews were all either small (fewer than 300 words) or medium length (400–900 words). These reviews were, however, strongly evaluative. The reviewer in *The Saturday Paper* writes: "the book is Australian realist-Gothic, the genre that defines the national culture as a crushing of the human spirit... It is very good; it may be a classic."[43] *The Australian* describes it as an "extraordinarily powerful debut novel" that is "masterful" and "clawingly brutal".[44] *The Sydney Morning Herald* review is even more positive:

41 Emmett Stinson, "The Miles Franklin and the Small Press." *Overland* (August 30, 2016).

42 "A. S. Patrić," Auslit.

43 XS, "A. S. Patrić *Black Rock White City*," *The Saturday Paper* (April 11–17, 2015).

44 Ashley Hay, "*Black Rock White City*: An Intimate Study of Life, Love and Grief," *The Australian* (April 4, 2015).

He is a writer who, deliberately or not, continues Patrick White's mission to bring European modernism to the Australian suburbs.

Formally rigorous and emotionally powerful, his new novel can only add to his stature as one of the most fascinating writers in this part of the world.[45]

In aligning Patrić with canonical Australian writer *par excellence* White, and both the forms (modernism, realism, gothic) and subject matter (suburbs) associated with the Australian literary tradition, as well as the notion of the 'classic', these reviews are clearly performing a consecrating function prior to the novel's Miles Franklin success in 2016.

De Nooy notes that prize juries "pronounce upon the literary quality of a text or of a body of works. Therefore, they function as instances of consecration: they attribute literary value to objects and, in doing so, they contribute to the harmonisation of opinions concerning literature."[46] In the case of both Wood and Patrić, the judges' comments strongly echoed the concerns and language of the preceding reviews. In Patrić's case, they all focus on realism, power and difficulty: the novel is described as "brutal, and frequently challenging, yet a deft poetry underlies its cinematic reach".[47] The Stella Prize judges' report on *The Natural Way of Things* describes it as "a novel of—and for—our times", repeating the reviews' emphasis on her critique of gender relations. This report also repeats a quotation from the novel that is included both in the publisher's book trailer and multiple reviews: "In the novel, women are told, with some hostility, that 'you need to know what you are'." In the case of the Stella Prize, the judges' report is

---

45 Owen Richardson, "Across the Borders from the Suburban to the Surreal: Fiction," *Sydney Morning Herald* (May 9, 2015).

46 De Nooy, "Gentlemen of the Jury," 532.

47 "About the Award," Perpetual, Miles Franklin Award, https://www.perpetual.com.au/milesfranklin/about-the-award.

literally aligned with reviews of Wood's novel. On the prize website, the report is followed by excerpts from, and links to, several reviews.[48] Judges' comments and book reviews are pieces of writing doing very similar kinds of evaluative work, although they circulate in different ways—reviews publicly and judges' comments semi-publicly as they are usually mediated by news reports on prize winners and sometimes accessible on prize websites after some searching. Judges' reports, then, can be thought of as synthesising earlier assessments of a novel's value or prestige, which further supports our argument about the interdependence of these two institutions.

Patrić is not the only early-career author included in our data. There are several debut novels listed in Table 2. Two writers, Fiona McFarlane and Emily Bitto, demonstrate two roads to how the usual priority of the review in the consecratory chain can be disrupted. One is well-trodden and has little to do with prizes; the other is new and has everything to do with them. McFarlane's novel follows an earlier model by which local cultural approval is achieved after international acclaim. Prior to the publication of *The Night Guest*, McFarlane had already come into the public eye through her short fiction—indeed, a single work of short fiction. Her story "Art Appreciation" was published in *The New Yorker* on May 13, 2013—an unusual, but not unprecedented, achievement for an emerging Australian writer.[49] McFarlane's *The Night Guest* was published by Penguin in August 2013 and received seven reviews stretched across the succeeding three months; was shortlisted for the Stella Prize in March 2014 and the Miles Franklin in May; and won the Glenda Adams Award for New Writing in the NSW Premier's Literary Awards, also in May. The longer timeline for her Australian reviews, plus the fact that her novel was also published in

---

48 "The Natural Way of Things," The Stella Prize, http://thestellaprize.com.au/prize/2016-prize/the-natural-way-of-things/.

49 Earlier examples of Australian writers whose stories have been published in *The New Yorker* include Cate Kennedy (2006), Amy Witting (1965) and Shirley Hazzard (1961).

the United States (by Faber) and the United Kingdom (by Sceptre), and was reviewed in the high profile *New York Times Book Review*, suggest that in her case reviews, amplified by international recognition, played a role in the subsequent success of her novel.

Emily Bitto's *The Strays* demonstrates how prize culture is beginning to disrupt the review's priority. As we mentioned previously, awards both precipitated and secured position in the public eye. *The Strays* was first shortlisted for the Prize for an Unpublished Manuscript by an Emerging Victorian Writer in the Victorian Premier's Literary Awards in November 2013, then published by Affirm Press, received seven reviews including longer pieces in *Sydney Review of Books* and *Australian Book Review*, and went on to win the 2015 Stella Prize. Melanie Cheng's debut short story collection *Australia Day* won the Victorian Premier's Literary Award for an Unpublished Manuscript in 2016, was published by Text in 2017, was reviewed six times, and then won the Victorian Premier's Literary Award for Fiction in 2018.

We should note that even without an unpublished prize, debut works by smaller presses can occasionally fare well across Australia's reviews and prizes. *Australia Day* is one of two debut short fiction collections in our data published by Text that did so; the other is Sonja Dechian's *An Astronaut's Life*, which was widely reviewed for both a first book and a collection of short fiction, with six reviews. It then went on to win the Glenda Adams Award for New Writing. We might speculate that short fiction, a previously marginalised genre, has, since the success of Nam Le's *The Boat*, gained a new level of prestige and commercial potential in Australia. Lachlan Brown notes that the opinion of the judges of the Dylan Thomas Prize—of Le as a phenomenal literary talent—in 2008 "turned a trickle of favourable early reviews in Australia and North America into a torrent of publicity" and set Le on the course for later prize successes.[50] The

---

50   Lachlan Brown, "Globalised Fiction Becomes a Fact: Nam Le Launches *The Boat*," in *Telling Stories: Australian Life and Literature 1935–2013*, eds. Tanya Dalziell and

iterative processes between prizes and reviews that we describe in this chapter were clearly also important to Le's astonishing success, and the prestige of the contemporary short story collection in Australia.

In the case of both established and early career writers, prizes offer books—and indeed book reviews—an afterlife. Prizes are crucial to a book's longevity post-publication. They create hype and increase the likelihood of further book reviews. And the assessments made in book reviews preceding the bestowal of prizes cast a long and enduring shadow.

Prizes, Book Reviews and Judges

If it is true, as James English says, that "it is the first axiom among prize administrators that the prestige of a prize is reciprocally dependent upon the prestige of its judges", then our study suggests that the book reviewing field is where that prestige is acquired or enhanced.[51] Our findings accord with those of Wouter De Nooy who, in the context of the Netherlands' literary world in the late 1980s, found that the judges of prizes were drawn from a heterogeneous community of critics, authors, scholars, publishers, booksellers, librarians, journalists and arts workers.[52] Australia's judges also constitute a large group: there are more individuals in the pool of judges than individual book titles in the pool of prize winners in our survey.

That judges' comments echo book reviews in form and content is unsurprising when you consider how many judges also write book reviews. Of the ninety-four judges of the prizes in our study, 34% of them appear in the book pages as a reviewer between 2014 and 2017. Indeed, judges are often reviewing books and determining prizes simultaneously: our data shows a correlation between judges and reviewers

---

Paul Genoni (Melbourne: Monash University Publishing, 2013), 566.

51   English, *The Economy of Prestige*, 122.

52   De Nooy, "Gentlemen of the Jury," 539.

in the same year at a rate of 23% in 2014, 22% in 2015, 38% in 2016 and 20% in 2017. There is also significant crossover between judges and authors across the years of our survey at a rate of 32%.

Individuals who feature as authors of books reviewed or as reviewers in the literary pages or both between 2014 and 2017 make up 52% of the total number of judges responsible for determining the recipients of prizes in the same time period. It should be highlighted that these figures do not account for judges who also appear in the book pages directly or indirectly (for example, as literary editors and publishers) or who have appeared in them pre-2014 or in 2018 as reviewers or authors. In short, this proves that the book review pages are, arguably, the most significant catchment area from which judges are drawn. This is a key aspect of the interdependence of book reviews and literary prizes.

Conclusion

Claire Squires has argued that literary prizes have four crucial roles: they reward and recognise quality, help with distribution (including wider and more effective circulation), lead to the survival of books, and encourage national and regional literary production.[53] Our study has found that prizes perform these roles in ways that are underpinned by, and reassert the authority and influence of, the book reviewing sector. In the afterlife secured for a work by the effects of reviews and prizes, judges' comments and book reviews are circulating alongside one another online. Moreover, the relationship between reviews and prizes in the contemporary Australian literary field is interdependent and shifting. Reviews continue to play a key role in the early evaluation and promotion of Australian books. Works of fiction, even by debut or early career authors, are often widely reviewed in Australia before going on to win prizes. The important exception to this is the proliferation of prizes for unpublished manuscripts: books winning such

---

53 Squires, "A Common ground?," 43–44.

prizes experience a "headstart" effect, with a high level of attention in the reviews pages that sometimes parlays into a subsequent prize. The relationship between prizes and reviews works somewhat differently for nonfiction: with the exception of life writing and memoir, nonfiction works are less likely to be given repeat reviews, and so rely more heavily on prizes to secure their longevity in the public eye.

We should also note that the period of our study has seen dramatic changes in how the workings of both prizes and reviews in Australia are inflected by gender. The data on which this study draws was collected in collaboration with the Stella Count, which aims to document—and to shift—established gender biases in the book reviews pages. Over the same period discussions and activism around gender and specific segments of the literary sphere in Australia—especially prizes and publishing—have led to an increase in the number of prizes awarded to women authors, including the women's-only Stella Prize. It remains to be seen how the relationship between the workings of reviews and prizes will be impacted upon by these developments.

Works cited

Allan, Sophie, and Beth Driscoll. "Making the List: The Value of Prizes for Women Writers in the Construction of Educational Reading Lists." In *By the Book: Contemporary Publishing in Australia*, edited by Emmett Stinson, 127–140. Melbourne: Monash University Publishing, 2013.

Allington, Patrick. "'What *is* Australia Anyway?' The Glorious Limitations of the Miles Franklin Literary Award." *Australian Book Review.* (June 2011): 23–34.

Austlit. "A. S. Patrić." Accessed February 1, 2018, http://www.austlit.edu.au/austlit/page/A122412.

———. "Charlotte Wood." Accessed February 1, 2018, http://www.austlit.edu.au/austlit/page/A36080.

———. "Kim Scott." Accessed February 1, 2018, http://www.austlit.edu.au/austlit/page/A13678.

———. "Luke Carman." Accessed February 1, 2018, http://www.austlit.edu.au/austlit/page/A118240.

————. "Richard Flanagan." Accessed February 1, 2018, http://www.austlit.edu. au/austlit/page/A10641.

Bitto, Emily. *The Strays*. Melbourne: Affirm Press, 2014.

Blainey, Geoffrey. *The Story of Australia's People*. Melbourne: Viking, 2016.

Bradley, James. *Clade*. Melbourne: Hamish Hamilton. 2015.

Brown, Lachlan. "Globalised Fiction Becomes a Fact: Nam Le Launches *The Boat*." In *Telling Stories: Australian Life and Literature 1935–2013*, edited by Tanya Dalziell and Paul Genoni, 566–572. Melbourne: Monash University Publishing, 2013.

Carman, Luke. *An Elegant Young Man*. Sydney: Giramondo Press, 2013.

Cheng, Melanie. *Australia Day*. Melbourne: Text Publishing, 2017.

Clarke, Maxine Beneba. *The Hate Race*. Sydney: Hachette, 2016.

De Nooy, Wouter. "Gentlemen of the Jury… : The Features of Experts Awarding Literary Prizes." *Poetics* 17, no. 6 (1988): 531–545.

Dechian, Sonja. *An Astronaut's Life*. Melbourne: Text Publishing, 2015.

Driscoll, Beth. "Contemporary Australian Literary Culture." In *Oxford Research Encyclopedia of Literature*. Oxford: Oxford University Press, 2017. http:// oxfordre.com/literature.

English, James. *The Economy of Prestige: Prizes, Awards and the Circulation of Cultural Value*. Cambridge, MA: Harvard University Press, 2005.

Flanagan, Richard. *The Narrow Road to the Deep North*. Sydney: Penguin Random House, 2013.

Goldsworthy, Kerryn. "Food for Thought as Women Prove the Great Survivors." *The Sydney Morning Herald*, October, 10 2015.

Harvey, Melinda and Julieanne Lamond. "Taking the Measure of Gender Disparity in Australian Book Reviewing as a Field, 1985 and 2013." *Australian Humanities Review* 60 (2016). http:// australianhumanitiesreview.org/2016/11/15/taking-the-measure-of-gender-disparity-in-australian-book-reviewing-as-a-field-1985-and-2013.

Hay, Ashley. "*Black Rock White City*: an Intimate Study of Life, Love and Grief." *The Australian*, April 4, 2015.

Holland-Batt, Sarah. *The Hazards*. St. Lucia: University of Queensland Press, 2015.

Kent, Hannah. *The Good People*. Sydney: Pan MacMillan, 2016.

Krasnostein, Sarah. *The Trauma Cleaner: One Woman's Extraordinary Life in Death, Decay & Disaster*. Melbourne: Text Publishing, 2017.

Lindsay, Portia. "Fiction Reviews." *Books+Publishing* 95, no. 1 (July 2015): 21.

————. "Horrors of Misogyny in Charlotte Wood's *The Natural Way of Things*." *The Australian*, September 26, 2015.

McFarlane, Fiona. *The Night Guest*. Melbourne: Penguin, 2013.

Meyer-Lee, Robert J. "Toward a Theory and Practice of Literary Valuing." *New Literary History* 46, no. 2 (2015): 335–55.

Nolan, Sybil and Matthew Ricketson. "Parallel Fates: Structural Challenges in Newspaper Publishing and their Consequences for the Book Industry." *Sydney Review of Books,* February 22, 2013. https://sydneyreviewofbooks. com/parallel-fates-2/.

Pascoe, Bruce. *Dark Emu: Black Seeds: Agriculture or Accident?* Broome: Magabala Books, 2014.

Patrić, A. S. *Black Rock White City.* Melbourne: Transit Lounge, 2015.

Peterson-Ward, Jennifer. "Black Rock White City." *Books+Publishing* 94, no. 3 (February 2015): 20.

Pool, Gail. *Faint Praise: The Plight of Book Reviewing in America.* Columbia: University of Missouri Press, 2007.

Richardson, Owen. "Across the Borders from the Suburban to the Surreal: Fiction." *Sydney Morning Herald,* May 9, 2015.

Romei, Stephen. "Gripping from the Outset." *The Australian,* September 4, 2015.

Scott, Kim. *Taboo.* Sydney: Pan MacMillan, 2017.

Sorensen, Rosemary. "Listen to the Sirens: *The Natural Way of Things* by Charlotte Wood." *Sydney Review of Books,* October 2, 2015. https:// sydneyreviewofbooks.com/the-natural-way-of-things-charlotte-wood/.

Squires, Claire. "A Common Ground? Book Prize Culture in Europe." *Javnost—The Public* 11, no. 4 (2014): 37–47.

Stinson, Emmett. "The Miles Franklin and the Small Press." *Overland,* August 30, 2016. https://overland.org.au/2016/08/the-miles-franklin-and-the-small-press/.

———. "Small Publishers and the Miles Franklin Award." In *The Return of Print? Contemporary Australian Publishing,* edited by Aaron Mannion and Emmett Stinson. Melbourne: Monash University Publishing, 2016.

Thompson, John. B. *Merchants of Culture: The Publishing Business in the Twenty-First Century.* Cambridge: Polity Press, 2010.

Trinca, Helen. *Madeleine: A Life of Madeleine St John.* Melbourne: Text Publishing, 2013.

Van Rees, C. J. "How a Literary Work Becomes a Masterpiece: On the Threefold Selection Practised by Literary Criticism." *Poetics* 12 (1983): 397–417.

Wilson, Josephine. *Extinctions.* Crawley, WA: UWA Publishing, 2016.

Wood, Charlotte. *The Natural Way of Things.* Sydney: Allen and Unwin, 2015.

Wyld, Evie. *All the Birds, Singing.* Sydney: Random House, 2013.

XS. "A. S. Patrić *Black Rock White City.*" *The Saturday Paper,* April 11–17, 2015.

Contributor Biographies

Katherine Bode is Associate Professor of Literary and Textual Studies at the Australian National University and an Australian Research Council Future Fellow from 2018 to 2022. Her research uses large datasets and digital methods to investigate Australian literature and literature in Australia. She has published extensively in literary history and digital humanities including as author or co-editor of *A World of Fiction: Digital Collections and the Future of Literary History* (2018), *Advancing Digital Humanities: Research, Methods, Theories* (2014), *Reading by Numbers: Recalibrating the Literary Field* (2012) and *Resourceful Reading: The New Empiricism, eResearch and Australian Literary Culture* (2009).

Katherine Day has been working in the publishing industry for over fifteen years. She was an editor at Penguin Group (Australia) for eight years before freelancing for Penguin Random House, Allen and Unwin, University of Queensland Press, Rockpool Publishing, Working Title Press, and Thames and Hudson. She is currently a sessional course coordinator and lecturer in the School of Culture and Communications, University of Melbourne, and is a PhD Candidate at RMIT. Her area of interest is publishing contract negotiations.

Michelle Goldsmith is an author, editor and PhD candidate in Creative Writing and Publishing at the University of Melbourne. Her research investigates not only the content of books, but also how various external factors may affect a book's reception, as well as exploring the wider operations of contemporary fields of cultural production and how different participants in these fields interact. She is particularly interested in speculative fiction and non-realist texts. She has a BSc and a Masters of Publishing and Communications, and has worked in bookselling and publishing for over a decade. Her short fiction and academic papers have appeared in publications within Australia and overseas, and she has been short-listed for both the Aurealis Award and the Ditmar Award.

Jocelyn Hargrave teaches writing, editing and publishing at Monash University and the University of Melbourne. She has worked in the educational publishing industry for 22 years, 20 as an editor. Her forthcoming monograph, *The Evolution of Editorial Style in Early Modern England*, is scheduled for publication by Palgrave Macmillan in October 2019. Current research relates to colonial Australian print culture and to contemporary editorial pedagogy.

Melinda Harvey is Lecturer in Literary Studies at Monash University. She convened the 2015 symposium Critical Matters: Book Reviewing Now and co-edited the special section 'Book Reviewing in Australia' published in *Australian Humanities Review* in 2016. She works as a book critic in Australia and is a current judge of the Miles Franklin Literary Award.

Julieanne Lamond is Lecturer in Literary Studies at Australian National University. Her research focuses on literary reception in Australia. She has published essays on Australian writers (Rosa Praed, Barbara Baynton, Steele Rudd, Miles Franklin, Christos Tsiolkas), gender and Australian literary culture, digital approaches to studying the history of reading, mass market fiction at the turn of the twentieth century, and gender and book reviewing. She is currently writing a monograph on the work and reception of Amanda Lohrey. She a judge of the Patrick White Award and editor of *Australian Literary Studies*.

Brigid Magner is a Senior Lecturer in Literary Studies and founding member of the non/fictionLab research group at RMIT University. Her monograph *Locating Australian Literary Memory* (Anthem Press, 2019) is forthcoming.

Aaron Mannion is a writer, editor and academic. From 2015 to 2017, he was Vice President of the Small Press Network.

Born in Indonesia of French parents, and brought up in France and Australia, **Sophie Masson** is the award-winning and internationally-published author of over 60 books for children, young adults and adults. Sophie is also a founder and the publishing director of Christmas Press, a boutique children's publisher based in regional NSW. She has just finished a PhD at the University of New England in Australia, where she has been working on the creation of a young adult speculative fiction novel, *The Ghost Squad*, with an accompanying exegesis. She has presented her research work at conferences and her scholarly articles have been published in journals including *TEXT*, *M/C Journal*, *The Looking Glass*, *Bookbird*, *Papers*, and *New Writing*. Her book chapter, 'Going Over to the Other Side', was published in *Publishing Means Business* (Monash University Publishing, 2017).

Currently lecturer at RMIT, **Rose Michael** was previously commissioning editor at Hardie Grant Books and co-founded Arcade Publications in 2007. She has been published most recently in *Sydney Review of Books, Meanjin, Overland, The Conversation* and is the author of two novels: *The Asking Game* (Transit Lounge, 2007) and *The Art of Navigation* (UWA, 2017).

Tracy O'Shaughnessy is a publisher with over 25 years' experience in trade books. In 2016 she created RMIT's Master of Writing and Publishing and established The Bowen Street Press, a student-led press that forms the backbone of this program. She is also chair of Express Media board and a board member of the Small Press Network.

Emily Potter is a literary and cultural studies researcher in the areas of Australian literature, place-making, and postcolonial environments. Her books include *Writing Australia at the Millennium: Field Notes on Belonging* (Intellect, 2019). She is Associate Head of School (Research) and senior lecturer in Literary Studies at Deakin University.

Ronnie Scott is a lecturer at RMIT and founder of independent literary magazine *The Lifted Brow*. He is two-time recipient of MacDowell Colony Fellowships and a contributor to *The Believer*, *The Monthly*, and *Griffith Review*. His first novel, *The Adversary*, will be published by Penguin Random House Australia in 2020.

Emmett Stinson is a Lecturer in Writing and Literature at Deakin University. He is the author of *Satirizing Modernism* (Bloomsbury) and *Known Unknowns* (Affirm Press).

Millicent Weber is a Lecturer in English at the Australian National University. She researches the intersections between live and digital literary culture, and is the author of *Literary Festivals and Contemporary Book Culture* (Palgrave Macmillan, 2018). She has published articles in peer-reviewed journals including *Continuum* and *Convergence* and literary journal *Overland*, and co-edited *Publishing Means Business: Australian Perspectives* (Monash University Publishing, 2017).

Editors' Acknowledgements

We would like to thank the copyeditors: Travis Englefield, Rebecca Fletcher, Mackensie Freedman and Vidisha Srinivasan. Students in the publishing program at the University of Melbourne, they edited the book with care, skill and intelligence.

We would also like to thank everyone at Monash University Publishing for their support of this project.

Other books in the Monash Publishing Series

By the Book? Contemporary Publishing in Australia
Edited by Emmett Stinson (2013)

Publishing Means Business: Australian Perspectives
Edited by Aaron Mannion, Millicent Weber and Katherine Day (2017)

The Return of Print? Contemporary Australian Publishing
Edited by Aaron Mannion and Emmett Stinson (2016)

For more information see
http://www.publishing.monash.edu/series/publishing-series.html

CPSIA information can be obtained
at www.ICGtesting.com
Printed in the USA
FSHW011134160420
69235FS